Anishinaabe syndicated

# Anishinaabe syndicated

## A View from the Rez

Jim Northrup

*12-8-11*

Introduction by Margaret Noori

*ERIC
TO THE FULL
MONTE TUSEN TAKK
MII GWECH

Jim Northrup*

MINNESOTA HISTORICAL SOCIETY PRESS

www.mhspress.org

The Minnesota Historical Society Press is a member of the Association of
American University Presses.

Manufactured in the United States of America

10 9 8 7 6 5 4 3 2 1

∞ The paper used in this publication meets the minimum requirements of the
American National Standard for Information Sciences—Permanence for Printed
Library Materials, ANSI Z39.48-1984.


International Standard Book Number
ISBN: 978-0-87351-823-9 (paper)
ISBN: 978-0-87351-831-4 (e-book)

Library of Congress Cataloging-in-Publication Data

Northrup, Jim, 1943-
    Anishinaabe syndicated : a view from the rez / Jim Northrup.
        p. cm.
    ISBN 978-0-87351-823-9 (pbk. : alk. paper)
    1. Northrup, Jim, 1943- 2. Ojibwa Indians—Biography. 3. Ojibwa Indians—Social
life and customs. 4. Fond du Lac Indian Reservation (Minn.)—Social life and
customs. 5. Ojibwa wit and humor. I. Title.
    E99.C6N65 2011
    305.897—dc22
                                                                    2010042708

# contents

*To Umpaowastewin and Giiwedin Noodin*

# Introduction
## Awenen Aawaad

Chibinesi ezhinkaazo.
Makwa dodem debendagozi.
Nagaajiwanaang onjibad.
Ogichidaa gii miigaazo Vietnamong.
Ogichidaa gii giiwekii.
Nitaadibaajimo miinawaa nitaa'ezhibiige.
Weweni Anishinaabemo ensa giizhigag.
Manaajitoonan gakina gegoo akiing.
Manaaji'iaan gakina goya maampii.
Weweni bimaadizi .
Weweni iskigamizige.
Weweni nooshkaachinaagananke.
Weweni manoominike.
Booch igo gda'bizindawaanaan
    ji-nisidotan bimaadiziwin.
Ogashkitoon gikinoo'amawiyangid,
aanii ezhi-pindaakojigaamaang asemaa
aanii ezhi-anami'aaying
aanii ezhi-bizindamoying
aanii ezhi-minobimaadiziying.
G'miigwetchin, Jim.
G'miigwetchaawan chigete Anishinaabeg
G'miigwetchaawan gdindawemaaganag.
G'miigwetchwigo, Jim.

To truly introduce Jim Northrup properly, I would use the words above. He is a member of the bear clan, which explains the fierce and firm way he protects those he loves—their collective culture and their individual everyday lives. He is a warrior, a marine who fought in Vietnam, and he is one who came home bearing the physical and mental memories of battle. He is a fine storyteller, an accomplished writer, and a constant steward and student of the Anishinaabe language. His respect for the earth and her people is immense. It shows in everything he does, whether it is boiling sap for syrup, making baskets, or ricing on the lakes. Listening to him, we gain an understanding of life on and off the reservation because he teaches what is important. As a lifelong friend I owe him great thanks. I am certain the ancestors thank him along with all the relatives on and near Northrup Road.

This "distillation" of the Fond du Lac Follies is an edit of the first twelve years of an ongoing series of newspaper columns. Readers will find in the circle of each year literature, history, community beliefs, shared traditions, and facts about America from the rez perspective. Like the baskets Jim makes, his writing reflects a circular tracing of detail, an attention to both purpose and aesthetics. He finds new shapes in the familiar and makes art out of the ordinary. Each chapter presents selections from a year's worth of monthly columns, originally published in *The Circle* Native American newspaper in Minneapolis, Minnesota, and *News from Indian Country,* based in Hayward, Wisconsin.

Although each column ends with a disclaimer, "The views expressed in this column belong to the writer alone," Jim writes more than just his opinions or his autobiography. The Follies could best be called "auto-commun-ography." Much more than autobiography, this series reveals a network of reservation relations across lakes and land, through woods and words, as the entire community survives one day, one month, one year, one generation at a time. Children are born, languages are lost and revived, the arts of basket making and bingo gaming develop, and all the while Jim bears witness. He allows readers to see the strange world in which we live from a new angle. Friends and family read his words for updates and honesty. Citizens from other Native nations read for comparison and contrast. Fellow citizens of the United States read to find out what wasn't in their history books. And because he travels widely, it is clear his readership is international. As new readers journey with Jim through this collection, they are able to see the ways in which life has changed radically in recent years as well as the ways in which it has remained remarkably the same.

The Follies first appeared in 1989, a year marked by a series of revolutions starting in Poland, the fall of the Berlin Wall, and eventually the death of the Soviet Union, which signaled the end of the Cold War. It was also a time when much was changing in Indian country. In 1988 Ronald Reagan signed the Indian Gaming Regulatory Act, which began an avalanche of issues related to tribal sovereignty and brought new dollars to tribal communities. The Native American Graves Protection and Repatriation Act became law in November 1990 and began requiring federal museums, schools, and libraries to return cultural items and human remains to their respective peoples. In 1992 Congress passed the Native American Languages Act to promote and preserve the languages now dying as a result of colonization and forced assimilation. The Follies follows all of these developments and reports on the ways life on the reservation changes—and the ways it does not. Casinos were built and bones were sent home, but Jim finds evidence that not all federal intentions are understood in small towns, and he repeatedly wishes for more students around the language table. He is honest about both the past and the future and is engaged in both re-recording the past and building the future his grandchildren will inherit.

Jim's columns offer an alternate view of history. During the late 1980s and throughout the 1990s, a series of court cases addressed the question of exactly how to interpret the 1837 and 1854 treaties between the United States and several bands of Lake Superior Chippewa. At stake were millions of dollars in payment from the state and the right to hunt and harvest in ceded territory. The sportsmen in Minnesota and Wisconsin who enacted and enforced gaming regulations felt the state guidelines should apply to everyone. However, Article 5 of the 1837 Treaty provides that "The privilege of hunting, fishing, and gathering the wild rice, upon the lands, the rivers and the lakes included in the territory ceded, is guaranteed to the Indians." Furthermore, Article 11 of the 1854 Treaty says, "And such of them as resides in the territory hereby ceded, shall have the right to hunt and fish therein." For awhile, a fee was paid to compensate the Lake Superior bands for the limitation of their rights, but when the enrollees of Fond du Lac decided their rights were not for sale, old wounds were opened. Jim's record of this period is one that was not published in the mainstream.

This is a book to hand anyone curious about reservation life, about treaty rights, about global issues viewed through a local lens, about life and death and the ups and downs that chase us from one end of that journey to the other. There is cultural value in walking the rez road with Jim, but there is great literary value as well. He talks about his writing roots and how writing has the power to help process even the most difficult experiences. His voice has developed over time, and it now possesses the power, grace, and individuality of a valued nooskaachanagan, used to winnow the hulls from the tastiest rice. He sifts through the words and phrases of his two worlds, sometimes writing in Ojibwe, mostly writing in English with the kind of irreverence that would make the hair on the back of a composition teacher's neck stand on end.

Jim doesn't so much break writing rules as make his own. Alliteration, metaphor, syntax, and meter all work to gently untie a reader's expectations. If you think you know which simile he'll reach for or which adjective he'll use, you'll most often be wrong and happily, most often humorously, surprised. The slang of the rez (reservation) reflects the views of the Shinnobs (Anishinaabe people), specifically the Fonjalackers (Fond du Lac-ers). Rez cars say "gaawiin" (no) some days. And just when you think you've caught on that "snagging" is the art of finding a mate (or at least a mate for the night), he'll tell you that negotiations hit "snags" and someone was arrested for "snagging" a salmon. Rather than leave readers sitting outside the punch line, not knowing when to laugh, he gradually teaches the terms needed to find humor in Indian country.

Another important lesson in Jim's work is the ability to relax and revel in the Anishinaabe aesthetic of repetition. Years roll by and stories seem at first to repeat now and then, and yet the stories are never really the same. Some powwows are small and intimate, others include exploding garbage trucks. Some years the rice is plentiful, some years there is less, but always there is enough. Jim's journeys as a writer always begin with the point of departure and end with the point of rez reentry. What and who we see in between is anybody's guess, but it usually involves a check for far-flung friends and relatives and a bit of educating the masses. Although the modern editorial stance would be to trim and remove these echoes and repeats, allowing them to serve their purpose as harmony to the melody of events invites readers to truly understand not only what happens on the rez but also the way it happens. Mii sa aanii dash boochigo gindaasiig, ji-nsostaamiig ezhi-bimaadziwaad Anishinaabemjig ishigonigong noongo. And that would be the reason to read the Follies, to understand Anishinaabe life on the rez today.

Margaret Noori
*Program in American Culture*
*Ojibwe Language & Literature*
UNIVERSITY OF MICHIGAN, ANN ARBOR

# Preface
## Fond du Lac Follies
## and a writer's Life

I write how it is on the reservation. The usual term for this place is the rez—specifically, the Fond du Lac Reservation in what is now called Minnesota. In the Ojibwe language, Nagaajiwanaang.

I rely on the oral tradition to tell my stories, so I move from one topic to another. This approach lets me include many different stories, from beginning businesses to failed businesses, from personal travels to seasonal traditional activities.

I was born at a very early age in the government hospital on the reservation. I am one of twelve children because it's cold during those long Minnesota winter nights. I began my writing career as a lonely six-year-old boy in a federal boarding school. Writing letters was the only way to stay connected with my family back at Nagaajiwanaang. I knew from the family stories that my grandfather Joseph Northrup wrote stories back in the 1920s and 1930s. His pen name was Nodin. It was as if he broke the trail for me, and anyone who has walked in knee-deep snow understands what breaking trail means.

I am also one of the Anishinaabe who survived Agwaajing (they call it Ah-Gwah-Ching), the tuberculosis sanitarium at Walker, Minnesota, when I was age three, then the federal boarding school in Pipestone, Minnesota, when I was six to ten years old. From grades six to eight I went to Brainerd Indian Training School in Hot Springs, South Dakota, which was run by the Wesleyan Methodists. I've survived years of attempted assimilation.

I finally left the American Indian boarding-school system when Alvin Broken Rope and I went along with some Onadaga girls who were trying to escape. We eventually convinced them to return to the school and wait for a bus ticket home. Since we were the only boys in the group, we were arrested and locked up in the county jail. After jail they cut my hair and demanded an apology to the entire school. I refused, thinking I had done nothing wrong.

I called home and told them to send me a bus ticket or I was walking home. Once I got home it wasn't long before I was sent to reform school in Red Wing, Minnesota. I usually say it was because I stole a pig and it squealed, but the real reason was because I was in a high-speed chase involving a stolen car.

It was at the reform school that I began asking questions and publishing them for others. Some of the questions I asked in a journalism class were:

> *How tall is the bluff behind the school?*
> *How deep is the Mississippi in front of the school?*
> *Which building has the lowest ceiling?*

I published these imaginative questions on the front page of the newspaper and wrote "Answers on page nine" on the bottom of the list. It was an eight-page newspaper. For months people were asking me, "Where is page nine?" I learned from this that my imagination could make people laugh.

The last school I attended was the public high school in Carlton, Minnesota, just twelve miles from home. In 1961, according to the principal, I became the first Indian to graduate from that school.

I joined the marines right out of high school. I traveled around the Gulf of Mexico, stopping at a few different countries. I next traveled to the Far East, visiting six different countries there, and finished my military service with a tour in Vietnam in a rifle company. Once again I used letters to stay in touch with my family.

I returned to the reservation, as I always knew I would, in the late 1970s. There was a shortage of housing on the Fond du Lac Reservation, so I lived in a tipi on a remote reservation lake. It was a long hike from the tar road to my house deep in the woods. It was primitive living but rewarding. After meeting the basic requirements of food, water, and shelter, I had it easy. Clocks didn't exist in the woods.

I used to entertain my visitors with stories while sitting around the fire or watching the sun go down across the lake.

One day I was making notes about a story I wanted to tell the next time I had company. Then I realized they didn't look too different from a story you could read in a book. That is, if a book existed about current-day Anishinaabe life on the rez.

I invented a character named Luke Warmwater and rewrote the story using events and history from my life.

I read the story the next time I had visitors to my home, and their response told me I was doing something right. I wrote another story, then another. I continued writing, and a lot of people helped me along the way. Gerald Vizenor published fourteen stories of mine. Louise Erdrich wrote me an encouraging letter.

My monthly column, Fond du Lac Follies, came about in 1989 as a result of a conversation I had with Rod Greengrass, the editor of *The Circle,* a newspaper published in Minneapolis for the Native American community. My first book, *Walking the Rez Road,* was published four years later. The book and the newspaper column gave me exposure to many more readers, including people in bookstores and on college campuses and some who heard me on the radio.

Then I was given an opportunity to do a one-man show about my life. I performed that play on Broadway—Broadway Street in Albert Lea, Minnesota. We then staged the play at the Illusion Theater in Minneapolis and the History Theatre in St. Paul.

I was given a chance to assist in making documentaries about Anishinaabe life that included *Warriors,* a film about Native American Vietnam veterans directed by Deb Walwork for Prairie Public Television; *Jim Northrup: With Reservations,* which focused on the seasonal life of the Anishinaabe, made by Mike Hazard and Mike Rivard; and *Way of the Warrior,* whose director, Patty Loew, says she included me and my poetry because I am her second-favorite veteran (her dad is her first). In the PBS after-school special *Zero Street,* I played an Indian activist. And then Hollywood came to visit when Georgina Lightning filmed parts of *Older Than America* on the Fond du Lac Reservation and at my home on Northrup Road.

As a result of these opportunities, I hear from people all the time who are moved by my stories and words. I realized that I had seen some big changes happening on the Fond du Lac Reservation, for its history and its people, over the time I've been writing my column. These extracts show what life was like from 1989 through 2001.

I've heard many questions over the years as I have traveled. People start by noticing I am not a white American, and they ask me what I am. Once we establish that I am an Indian, an Anishinaabe man, they feel they have a license to ask anything about me and mine. Their questions are sometimes silly, sometimes dumb, sometimes cruel. I respond in kind. I will answer well-meaning questions to the best of my ability. Absurd questions deserve absurd answers. There are no rules about how often questions can be asked.

My hope is that *Anishinaabe Syndicated* will lead you to questions of your own.

Jim Northrup
*Northrup Road, Sawyer, Minnesota*
FOND DU LAC BAND OF LAKE SUPERIOR CHIPPEWA

# Anishinaabe syndicated

# 1.
# Didja Ever Notice?

## 1989

Didja ever notice the bingo hall seems to be full of ex-drunks? At the end of the evening the bingo players have something to show for their money—dauber juice stains on their fingers. The bingo players also have a chance to win thousands of dollars. Didja ever notice? Bingo money doesn't seem to last as long as regular money. It's got an attitude of "easy come, easier go." Now, what was that last number he called?

In traveling around the rez, it's hard not to notice the two hundred-some new homes built in the last six years. Some of the houses look pretty bare. We're thinking of forming a committee to study the feasibility of putting at least one junk car in every yard.

Jim Weaver of White Earth is on a fast. Jim is well known in these parts. He usually has a stand at the powwows called Iron Legs Shirts. He is protesting the leadership of his band at White Earth. He must have strong feelings about it to put his life on the line for his children and grandchildren. Didn't the Irish Republican Army do something like this a few years back? Good luck, Jim. I hope your spirit is as strong as your legs.

It's not too early to begin thinking how we can commemorate the five hundredth anniversary of Columbus's arrival here. My cousin told me he started off with four ships but one of them fell off the edge.

*QUESTION: Are you really an Indian?*
*ANSWER: No, I'm a spirit. I just look real to you.*

The powwow at Sawyer was the social event of the summer. The people at Mashkawisen Treatment Center, where the powwow grounds are located, fed a couple thousand people during the feast. The grand entries were grand. Walt Bressette of Bayfield, Wisconsin, was selling shirts that read, "I will snag no more forever." He quickly sold out his stock but promised to have more available. The drummers and singers were surrounded by the traditional tape recorders. The dancers circled the drums, looking good in their outfits. I know I am not supposed to call them costumes because clowns wear costumes. The tall guy wearing the military green army blanket stood out in contrast to the other dancers in their colorful regalia.

Powwows are great for shaking hands. It's nice to greet people you haven't seen for a while. It does bring up a decision: Do I shake hands like an old person, a gentle pressing of the flesh, almost a caress? Do I do a militant, wrist-twisting, soul-brother handshake? I know I don't shake hands like a white guy, which turns into a physical contest to see who can squeeze the hardest. Maybe I'll just settle for a wave across the arena.

The moccasin game was how Indians gambled before bingo and pull-tabs were invented. The sound of the small drum caught the ear and pulled some people over to watch. The pull-tabs exerted a stronger pull, because the boxes had people three deep in front of them. There were fifty-five-gallon barrels full of dashed dreams and losing pull-tabs.

We are rapidly building a new tradition, and I'm not sure how it fits with the old ways. Princess contests are now popular at most powwows. At some gatherings, it is not uncommon to see four or five young women wearing a crown and a sash, a sash that identifies them as the current princess representing their school, rez, powwow, or tribe. On the one hand, I think our young women should be recognized for their accomplishments, but maybe, just maybe, we are doing it the wrong way. First, why a princess? Isn't it borrowed from the Europeans? The royalty ranking system came from across the ocean. In fact, it was one of the major reasons many of the Europeans came to this country. They came to escape the rigid class structure of their homeland, where birth counted for more than individual merit. Are we so hard up for traditions we use one of their discarded ideas?

Who started the princess contest tradition, anyway? Is it a dusky Miss America contest? If so, why do our young women never go on to compete in the real Miss America, Miss World, and Miss Universe contests? For many of the children growing up now, we have had a princess contest as long as they can remember. It's traditional in their lives. If we are buying into the princess concept, shouldn't we also have a prince contest? There must be a better way to honor our young women, the life-givers of the next generation.

It was the eleventh annual powwow for the Mashkawisen Treatment Center. I wonder how many people know about the free beer rock concert held there before Mash opened up to begin treating Indians? See you next year?

> QUESTION: *How could you tell they were real Americans?*
> ANSWER: *She used synthetic oil in her German car.*
> *He used unleaded gas in his Japanese car.*
> *She drank reconstituted orange juice.*
> *He drank decaf coffee with nondairy creamer.*
> *She had a perm that wasn't, silicone breasts*
> *    that were.*
> *He wore a Willard Scott–style hairpiece.*
> *She believed the weatherman.*
> *He believed the president.*

I saw federal money being put to good use the other day at the Sawyer Center. It was foot clinic time. Elders from the community were being treated to total foot care. First their feet were soaked, then toenails were trimmed, and lastly, their feet were massaged. The people providing the care were from the rez health clinic. They were cheerful as they trimmed and massaged. The elders seemed to enjoy the attention. Makwa Lyons remarked that he was waiting for the blacksmith as he soaked his feet. The money spent on foot care for the elders would probably pay for two or three shells for the USS *Iowa*.

Gossip from the moccasin telegraph also showed another use of federal money. It seems the BIA gave a workshop in Reno for some of the rez employees. The workshop was canceled but the employees still went to Reno. I wonder if the BIA would send some of the unemployed rez residents next time. They have the time and usually don't get to go anywhere like Reno.

The Fond du Lac Community College is making quite an impact on the rez. Dr. Tom Peacock is now the superintendent of schools for the rez. He recently got his degree from Harvard. For those of us who have been watching his career over the years, since his rez name is Auk, it's time to say, "Well done, Doc Auk." There are now former dropouts walking around talking about midterms, grade-point averages, and class schedules. These are some of the same people who used to scoff at the idea of education beyond the eighth grade. I was by there last week and I saw one of the best deer hunters from the rez interfacing with a computer. It looks like the community is taking advantage of the educational opportunities. A few more generations of this and we will consider higher education a normal state instead of a rarity.

Chief Plenty Coups (Aleek-chea-ahoosh), a visionary leader of the Aapsalooke (Crow) Nation who lived from 1848 to 1932, once said, "Education is your greatest weapon. With education you are the white man's equal, without education you are his victim and so shall remain all of your lives. Study, learn, help one another always. Remember there is only poverty and misery in idleness and dreams—but in work there is self-respect and independence."

It rained during the something-annual Protect the Earth festival. It was kind of fitting with all this talk about drought. It was a good time for establishing networks. The environmentalists and the Indians have a lot in common, that is, protecting the earth. Witnesses from the boat landings were there with their war stories of the past spearing season. During the rainstorm, an environmental type went outside and checked the pH level of the puddles. According to his gauge, the mud puddle was full of acid rain. The witnesses are expecting more violence than last year. On the one hand, I appreciate their help, but on the other, I can do without the fear-mongering. Indians have faced racists before. I learned that the guy who is doing the negotiating for the state of Wisconsin was formerly associated with Exxon. I wonder how many PARR (Protect America's Rights and Resources) secret agents were circulating in the Protect the Earth crowd at Ladysmith, Wisconsin. Who is paranoid?

It's easy to complain about what we don't have on the rez, like jobs. Let's look at what else we don't have. We don't have poisonous snakes, street gangs (would they call them "trail gangs"?), wide-scale political corruption, car bombings, traffic lights, rush hour, smog and water pollution, a thousand strangers per square mile, paper-mill riots, boat landing rednecks and their Treaty beer, hourly sirens, Jim and Tammy Bakker, crack houses, wire cages around our bald eagles, streetlights, locked doors, and noise. To name just a few.

The rez has a negotiated settlement with the state of Minnesota for the taxes paid by rez residents on liquor and cigarettes. According to Henry Buffalo, the rez attorney, Fond du Lac will get $438,000. Don't get happy. The RBC (Reservation Business Committee) doesn't know when they will get it but it has already been allocated. A suggestion was made by a member of the audience to use some of that money to buy teeth for the Fonjalackers who are walking around toothless. That suggestion was appreciated but no, no money will filter down to the people. Is this taxation without representation? Wasn't a war fought over something like this?

*QUESTION: What do you use for streetlights in Sawyer?*
*ANSWER: The stars, and once in a while, the moon.*

Two Fonjalackers, Sulu and Steve, are working for the rez and their people. They are going from house to house checking and cleaning the heating systems. The gas furnaces are cleaned and new thermo couplings are installed. Chimney inspections and smoke alarms are also a part of the service.

The old way was to pay a Chimook. Chimook is short for Chimookimanan, meaning "the long knives" in Ojibwe, which is what the cavalry soldiers carried during the Indian Wars. Not all Chimooks have long knives, or clean chimneys, but those who gave them the name have long memories.

The two Fonjalackers are paid with Reservation Housing Authority money originally funded by the U.S. government. I wonder if we have found one good use for HUD money? Sulu and Steve charge twelve bucks a house, and the Chimook price was sixty bucks a house, for two hundred houses. By hiring on the Rez, the Housing Authority is saving money and providing jobs.

We need parity in our pedigree. There are some Indians on the rez who are more equal than others. In some situations, the residents are counted as Indians, in others they are not. Let me explain. According to the Indian health service, the housing authority, and the education division, federal and state programs, and rednecks, we are all Indians regardless of where we are enrolled. The unfortunates lose their Indian-ness when they try to hunt, fish, and gather off the rez. They're still Indians on the rez, but once they go off they are no longer Indians. They must comply with state laws. There is a paradox here. You're an Indian until you cross an imaginary line separating the rez from ceded territory. Meanwhile, the whites can hunt or fish on or off the rez. Somewhere in the complex rules of being an Indian, some of us—to borrow from George Orwell—are more equal than others.

The recent snowfall gave me a good excuse not to cut my lawn. The deer and moose hunters are happy. It makes for easier tracking, easier seeing. But if you really want to see deer, go to the ceded territory in northern Wisconsin. During a recent drive down Highway 2 we were weaving in and out of the herd for two hours straight. The scary ones were those that were looking away from the headlights. I don't suppose the deer carry liability insurance when they use the highways.

It's a good feeling to see a Fond du Lac license plate when you are driving around. The familiar orange and black plates are easy to see. If something breaks on your car, help is as close as the next FDL plate. Even if you don't know the other driver, they know someone that you do. In this hurly-burly world, it's good to see someone else from the rez.

*QUESTION: What did they call Duluth before the white man came?*
*ANSWER: Home.*

The rez bought a building from the Catholic Diocese of Duluth. The building houses health services, Indian legal aid, and the Minnesota Council of Churches. There were over a hundred people there for the opening pipe ceremony, done by Jimmy Jackson. A drum group provided an honor song. There will be fourteen full-time staff working at the new place. The Fond du Lac Reservation Business Committee provided the traditional ham, turkey, and cheese sandwich feast.

Some Indians were out spearing at Round Lake in Price County, Wisconsin, a couple of weeks ago. One of the fish speared had Frankenstein stitches in his belly. The big zigzag stitches held a radio transmitter in. The antenna stuck out a foot. One of the Indians remarked, "Careful boys. This one may be wearing a wire." The fish fuzz wanted their fish back. The Indians didn't want to give it up. After a brief scuffle involving six badges and one Indian, the fish fuzz got their fish back.

There are approximately one hundred and eleven highway signs between the interstate and Sawyer along Highway 210. Do I really need one hundred and eleven pieces of information as I make the seven-mile drive from the truck stop to the Sawyer Mall?

Oh no, Christmas is coming. We now have months and months of Christmas sales, followed by Christmas, then another month of after-Christmas sales. The former religious ceremony has been turned into a vast commercial enterprise. A Sawyer Shinnob was assigned some community service hours at the Sawyer Center. One part of his duties was to put up the Christmas tree. He stood the tree up, replaced the defective bulbs, strung the lights, and made the tree look nice. He finished the job by hanging a rabbit snare from one of the lower branches. As one of the pagans, I'm glad we don't buy into Christmas.

## 2.

# I WILL SNAG NO MORE FOREVER

## 1990

*QUESTION: What is the past tense of snag?*
*ANSWER: Snug.*

Fond du Lac Follies went on the road. We motored to Minny, which is Rez slang for Minneapolis, to see the Rolling Stones. We had ordered the tickets last ricing season and the day had finally arrived. We waded into the crowd. After checking the tickets, we found the right gate. On the way in we saw people who wanted to scalp our tickets. Scalp an Indian's tickets? After finding the right section, we walked into the Hump, aka the Humphrey Metrodome. Thousands of people, ten thousands of people, flowing by like a river. Someone said 60,000 people. I only counted 59,786.

Indians always find each other in a crowd. Sure enough, the first people we recognized were from Fond du Lac. We met and greeted ten other Indians as we walked through the concert crowd. One guy who worked for the Hump pushing garbage cans yelled, "Indians!" when he saw us. He yelled it with pride in his voice. A nod, a smile, or both were exchanged as Indians met each other in the river of people. The concert was over after one encore. We waved good-bye to Mick and the other Stones. I doubt if they saw us. We became the crowd walking out. I quit tapping my foot just north of Hinckley (also known as Hinckles).

We have Irish Americans, Mexican Americans, German Americans, Swedish Americans, Japanese Americans, and so on. What does that make us? American Americans?

We can see all the other Americans on TV. In Sawyer, Minnesota, we get four TV stations. I wonder about the message we are getting from the tube. As a self-confessed TV-holic ("My name is Jim and I'm a TV-holic"), I very rarely see Shinnobs on the tube. I would like to see Shinnobs on the commercials or delivering the news, sports, or weather. It makes us invisible with no Indians on the tube. I think in these days of treaty rights and other important issues, we need more of a regularly scheduled program.

Speaking of weather, the other night I saw an earnest young Chimook say last night was the coldest ever. Does he really think we didn't have weather before the white man came and began keeping records?

Winter and cars, they go together as well as an empty bingo dauber and the final blackout game. The rez is littered with winter-kill cars. Everyone who drives has a dead car story. Just looking at the blood-red transmission fluid on the white snow is chilling. Plastic antifreeze jugs of different colors are accumulating. There is something about thirty below that tests the mettle of the driver and the metal of the car.

While changing a starter the other day, we discovered that a kid's red plastic toboggan makes a good mechanic's creeper. It would be tough sledding in June, but cars never break down in the summer. We can get a lot of use out of it.

Over the years I have learned to carry certain supplies in a winter emergency kit. I need: gas-line antifreeze, radiator antifreeze, jumper cables, battery charger, starting fluid, tow chain, shovel, blanket, ten-pound bag of paddy rice for traction, and a ten-pound box of twenty-dollar bills.

The Berlin Wall came tumbling down. Gorby is now our bestest friend. I'm having a hard time adjusting. It wasn't too long ago that Russia was called the Evil Empire by Ronald Reagan. Sister City projects, cultural exchanges are all the rage. I am waiting to hear the economic reasons for the invasion of Panama and the Berlin Wall collapse. Would a smart guy learn Spanish or Russian? Am I the only one who thinks that Russians look like Chimooks? Now if we could only remove that Berlin Wall of racism that surrounds most reservations.

Fond du Lac Follies went on the road again. We motored to Superior, Wisconsin, to see Sitting Bull's doorknob. It has been several years since we last saw the doorknob and hinges from his cabin. In addition to the door parts, the Fairlawn Museum has a collection of 2,500 pictures. They were taken by David Francis Barry (a guy with three front names). They span the years 1874 to 1890. A lot of them were from the Dakotas.

Someone gave the relics to the photographer. We wanted to see the doorknob and hinges again. They were not to be found. The door parts were no longer on display. They were not in the storage closet.

While prowling around, we found an old prayer book. It was written in Chippewa in 1851. The prayer book also contained two four-leaf clovers, a lock of brown hair, and prayer cards. The seven hundred-page book had a brownish leather binding. It looked old. It was full of old words, old prayers.

FDL Follies went to a PARR meeting. PARR is the acronym of a group that says it wants to Protect America's Rights and Resources. The key word in that statement is America. It was a chance to see, up close, those with necks of red.

We formed a two-car convoy and motored to the meeting. It was held at the Superior Town Hall. As we drove down dark Highway 35, the street lights got farther and farther apart. We found the hall and locked our cars in the dim parking lot.

Inside, Mr. PARR himself, Larry Peterson, was greeting those who were walking in. He seemed like a pastor welcoming the faithful. He went out of his way to be phony friendly to the Chippewa. The room was large and well lit. Folding chairs were arranged with a center aisle of about six feet. PARR newspapers were displayed on a side table. The head table was under the flags of the Rotary Club, the Lions Club, and the United States.

A white man, later introduced as Wayne Powers, was sitting at the head table. When the people coming in sat at the back, like church, Powers said, "C'mon up front. We don't have our white sheets on tonight. Move up front. We don't bite."

Larry Peterson went to the front of the hall to promptly open the meeting. Apparently PARR doesn't run on Indian time. Peterson is a tall, thin white man. He waves his skinny fingers around as he talks. He wore Kmart kind of clothes. Ironically, he also wore a turquoise belt buckle. He seemed at ease, as if preaching to the converted. About fifty people were listening to his words. Some of them were Chippewa. The right-wing types sat on the right side of the center aisle. The Chippewa were on the left.

Larry Peterson filled the hall with propaganda, half truths, and lies. He gave PARR's version of history, PARR's interpretation of federal court orders. He used fear and scare tactics. The center aisle seemed to grow wider as he talked. We laughed in Chippewa at some of his bald-faced lies.

Peterson identified all those who were responsible for the "treaty problem." Among those blamed were the liberal judges of the federal court, the cops with their dogs, the paper mills for sitting back, the media, Senator Inouye, and Governor Thompson.

The Chippewa were blamed for depleting the resources, potential harm to tourism, loss of timber, clouded land titles, and declining property values. The only things we didn't get blamed for were starting the Civil War and running the *Exxon Valdez* aground. Peterson introduced PARR member Wayne Powers. Powers, who earlier talked about white sheets, claims to be one-eighth Cherokee. He said his fight is not with the Chippewa but with the federal government. He does not favor abrogating the treaties, just modifying them to bring them up to modern times. He didn't say how wearing white sheets would help.

The local TV crews arrived and Peterson went out to face the lights and cameras. Apparently the electronic media does run on Indian time. While Peterson was gone, Powers continued shoveling out the propaganda, half truths, and lies. Larry Peterson came back and resumed placing blame for the treaty "problem." He said one part of the "problem" is the person who carries the fake Indian head on a spear at protest rallies. "It's crap. It's bullshit. We will find out if this person is a member of PARR. He represents right-wing idiots," Peterson said. In response to a question on what was a greater threat to the resources, Indians or pollution, Peterson replied, "Treaties are the worst form of pollution."

Peterson concluded the meeting by telling the right half of the hall that PARR needs grassroots volunteers. He asked them to join and buy memberships, T-shirts, jackets, and hats. The right half of the hall got up to sign up. It is assumed that PARR member Wayne Powers will tell them where and when to wear the white sheets.

FDL Follies left the hall. We had seen enough necks of red. We drove the dark highway toward the lights of Duluth-Superior.

*QUESTION: Do you speak your language?*
*ANSWER: Yup, yours too.*

Land . . . Will Rogers, a real one-quarter Cherokee, said something like, "Invest in land. They're not making any more." On the rez, out of the original 100,000 acres, we own or control 22,000 acres. That means we have lost almost four-fifths of our land base since the Treaty of 1854 was signed. Where did it go? An article in the *Cloquet Pine Knot* estimated that the state and county own 20,000 acres, the University of Minnesota has 3,700 acres, and 51,300 acres are owned privately. How did that happen? The Dawes General Allotment Act of 1877 opened the rez up to homesteading.

We suspect fraudulent land deals throughout the years since the treaty days. The only recent addition of land to the rez was a corner of a city block in Duluth where the Fond-du-Luth Casino is. That little corner is rez, I guess.

I don't know why our tribal government hasn't made returning land a priority. It might take two to three hundred years, but wouldn't it be nice? Wouldn't it be worth it for the future generations? Surprise! The Reservation Business Committee is getting some land back from the white man. The RBC has purchased 350 acres of land. It's located northwest of the intersection of Highway 210 and Interstate 35. The purchase price and plans for the property have not been made public. The RBC should be congratulated for getting some of the land back from the white man.

The recent thaw brought out the little boy in two grown-up Sawyer Shinnobs. The melted snow wanted to flow, but couldn't. One of them saw the reason. The river was plugged by a large gray piece of ice. They carved a channel with a splitting maul. The river was opened up and began to flow. Of course they had to race little pretend boats down the river. One Sawyer Shinnob went home with wet feet because he didn't listen to his ma thirty years ago. She told him to put his rubbers on when playing in the water.

Easter? I'm having a hard time understanding that one. I grew up hearing the Christian reason for the holiday. The way it is celebrated now confuses me. Let me see if I got this straight. It all begins with an Easter sale in the retail stores. An unusual rabbit lays and delivers pastel-colored chicken eggs. This waabooz also lays chocolate eggs. The gender of the strange rabbit is never mentioned. Green plastic grass is part of it somewhere.

The kids are teased by hiding the food. They look for and collect the bunny's leavings. Sometimes the pastel-colored chicken eggs are rolled down the White House lawn. Everyone gets new clothes and the ladies get a bonnet to wear in a parade. The doings are concluded with an after-Easter sale in the retail stores. I wish that Easter bunny would come hop-hopping by this rez. I got a snare with his name on it.

FDL Follies went spearing in the ceded territory in Minnesota. We were looking for the wily walleye. We entered the food gathering in a spiritual mood. We smudged and offered tobacco before we left. The Shinnobs wanted to think good thoughts when we were out on the lake. It felt good to be doing what other Anishinaabe have done down through the years.

When we first got to the lake, we woke up the loons because they welcomed us with their songs. It was quiet on the lake. In the distance, we could hear semitrucks and trains. Patchy drifting fog surrounded us as we paddled along. We woke up a total of four blue herons. A kingfisher didn't wake up as we passed by. He was sleeping so good, he should have been snoring. A beaver came swimming up to the light. A muskrat showed us his hind end as he dove in front of the canoe. The frogs croaked their welcome. Bullheads and suckers went by like they knew we were only after walleye.

We saw and speared some walleye. After a few strokes of the paddle, we decided to rename the lake. From now on, in our memories, it will be known as Lake Beer Can. The bottom of the lake was littered with beer cans. There were so many we had trouble seeing the walleye. We decided to pick up the beer cans the next time we go to Lake Beer Can. We'll use the same walleye spears to help clean the lake as we fish. When we came to the end of the evening spearing, the owls welcomed us back with their song. When asked how many walleye we got, we always answer—enough for a Shinnob, not enough for a Chimook.

A couple of weeks later, we went off the rez again to exercise our 1854 treaty rights. The spearing was done without the tribal government knowing about it. When they found out, they called a meeting. At the meeting, tribal government chairman Robert "Sonny" Peacock told us we were going to be thrown to the wolves. He said that Fond du Lac couldn't protect us because of a verbal agreement with the state. We were offered fish by the Minnesota Department of Natural Resources to give up our existing treaty rights to go off the rez to spear. If FDL wouldn't accept almost $2 million for treaty rights, why did they think a few fish would do it? Fish that already belonged to FDL.

Another meeting produced a permit to gather food for a ceremony. Permit #001 was issued by the RBC. The first night of permit spearing was uneventful unless you count the twelve gunshots we heard. The game wardens didn't hear the shots. They thought the muzzle flashes were from someone with a flashlight. The second night of permit spearing was more interesting. There were about fifteen protesters, one of them masked, at the boat landing. They were counterbalanced by fifteen trained witnesses. About fifteen law-enforcement officers watched the two groups. The lights of a

TV crew added to the confusion. Two canoes with a total of six Shinnobs went out on the lake. The canoe with the permit was ordered
back to shore because there were three people in the canoe. The permitless canoe was brought back to the landing by the game wardens. Two FDL residents from different bands in Minnesota were
cited and had to go to state court. The skin from FDL was sent to
tribal court. The Indians who were cited by the state had their gear
confiscated and got a free boat ride back to the landing.

Those of us with the permit continued to look for fish. We didn't
see anything worth eating and wondered who picked this lake for
spearing. We only saw beer cans on the bottom of the lake. Someone had also left a huge wooden door floating in the lake. After the
arrest of the permitless FDL residents, permit #001 was revoked.
Chairman Peacock said the ceremony was turning into a circus. It
was felt that the chairman knew more about circuses than ceremonies. We continued looking for fish in the ceded territory.

A couple of days later, the RBC decided to allow spearing for any
members of a band that signed the 1837, 1842, and 1854 treaties.
This permission included those Indians who reside in Michigan and
Wisconsin. After checking with legal counsel, the RBC decided they
couldn't give that kind of blanket permission. The RBC could only
protect those from FDL. Permits were no longer needed. We only
had to let the game wardens know which lake in the ceded territory
was going to be used. FDL spearers continued looking for fish until
Governor Perpich and other Minnesota citizens opened the regular
state fishing season.

In this exercise of treaty rights, the news media seemed to want
a confrontational story. They chose to ignore the greater story of
pollution in the lakes. The elders from Sawyer received a walleye
dinner donated by the spearers. The fish came from the ceded territory. FDL spearers would like to thank the Creator for the fish; the
game wardens, deputies, and rescue squad for protection; the witnesses for their time and courage; the protesters for their simple-
minded opposition; and all Indians who supported the spearers' actions. The spearers would like to especially thank the RBC for their
firm "no, yes, no, yes, maybe" decision to allow spearing off the rez.

Fond du Lac Follies traveled to Lame Deer, Montana. We went to the Ninth Annual Vietnam-Era Veterans Inter-Tribal Association Powwow. The event was hosted by the Morning Star chapter led by Windy Shoulderblade. We motored to Montana in our 1967 Buick. The big blue car was originally a rez car, but has survived to become a classic, almost a collector's item.

A USMC Vietnam vet was the navigator on the 861-mile trip to Lame Deer. His directions were precise and flawless: "Get on 94, hang a left just past Forsyth, Montana." To do that we had to go through North Dakota. Along the way we passed through the North Dakota state forest. We saw both trees. In Jamestown, we saw the world's largest buffalo. Somewhere along the interstate was the world's largest Holstein cow. We wondered who had to clean up after those huge critters. There were the usual summertime construction zones with the orange-clad workers. We saw an airplane spraying the crops. Other than that, there wasn't too much to see in North Dakota.

After we hung a left just past Forsyth, Montana, we got to the powwow grounds in Lame Deer. Everyone was still sleeping, so we took a side trip to Custer Battlefield National Monument. It was a forty-mile ride through the Rosebud Mountains. It cost three bucks to get the big blue Buick through the gates of the Custer battlefield. "Cheap at twice the price," came the comment from the back seat.

We parked next to a tourist driving a Winnebago camper. He was pulling a Dakota truck behind the RV . . . the site of the Sioux and Cheyenne's best-known battle is visited by Winnebagos with Dakotas. We toured the museum, took pictures, and generally basked in reflected glory. We honored the Sioux and Cheyenne warriors who fought here. At one point I wanted to yell, "Way to go, Indians!" Yelling would have disturbed the somber-looking tourists. The RV drivers were walking around like they were in church. Most of their faces were set in a half frown. They were talking quietly among themselves. Meanwhile the Minnesota Indians were enjoying the battlefield tour. The Vietnam combat vets studied the terrain. It looked like a classic double envelopment was pulled on Custer. Chief Gall led one side and Chief Crazy Horse led the other.

The U.S. army troopers were buried where they fell. The white stone markers were scattered in the rolling hills. "Look, two more got it over there," said a Chippewa. While touring the battlefield, I remembered that old joke about Custer being well dressed for the occasion. He was wearing an Arrow shirt. Inside the museum was a huge steel plate. It was a memorial for the Indian warriors who fought at this battlefield. According to the placard, the memorial was erected by Indian activists.

We left the dead at the battlefield and joined the living at the pow-wow. We picked sage on the way back. We got there just in time for the parade down the main drag of Lame Deer. The Cheyenne people lined the street in the drizzling rain. A little rain didn't stop them from honoring their veterans. Camouflage jackets and ribbon shirts marched together in the parade. American and tribal flags were carried by the veterans. There were a couple of Marine Corps flags. Somehow the big blue Buick brought up the rear of the parade.

At the end of the parade the marchers mingled around until some-one said, "Let's get out of this rain." After the rain ended, the danc-ing began at the Kenneth Beartusk Memorial Powwow Grounds. It was a good celebration. There were honoring ceremonies and give-aways all afternoon. There were almost thirteen straight hours of honoring veterans. There was a horseshoe tournament. Fond du Lac Follies placed a distant fourth. The eating, singing, and dancing continued long past dark in the mountains of the Cheyenne.

We felt good and bad as we left. Good because of the way we were honored as veterans. Bad because we had to drive through North Dakota again to get home. Good because we had the big blue Buick to drive. Bad because we have a whole year to wait for the next vet-erans' powwow, in Colville, Washington.

Bingo is the only business that consistently makes money for FDL. Except that golden goose was cut in half. We are in the bingo busi-ness with the City of Duluth at Fond-du-Luth Casino in downtown Duluth. Any money that Fond-du-Luth makes is snagged up in the parking-ramp dispute. I hear of other reservations in Minnesota that are paying their tribal members a monthly sum. We started the first bingo game in the state and have yet to see a dime of the money. The RBC does pay for some programs with bingo money, but the bulk of it goes to the god called economic development. I still think we are in the money-laundering business.

The annual Honor the Earth powwow was just good. FDL Follies motored to the doings in the old Buick. My cousin calls it a grampa Buick. The LCO (Lac Courte Oreilles) rez and people always make you feel welcome. Hayward was plumb full of tourists, but we caught the feeling of the powwow long before we got there. The names of the drum groups were talked about, the lead singers were identified. We knew what we were going to see and hear.

There were blue tarps everywhere. Some of the blue tarps covered the food stands, others covered turquoise ring and earring stands. We found two boxes of pull-tabs. We stopped and ate at the Long Fox food stand. After that meal, we didn't try any others. No need to, we got lucky and found good food right away. We walked around and said, "Hi, how are you, hi, how are you" a couple hundred times. We carried our powwow chairs. We smiled at a lot of familiar faces. We told lies and stories. We laughed as we listened to lies and stories. The sun was shining and the breeze was making it comfortable. During some of the dances we didn't know whether to look at faces or feet. The sound of the drums and singers recharged our Indian batteries.

The '67 Buick made the trip easily. The only problem was a tire that committed suicide. A fender brace came loose and rubbed the rubber until it got to the air inside. There are not many thrills like changing a tire on a narrow, slope-shouldered, high-speed highway filled with tourists.

A retrospective of artist George Morrison's work, called Standing in the Northern Lights, will be shown at the Tweed Museum of Art at the University of Minnesota, Duluth. The exhibition spans forty-four years of the artist's career. George Morrison is one of the living treasures of the Ojibwe. When I went to the show, I was most interested in George Morrison the artist meeting his fans, his public. His black hair was mostly gray and thinning. His speech sounded Ojibwe. George's strong hands were adorned with turquoise rings.

He put people at ease when they came up to shake his hand or ask for an autograph. I listened as he explained how he works. He said he first establishes the idea of what he wants to create in his head. He then plays it by ear until he gets it right.

There was a circle of people waiting to talk to George Morrison. It was a mix of art students and art patrons. He introduced old friends to new friends. George put them in a mood to visit with each other. I learned more about George Morrison the elder than I did about George Morrison the artist.

During the Grand Portage powwow, the Russian flag was flying over the Grand Portage Lodge. It was right up there with the American and Canadian flags. After forty years of the Cold War we were curious. Fond du Lac Follies met the Russians. There were Russian vets of the Afghan war traveling with Vietnam vets. We got there in time to join the banquet at the lodge. Everyone else was on the dessert course, but after some fancy knife and fork work, we caught up. We all went to the powwow grounds to be honored by the dancers and spectators. The Russians danced one round and split up to watch the doings. We found one thing we had in common with the Russians. We both understood the turtle reflex. That is the involuntary act of trying to pull your head down into your chest cavity when a loud noise is heard.

The Russians had read about Indians but had never met any. They were curious about the dancing, the outfits, and the language. There were more questions asked about Indians than Vietnam vets. The Russian vets and American vets asked questions about each other's war. War stories were told in many languages. There was a bond forged among the vets. Bullets and shrapnel are the same regardless of the ideological cause or location of the war. We learned that Russian vets were treated the same as Vietnam vets when they returned from their two-year tour of duty. Through an interpreter, we traded fry bread for postcards. We traded American money for Russian money. The Russians said they will tell their people about the skins they met at Grand Portage.

FOR SALE: One Russian Ruble—make me an offer, comrade.

The Mashkawisen powwow brought 2,500 Indians together. It was a good dance with one problem. After the dance was over it looked like several garbage trucks had exploded. The trash on the ground was sickening. What are we teaching our children? Is it okay to throw garbage on the ground if it's at a powwow? Plastic plates, pop cups, envelopes used to pay the dancers, broken powwow chairs, plastic silverware, cigarette packs, tent boxes, broken tent pegs, flyers for the next powwow, and food were lying on the ground. There was a garbage fire still smoldering by the sweat lodge. Respect for Mother Earth, what a joke. We talk the talk but don't walk the walk. The trail of litter continued down Mission Road, a reminder of the 2,500 Indians that gathered to celebrate. The staff at Mash tried to keep up with the avalanche of garbage but were unable to pick the garbage up fast enough. We must pick up after ourselves. We can't expect others to clean our mess. We must show respect.

Fond du Lac Follies went to the rez bingo hall to hear four white guys talk about their future plans for the rez. It seemed kind of fitting to meet in the bingo hall, the place of so many big gambles and failed dreams. Big doings. A new bingo hall, a thirty-six-bed motel, a 150-seat restaurant, a cultural center, arts and crafts, a museum and education center, a gas station and convenience store, nature trails, cross-country ski trails, an amphitheater, and individually owned shops are all on the drawing boards.

It gets scary when the planners drip millions of dollars from their lips when explaining the project. The overall cost will be $8 to $10 million. They have started the project with a $200,000 state Community Development Block Grant. Out of the 320 acres involved, about fifty will be used for commercial development. The rest is called wetlands, what we used to call swamps. Otter Creek, a trout stream, bisects the property.

My head was reeling after listening to the white guys talk about their plans for our rez—reeling like I had ten "outs" on a big-money blackout game. I left the bingo hall with hopes that their plans would work, but I have seen so many sins committed in the name of economic development in the past. I guess we will wait and see.

*QUESTION: How did Shinnobs survive the Great Depression?*
*ANSWER: I didn't know it was over.*

I can see the yellow and red of the maple trees. The leaves of the maple always let me know that winter is coming. As the price of heating oil goes up, more and more maple trees are coming down. As my friend the firewood merchant told me, "We cut 'em down then cut 'em up." The cutting of maple trees for firewood is shortsighted. We need the trees for the sap. As sugar producers, we can use the trees year after year. As fuel, we only use them once.

The Protect the Earth Festival in Hayward was well organized, well attended. People who were concerned about the environment showed up to talk, eat, talk, camp, and talk. The talking circles were productive and added to the doings. Women's issues, the air, the water, mining, hazardous wastes, and treaty rights were discussed in the circles.

John Trudell and Floyd Westerman were the headliners for the entertainment. After listening to Trudell's powerful words, I couldn't stop talking like this, like this, like this. Walt Bressette was the emcee who kept things rolling along, rolling along. Floyd Westerman sang some of his songs. My personal favorite was "Custer Died for Your Sins." After Floyd sang we talked with him while he ate fry bread from the Northsky food stand. While the melted butter ran down his arm, we talked about his movie career. He said he has eight movies to his credit and is working on more. Wouldn't it be great to see Floyd in a tux at the Academy Award doings?

The AIM powwow was Floyd's previous stop before Hayward. He was on his way to Grand Portage. We later learned that Floyd Westerman was in boarding school with some people from Sawyer. The gathering area was clean. The earth was protected at LCO.

Ricing was not so pretty good this year. We got enough for the year, but it was a lot of work. Of course if it was easy then everyone would be doing it. Whenever we're asked how much rice we have, we always answer, "Enough for a Shinnob, not enough for a Chimook."

I remember the good old days of ricing. Then there was a forty-boat limit on Perch Lake. The rice was tall and green all the way across the lake. There was only a room-sized patch of open water near the landing. Today there is mostly open water on Perch Lake. The moose-ear plants have taken over the lake. We still don't have a recipe for cooking moose-ear plants. We have game wardens, rice committees, natural-resource managers, conservation committees, and tribal government. It seems like the more people we pay to watch the rice, the worse it gets. Allowing motorboats in the rice beds isn't a good idea. Would you rather have butter or motor oil on your wild rice?

The rice we did get parched good. Since we parch the same day it comes off the lake, it stays green. I think the wood smoke mixes with the rice in the cast-iron kettle. The smell of the parching rice was familiar. It reminded me of my youth when that smell was all over town. We ate rice all day while we worked on our share of the Creator's gift. We danced on the rice and fanned it. We spent a lot of time cleaning rice. I know it would be easier processing the rice in machines, but I don't think it would look or taste the same.

The other day there were six canoes out on Perch Lake. Three of the canoes had white people ricing. They were from the natural resources class on the rez. The game wardens, the rice committee, and the Reservation Business Committee didn't know they were out there. It is hard enough finding rice without competing with white people. Whose lake is it, anyway? I'm all in favor of learning, but I think they should learn on the state lakes and rivers. Those are open to anyone.

QUESTION: *How could you tell she was a tradish' Shinnob?*
ANSWER: *Her perfume was called Eau de Parched Rice.*

The Minnesota Vietnam Veterans Memorial groundbreaking ceremony was held on Saturday, 22 September 1990, at 1200 hours. The design was chosen from among hundreds submitted. It is a silhouette of the state of Minnesota. The names of the fallen warriors will be etched in the walls. Lake Superior is a part of the design. Construction is expected to begin next spring. Governor Perpich promised to send letters to help raise the funds. I hope it was more than a campaign promise. I and some other veterans of that war would like to say, "It's about #@&*(+%@!\| = time."

Then on a national scale, Fond du Lac Follies jetted to Washington, DC, for the Veterans Day ceremonies and the Marine Corps birthday. On the flight we noticed a screw was loose on top of the wing. We knew it was loose because we had memorized all of the screws and their locations before we took off. We watched the screw for a couple hundred miles. It didn't seem to be coming out any further. We informed the flight attendant. She didn't seem too concerned. Other passengers who heard us tell the flight attendant about the loose screw helped watch for the rest of the flight. There were even some people on the other side of the aisle who helped watch our wing. The flight attendant wasn't looking for a screwdriver, so we just watched until the plane landed in Cleveland. We knew it was our combined willpower that held the wing together. The connecting flight was uneventful.

On November 10, the Marine Corps' birthday, we set up camp in a motel and went out to eat. We found Blackies. We ate prime rib that was thisssssss big. We rubbed shoulders, knees, and hips with others who like eating at Blackies. There might have been some famous people in there, but we didn't notice. After eating, we went to the Wall, the Vietnam Veterans Memorial. There we talked with the living vets and honored the fallen. There was a lot of camaraderie among the proud, getting old, Vietnam vets. The reflecting pool in front of the Lincoln Memorial was half full of grenade pins by the time we were done telling war stories. We exchanged birthday greetings with other marines.

After honoring the warriors, living and dead, we went to the Smithsonian. We walked through like we were late for a bingo game. One display that turned us off was the Columbus exhibit. There was a map that showed where Chris what's-his-name landed. With the map was an Indian's skull. We saw that and left. As we taxied around, we could see most places had jailhouse bars over the windows and doors. After hearing about the three to twelve people murdered every night, we knew why the citizens put themselves in jail.

The next day, Veterans Day, we saw the Northern Cheyenne warriors at the Wall during the ceremonies. The honor guard all wore eagle feathers. There were Shinnobs from Mille Lacs, Red Lake, Leech Lake, and Fond du Lac at the doings. On the last day in town we visited Arlington Cemetery. We saw the graves of the Kennedy brothers. In contrast to the elaborate eternal-flame tomb for John, Robert's was marked by a simple white cross. The Grandfather Plaque was still intact. The tree planted during the dedication was growing well. Its trunk was as big as a baseball bat. The Grandfather Plaque honors all Native American warriors. We watched the twenty-one measured steps of the soldier guarding the Tomb of the Unknown Soldier. In the building near the Tomb we saw a coup stick and war bonnet from Chief Plenty Coups of the Crow tribe. One cynical vet said he saw the parents of the Unknown Soldier outside. We all rushed out to look before we realized what he had said.

On the way to National Airport, we crossed the bridge that was the scene of a plane crash. The middle span was a different color than the rest of it. We didn't get a chance to check and count the screws in the wing on the way home. It was dark so we just held our breath during the flight back to Minnesota.

> QUESTION: How does the Declaration
> of Independence describe Indians?
> ANSWER: "... the merciless Indian Savages,
> whose known rule of warfare, is an undistinguished
> destruction of all ages, sexes, and conditions."*

---

*This aggressive phrase appears in the U.S. Declaration of Independence as adopted by the Second Continental Congress on July 4, 1776. It is part of a litany of grievances against "the present King of Great Britain." He is accused of having engaged in what would today be labeled acts of terrorism. The full quote is: "He has excited domestic insurrections amongst us, and has endeavored to bring on the inhabitants of our frontiers, the merciless Indian Savages, whose known rule of warfare, is an undistinguished destruction of all ages, sexes and conditions."

# 3.
# American Americans

## 1991

It was tribal court time on the Fond du Lac Reservation. Before the wheels of justice began to turn, the Shinnobs smoked red willow. Anishinaabe Judge Dee Fairbanks came in. She seemed upset about the smell. The first order of business was to outlaw smoking in the courtroom a half hour before she arrived because of her asthmatic condition. She told one Shinnob to put out her cigarette. The Shinnob showed the judge the pen she was holding.

A Fonjalacker named Napoleon Ross was in court. He was charged with snagging (not that kind of snagging) a salmon from the Lester River in the ceded territory. Fond du Lac was not in an agreement with the state about treaty rights at the time of the snagging. Nappy said he never received notice of a court date. He had been found guilty when he didn't show up for tribal court the first time. Nappy said he had been out of state attending a ceremony. He was fined seventy-five dollars for the snagged salmon.

In this latest hearing he was ordered to show cause why he didn't pay the fine. Nappy explained his reasons. He thought he shouldn't have been found guilty for exercising his treaty rights. The judge listened to his reasons and ruled against him. His hunting, fishing, and gathering rights were taken away. Until the fine is paid, Nappy can't legally gather medicine from the woods.

The prosecution was handled by the rez lawyers, Henry Buffalo and his new sidekick Dennis Peterson. We wonder if justice was served in this case. We know there is no appeal process from tribal court. Are the wheels of justice attached to a locomotive?

Sitting Bull's doorknob and hinges are still missing. The Fairlawn Museum in Superior was recently given two dance shields recovered by the FBI in St. Louis, Missouri. The artifacts were stolen in 1978, and the museum received $30,500 from the insurance company for their loss. The museum spent their money on repairing the roof and buying more David Francis Barry pictures. Other items missing from the museum's collection include Sitting Bull's rifle and war shield, a Lakota ceremonial dress, and other war clubs. The doorknob and hinges are still missing.

Harold Gronquist, president of the historical society, said that security has been increased since the theft. He also said, "They're back where they belong." Ownership of the two dance shields passed to the insurance company when they were recovered. The insurance company donated them back to the Fairlawn Museum. No one thought to ask the Lakota people if they would be interested in getting the dance shields back. We are still wondering what happened to the missing doorknob and hinges.

I have been trying to avoid writing about the war but that has proved to be impossible. Here are some rambling, disconnected war thoughts. I speak as a Vietnam veteran, an Anishinaabe, and a father. Honor the warriors but not the war makers. A very difficult concept. How can we support the troops without letting George Bush (president number forty-one) do anything he wants with them? We have sent our best and brightest to the Gulf. Now that the ground war has started, how many will we get back undamaged in body or mind? Only time will tell if the sacrifice will be worth it.

*Gulf Oil.*

The start of the war was big news last month. It was on all the stations for three whole days. They didn't even break for commercials. After three days the regular programming came back on. It started with the soap operas. I wondered about that, then the titles of soaps jumped out at me.

ALL MY CHILDREN *have but* ONE LIFE TO LIVE.
*We know they need a strong* GUIDING LIGHT *in these*
DAYS OF OUR LIVES.

But *AS THE WORLD TURNS, we don't want them to end
up in a GENERAL HOSPITAL in SANTA BARBARA or
anywhere else.
We know they are THE YOUNG AND RESTLESS
and the BOLD AND BEAUTIFUL,
but we pray they come home safe and soon.*

I feel like we have been stroked into this war by the media. It has been interesting to see how the war has been portrayed. At first we were just there to defend Saudi Arabia. The goals have shifted. We are now liberating Kuwait. We are also going to remove Saddam as a military influence in the region. I am waiting to hear our next goals. It's been said many times, but I will say it again. The first casualty in war is truth.

I dislike being manipulated into war. Where is that buffoon Willard Scott? I remember seeing him on the tube giving the weather report from the Gulf. He was wearing desert cammies and carrying an M-16 rifle. No one bothered to tell him he was carrying the rifle backward. Where is he and his cammies and rifle now that the shooting has started? Maybe it was just a media ploy to get us used to seeing desert cammies. I wondered what he was going to do with that rifle. Was he going to shoot someone from the National Weather Service or another network? Maybe he should stick to honoring the elders instead of trying to whip up patriotic fever.

Let's get rid of those silly yellow ribbons. If we want to show support for the troops, there are better ways. Donate food for the hungry, send money to help the homeless, visit an elder, teach someone to read, be a volunteer driver, donate blood, or something besides those yellow ribbons that don't really mean anything.

A couple of other Vietnam vets and I were talking. First, we decided that no one can hate war as much as someone who has been in one. While talking we discussed ways to end the war. One idea was to ban all sports until the hostilities cease. Think about it. If your kid can't play hockey until the shooting stops, it would help make us aware that there is a war. If Michael Jordan is earthbound for the duration, we would be making a sacrifice for the war. No NFL,

NHL, or spring training until people quit dying in the desert. Would Americans be willing to make that much of a sacrifice?

Since it is man's nature to make war, we also thought maybe no wars should be allowed until all the veterans from the last one have died of old age. That would give us a few more years of peace instead of the way we do it now.

QUESTION: *Why do we still need to ask questions*
*after three hundred years of living together?*
ANSWER: *Slow learners.*

I read in the local newspaper that Judge Barbara Crabb reversed herself in the Chippewa treaty case. In attempting to understand her convoluted legal reasoning, I can only think Mitch Walking Elk was right in one of his songs when he sang, "when they want what we got, they just change the laws." Judge Crabb said that Indians were not logging in treaty times, so they shouldn't be allowed to log today. In other words, use it or lose it. If we continue that reasoning, I'd like to remind her that Indians were not paying taxes, were not breathing bad air, were not drinking contaminated water, and were not eating fish that had enough mercury to be a thermometer. Okay, keep the timber. You were going to anyway. As we hear more about the drought in California, I wonder if Lake Superior will be next.

Fond du Lac Follies motored to Denver for the annual get-together of the Native American Journalists Association. We drove through a spring snowstorm to get there. The snow was heavy at times. The first to go were the white lines on the highway. We could see the semitrucks herding up at the truck stops. The ones that didn't were in the ditches waiting for the wreckers so they could finish their trips. At one point, somewhere in Iowa, we went sideways. All those hours spent playing on the frozen lakes of Minnesota came in handy. We were able to pull out of the slide and continue our trip. My wife relaxed her death grip on the dashboard fifty miles later.

We were not very good tourists. We didn't stop for any of the many museums. We only stopped for coffee, for gasoline, and to drain the coffee. Other than the fifty feet in front of the headlights, we didn't see much of Iowa, Nebraska, and Colorado. Then we saw a bank of clouds on the horizon. Under the clouds we could make out the Rocky Mountains.

While we were out there we went to the Seventeenth Annual Denver Powwow. It was said that there were fifty-six drums there. It reminded me of the time I asked my grampa if he was going to the powwow at one of the local colleges. He asked how many drums. I answered sixteen or seventeen. After thinking about it for a while, he told me they only need one.

The Denver Coliseum was lined with wall-to-wall trader's booths. There were enough jingle dresses there to build a B-52 bomber. The networking at the doings was worth the hazards of the spring storm.

Fonjalackers who are found in contempt of tribal court can now be incarcerated. A resolution passed by the Reservation Business Committee now provides for a ten-day jail sentence. Those convicted of contempt will spend ten days in the Nett Lake cooler. Why are we so willing to punish ourselves? Isn't the white man doing a good enough job locking up Indians? Instead of finding out why Indians are incarcerated in larger numbers than the general population, we have a new way to lock up Indians. I wonder if the state patted the RBC on the head and called them good boys for agreeing to lock up Indians.

What would reservation legal do if they were hit with a writ from federal court about incarcerating Indians? We are watching to see who goes to jail first for this new crime. What's next? Jail time for those found guilty of aggravated buffoonery with intent to mope?

The rez bingo hall now has coin slot machines just like Las Vegas. We were in there the other night feeding quarters so we could hear the *boing, boing* sound of the machine. Just for old times' sake we pulled the arm of the one-armed bandit. Seeing all the money going in makes me wonder where it comes OUT. What do they do with the profits from Big Bucks Bingo and Fond-du-Luth? Some smaller reservations are paying their members thousands a month from their casino and bingo operations. We just know that there is a profit but we don't know where it goes. Election time is not too far off. Maybe we'll get more answers then.

Check out the April 24, 1991, issue of the Minneapolis alternative newspaper *City Pages.* The front page has a picture of a person giving a clenched-fist salute. His hat reads "Save a walleye—spear a Indian," He should have been run through school before he went out to the landings. Say it right fella, it's "Spear an Indian."

> *QUESTION: What was the state motto of Minnesota when it was a territory?*
> *ANSWER:* Civilitas successit barbarum.
> *(Civilization has replaced the barbarian.)*

FDL Follies went to tribal court to watch the doings. It was a regularly scheduled session of the court. We wanted to know what would happen to Nappy Ross and Charles Nahganub. They were charged with possessing a spear and spearing a fish. They were charged with violating a code that was voted down twice by the Fond du Lac people. The first thing we noticed when we walked in was a poster that listed the rules of decorum for the court. The rules said no tape players or video equipment, no gum chewing, no drinking, no eating, no ceremonial smudging, no smoking, no smoking a half hour before court commences. The poster further warned that violating these rules could result in a charge of contempt of court.

The former Knife Falls Township office building now houses the court and the game wardens. The green block building was nice on the inside. It had light brown paneling and carpet. There was an American flag, but no reservation flag. The walls were decorated with stuffed animals and wildlife pictures. In addition to the defendants, thirty-five people came to watch the proceedings. Three game wardens lined up along the south wall.

Judge Dee Fairbanks walked in chewing gum. She had to step over the spectators to get to the bench. The bench was actually a bingo-hall kind of table. She faced Dennis Peterson, the rez lawyer who was prosecuting the cases. Wes Martins of Indian Legal Assistance sat next to Peterson. These two wore the only neckties in the place. A spectator named Val Ross asked the judge to spit out her gum. The judge bristled and asked Ross if she wanted to leave the room. Ross said no. Judge Fairbanks said she didn't know about the rule concerning gum chewing.

The ceded territory cases came next. There were only two of them. Wes Martins represented the two charged with spearing and possessing a spear. Nappy Ross and Charlie Nahganub pled not guilty. Ross said he will be out of town in June and July. The witness against the two will be out of town in August. The hearing is scheduled for September. Martins asked for a preliminary hearing and the possibility of a jury trial. He also said he will be filing motions in regards to jurisdiction and probable cause. The judge granted the continuance and the session was over. Friends and relative gathered outside to talk with and show support for the two spearers.

> The more corrupt the state, the more numerous the laws.
> Tacitus *Annals* 3.27

Through a friend of a friend of a friend, Fond du Lac Follies was able to obtain tickets for the George Carlin performance in Duluth. We have been fans of Carlin since he first came out as a comedian. His irreverent humor has always chuckled us. In the lobby of the Duluth Entertainment Convention Center we looked at the various items for sale. In addition to the booze, coffee, and soda pop there were T-shirts, a poster, and a book. The T-shirts had Carlin's pictures and words. One said, "When the going gets tough, the tough get f****d." Another T-shirt said, "Sometimes a little brain damage helps." The book cost five dollars and was titled *An Incomplete List of Impolite Words: 2,443 Filthy Words and Phrases.* It was compiled by George Carlin.

We went backstage to meet the performer. Carlin is friendly and gracious. He looks larger than he does on TV, maybe because our set only measures nineteen inches. Carlin was dressed in a loose black shirt and white pants. He wore gold: a necklace, a bracelet, and a thick ring. His gray hair was combed back and worn in a little ponytail. A slim black watch completed his outfit. Carlin is a master storyteller. While reminiscing with friends, he told a hilarious story of getting arrested in Chicago. Herb O'Brien, Lenny Bruce, and Carlin all went to jail because an underage girl was found in the audience. He talked fondly about his wife Brenda and daughter Kelly. He praised his wife for sticking with him all these years.

During the mostly one-sided conversation backstage, Carlin talked about his troubles with the IRS. Because of poor management, he once owed $3 million. He had to earn $6 million to pay them off. With the money he has since earned, he was able to buy a recording studio. The main reason for buying the studio was to recover his audio and video masters. He now owns all of his old material.

George Carlin describes his politics as somewhere between the Van Allen radiation belt and blowing up power lines. He doesn't vote — voting just encourages the politicians. George Carlin thinks Indians should be identified by their tribal names instead of the generic "Native American." This Anishinaabe agreed with him. He did think the FDL Follies term American Americans was acceptable.

In his nearly two-hour monologue Carlin joked about golf, the Gulf War, God, the media, baseball, football, dogs and cats, George Bush, airlines, and the homeless. He didn't call them homeless; he called them houseless. He suggests building housing on all the golf courses. Carlin tells jokes at the rate of twenty-five a minute with gusts up to forty. He physically acts out part of them. When joking about dogs, he wags his tail.

George Carlin is one of the few comedians who can make this observer laugh out loud. My cousin is another one. Both Carlin and my cousin say things most people just dare to think about. The audience reaction should convince Carlin to come back to Dull-tooth again. As we were leaving, we repeated some of his routines and laughed and laughed again.

Fond du Lac Follies was invited to an open house held by Senator Paul Wellstone. The open house, which looked more like an open office, was held at his Twin Cities digs on University Avenue. All visitors had to sign in and list their addresses. A name tag was issued, apparently so the senator would know who he was meeting. For just a moment we considered using the name George Bush but chickened out. A line formed and people chatted as they waited to meet their newest leader. Sheila Wellstone greeted the people before they got to the senator. She was charming, smiled a lot, and seemed to enjoy her role as the senator's wife and hostess. Senator Wellstone had a firm handshake and looked directly in the eyes of the citizens who filed past. He was warm and friendly as we spent our thirty seconds together. He was dressed in a conservative "going to Washington" suit.

Indians outnumbered any other minority group that came to meet the senator. The Indians and the senator's staff had a meeting after the open house. Chuck Robertson Jr. was the staff person soliciting opinions on some pending federal legislation. It was good to see an Indian on the senator's staff. Now let us see how he acts and what he does. The last we saw of the senator was when he was leaving with some other "going to Washington" suit-clad men. He was not riding in the famous green bus.

*QUESTION: Does it hurt the tree when you remove the birch bark?*
*ANSWER: No, but do you live in a wood house or read a newspaper?*

FDL Follies motored to Winnipeg in Manitoba, Canada, for the powwow ($11.50 admission) and an environmental meeting. The gathering was held at the Forks. We demonstrated birchbark-basket making at the doings. Others were demonstrating quill work, flute making, star quilts, and birchbark biting. It didn't take long for us to learn how to speak Canadian. Right away we noticed that we were ending every statement with a question, ay? Over six bucks for a pack of smokes, ay? The radio said that four of the six was for taxes, ay? Now it became clear why a lot of folks were rolling their own, ay?

Driving in Winnipeg was a little different than driving in Sawyer, Minnesota. The drivers have passed beyond assertive and drive aggressively. Every street was a speedway, every driver was in a race. We finally got to use the kilometer dial on the speedometer of our car. Gas was forty-seven cents a liter.

When we came back to the United States, we had to go through U.S. Customs. What a frightening experience. The guys with the guns ran our Fond du Lac plate through the computer, then invited us in for a search. The first thing we saw when we walked in was a large picture of George Bush. There were at least fifteen guys with guns milling around the office. It reminded me that this was the same outfit that just bombed the hell out of Iraq. It was intimidating. We knew we didn't do anything illegal or weren't trying to evade customs, but just being around those guys with guns was scary. What if one of them was having a bad day?

They didn't do a full body-cavity search. They just settled for looking in my pockets, moccasins, and wallet. My wife, Patricia, had to dump her purse. They looked at everything. One guy even looked down the length of a McDonald's coffee stirrer. They were very thorough. They didn't find anything wrong with us or the car, so they let us go. As we were leaving, they wished us a happy trip. We were just happy to get out of there, away from the guns.

Once we got far enough down the road, I started thinking about the experience. We should have had such a system in place when the white guys first got here. Chris Columbus would have had to declare that he was not carrying any drugs, weapons, or weird diseases. Every other white man would have had to do the same thing. It sure would be a different country if we had invented customs.

FDL Follies motored to Red Cliff for their annual summer powwow. It was a small gathering compared to the contest powwows in the area. The size didn't take away from the magic of the gathering of Indian people. It felt right to be there. The drum sounds synchronized everyone's heartbeat. The pride of the dancers was evident. The singers were good if one measures the number of tape recorders surrounding them. The taste of fry bread brought back many pleasant memories. It felt good to greet old friends and shake hands.

Walt Bressette and Eddie Benton handled the microphone chores. Both of them told jokes old and new to keep the crowd in a good mood. Eddie Benton has a new book out called *Generations to Generations.* The rain from the previous two weeks soaked the red clay of the dance arena. It made the ground user friendly. Kind of like dancing on a water bed, one dancer told me. At one point, Walt Bressette was going to raffle off the cars that were blocking traffic.

The Red Cliff people had a feast where they fed the people who came to visit. The powwow was dedicated to the memory of Victoria Gokee. The giveaway was the largest I have seen in quite a while. The part I liked was the gift of quarts of oil for those who were driving rez cars. Walt Bressette was calling for all mud wrestlers to gather at the speakers stand just before the rain started again. The drums, dancers, and singers moved into a nearby building for the rest of the dance. The crowd, including a busload of tourists from Denmark, followed.

Walt explained that researchers are running into a little problem in the development of Fry Bread Lite™. It seems one of them used a bag of commodity flour in the mix. The high protein content of the worms threw everything off. He said they will have to start from scratch again. Watch for it next year. As we were leaving, I suggested a name change to Walt. They could call their reservation Red Clay instead of Red Cliff. His laughter followed us down the highway.

> QUESTION: *What is the new Ojibwemowin word for bingo?*
> ANSWER: *Jer ma win? (Did your mother win?)*

Missing since July 17, 1991: approximately 3,000 FDL band enrollment cards. The three-by-five-inch white cards were last seen in RBC man George Dupis's office. The cards list every Fonjalacker and their current address, date of birth, and blood quantum. Finder, please return to any Reservation Business Committee candidate.

The rez conservation commission reports that Fonjalackers will be allowed to take five deer for each hunter. There is also going to be a moose season even though Minnesota will not have one. There might just be some advantages to being an Indian. Now we are glad we voted the 1854 treaty sale down twice.

The Russians and the Americans are talking about signing START (Strategic Arms Reduction Treaty). If history teaches us anything, I would begin to get worried if I were Russian.

*QUESTION: How could you tell they liked to play bingo?*
*ANSWER: Their dog was named Dauber, their kids were called*
*Early Bird, Postage Stamp, Four Corners, and Blackout.*

More sins have been committed in the name of economic development than Christianity on this rez. I've been hearing that same song sung for quite a few years on Fond du Lac. Economic development— Tra la la la, la la la la. Is economic development another name for what used to be called a slush fund? All of our failed businesses were started and ended with economic development. Economic development is fast becoming a swear word on this reservation. For example, "You dirty no-good economic developer." It isn't just the current administration. We've been getting hit over the head for the past twenty years. The sales tax that all rez residents pay to the state is sent back to the Reservation Business Committee and it disappears into economic development. Where do the profits from our two bingo halls go? Of course, into that sinkhole called economic development.

Where is all this development that we have been spending millions for? What do we have to show for this? Nothing but satisfied white guys who have been developing with our money. Is economic development another phrase that really means white guy development? Please RBC, no more electronics factories, no more furnace factories, no more splitting profits with the City of Duluth. We're eating surplus commodities while financing your schemes. If our economy ever gets developed, we'll be sitting pretty.

According to a recent article in *News from Indian Country,* Fond du Lac Follies won the PARR award for the year. We shared the honor with that same newspaper. First of all, I'd like to thank all the little people that made such a thing possible. You know who you are. You wear blaze orange in the spring at the boat landings. You swear at Indians while denying that you are a racist. In the letter that accompanied the award, PARR complained about the Follies to Wisconsin governor Tommy Thompson. Further on, they compared Fond du Lac Follies to Hitler. I don't think we look anything alike. He was Austrian German while I am Anishinaabe. Okay, he's got me in the mustache department. I'm still writing and he's not. I think I am taller than he was. Once again PARR, I'd like to thank you for the award. You keep showing your racism and I'll keep writing about you.

Fond du Lac Follies boated on the big lake—Lake Superior—with Curt Gagne. He was the captain of a herring net–setting vessel. Captain Curt was going to get food from the lake. We offered tobacco before we left. The boat was a sixteen-foot aluminum skiff. It was wide and deep. It looked lake-worthy. A ten-horse Johnson motor (never seen a Johnson worth ten horses, my cousin would say) pushed and pulled us around the lake. The lake was bumpy in places. It seemed like it was alive. At times the right combination of waves and boat gave us a light spanking. The color of the lake was gray and green and everything in between. It moved with a life force all its own. We could see all the way to Michigan—Isle Royale. The water was cold, the air was warm. There was no wind. The seagulls were talking in their language as we rode on the lake we shared. Some were flying around and others were bobbing on the lake, waiting for supper or something.

Captain Curt said we were in about 120 feet of water when we set the net. The net was eight feet tall and three hundred feet long. It was nylon and the mesh was 2⅞ inches square. The net had floats spaced about five feet apart and the sinkers were the same distance. A recycled antifreeze jug marked one end of the net. A rock anchor was on the other end. The dark gray rock looked like it came from the north shore of Lake Superior. Captain Curt played out the net from the stern of the boat. He stood with one foot braced on the gunwale. The net was sliding over his leg. The floats made a *clunk-clunk* sound as they hit against the net box. Captain Curt separated the floats and sinkers as the Johnson *putt-putted* along.

The sun was just going behind the trees when we finished setting the net. It was your standard beautiful Minnesota sunset. After we were done, Captain Curt made a side trip for the tourist in the boat. We looked at a cave on the lakeshore. He said there were stories associated with that spot. It felt like it should have stories. It was big enough to hold ten boats like the one we were riding in. As Captain Curt winched his boat out of the lake, I suggested a name for his boat. He could call it the USS *Enterprise.* The name just beamed into my head as we completed our trek on Lake Superior. The next morning Captain Curt brought in seventy pounds of food.

QUESTION: *Why do you call it a rez instead of a reservation?*
ANSWER: *'Cause the white man owns most of it.*

I am not Indian, I am Anishinaabe. For almost five hundred years my ancestors and I have been called something we're not. It started with Columbus, then continued with the Puritans and Cotton Mather. Along the way the United States government started using it. Hollywood and other forms of mass media have perpetuated the use of the word *Indian* to describe us. It has become so common we have internalized it. We have heard it so much we begin to think we are Indians. I'm not Indian, I'm Anishinaabe.

It has been almost five hundred years since Native people discovered Columbus wading ashore. Almost five hundred years of being identified by the wrong name. I have nothing to celebrate. Columbus was just the point man for the invasion of this hemisphere. A way of life that was ecologically sound was transformed into a poisoned, polluted existence. Christianity and the lust for gold replaced respect for the land, air, and water.

As my way of de-celebrating the Columbus event, the word *Indian* will not cross my lips for one year. Instead of saying the word, I will use silence. Instead of writing the word out, I will use dashes. I am banishing the word from my vocabulary for one year starting October 12, 1991.

According to the World Book encyclopedia, we are called —— because Columbus didn't know he had stumbled onto a new continent.

He was originally looking for a short sea route to the Indies, at that time India and China. Thinking that he had made it to the Indies, he called the inhabitants ——. He liked these people so much, he took some back as slaves. He called his slaves ——.

We have been using the word —— so long we have overdone it. For example: *The Circle,* 24 pages, 333 times; *News From —— Country,* 32 pages, 342 times; *Ojibwe News,* 12 pages, 417 times; *Fond du Lac News,* 2 pages, 26 times; Fond du Lac Follies, 12 pages, 19 times.

Dropping the word —— might have some interesting thoughts associated with it. I would have to call that Hoosier state ——a, its capital would be known as ——apolis. When talking about the American —— Movement, I'd have to use silence or dashes in the middle. What about the Bureau of —— Affairs? There are enough examples to keep it interesting. The —— Health Service, the National —— Gaming Act, the Cleveland ——s baseball team. The road sign on the edge of the rez would read Fond du Lac —— Reservation. My kids could still play, only now they'll play cowboys and ——s.

Out of thousands of English words, I can afford to give one a short vacation. I realize —— is a permanent part of the language. Giving it up for one year will be just my form of silent protest. I will get a chance to de-celebrate Columbus almost every day for a year. I am not ——, I am Anishinaabe.

We have a grandson and I just have to brag. His name is Aaron and he can scream loud enough to wake the neighbors. He is sixteen months old and doesn't know how to pee standing up. We call him Air and Water and he is just discovering the world. It makes me young to see it through his eyes. Air and Water gets up early so he can old-man around with his grampa. He climbs the stairs and greets me open armed. He is still sleepy as he tries to climb in my lap. We usually just sit for a few minutes feeling each other's heartbeat. Together we look around the yard to see if night has changed anything. We watch the birds flying by. We hear the train going by in downtown Sawyer. I am getting the joys of parenthood without the wet diaper part. I am enjoying him now because I know he will turn into a teenager. Being a grandparent is special. Do you want to see pictures of my grandson?

Anishinaabe were exercising their 1854 treaty rights in the ceded territory of what is now called Minnesota. Fond du Lac hunters register their kills with the Reservation Conservation Department. So far the largest moose I have heard of has an antler spread of sixty inches. The moose we got was average sized. Shinnobs are going to eat moose all winter. The Reservation Business Committee should be commended for their support of the 1854 treaty rights.

*QUESTION: How do you say "moose" in Ojibwe?*
*ANSWER: "Mooz."*

Charlie "Tuna" Nahganub and Nappy Ross were finally found not guilty in tribal court. Judge Dee Fairbanks thought the prosecution failed to prove they were violating the FDL band conservation code for possessing a spear in a closed season. When the prosecutor tried to refer to the Minnesota state conservation code, he was informed that the state of Minnesota did not exist when the 1854 Treaty was signed. The two Shinnobs celebrated by going out spearing after the court hearing. They speared fish in one of the rivers that empties into Lake Superior. Four salmon went to the Elderly Nutrition Program (ENP) in Cloquet (rhymes with okay and bouquet). Two fish went to the ENP in Sawyer. Elders were eating fish because two Shinnobs were willing to use their 1854 treaty rights. This case proves that the tribal court is aware of the 1854 Treaty.

I am not ——, I am Anishinaabe. It has been harder than I thought it would be to banish the "I" word from my vocabulary. At least twice a week I catch myself still using the word ——. My kids have made a game out of it. They mark the kitchen calendar every time they hear me using the word. There are stories about tricking someone into using the word.

We are learning how powerful words and labels are. Since I banished the word from my language, I have become aware of how pervasive the word is in our daily lives. We were watching a movie on TV the other night. In the first ten minutes of the film, we heard the word —— five times. The word —— is official. It is used in the Declaration of Independence. It's used in the many treaties. Rez government makes daily use of the word ——. Washington, DC, is one of the hotbeds for the use of the word ——. Public Law 102-123 is a recent example. Senate Joint Resolution 172 states that the months of November 1991 and 1992 are to be known as "National American —— Month." The joint resolution has some nice things to say about the natives of this continent. It is also a reminder of the overuse of the word ——. My copy of the joint resolution uses the word ten times in a little over a page.

We keep hearing the message that we are ——. It's everywhere, it's everywhere. If you call someone a name or label, pretty soon they think they are that name or label. I think it may take a year to completely banish the word from my vocabulary. By that time it will be time to start saying it again. The calendar will be all marked up by then. The exercise has raised my consciousness about labels. Just another reminder of the power of words. I am not ——, I am Anishinaabe.

·

# 4.
# A combat cornet

## 1992

Why is it that refugees of color end up in detention camps and federal lockups? The most recent example is the Haitians being held at the military base at Guantanamo, Cuba. Meanwhile Russians are welcomed with open arms and open pocketbooks. According to the Immigration and Naturalization Service, some 200,000 Russians have come to America. Does the color of a refugee's skin have anything to do with the decision on who gets to enter and who has to stay in a detention center?

I wonder who is making the policy decisions on these issues. I heard one U.S. government official say some people were being returned to their country because they were not political refugees but were economic refugees. Can we make that policy retroactive? Can we send back all those who came to America for economic reasons? If it were possible to do that, think how many people would have to leave. Can we add something to the Statue of Liberty that says, "Give me your tired, your poor, your huddled masses yearning to breathe free (as long as they can pass the skin color test)"?

*QUESTION: Why is America called the land of the free?*
*ANSWER: Because they never paid the original inhabitants for it.*

Coming from a large extended family means you go to a lot of funerals. I went to one this month. My older sister Judy Lafave died after a short illness. I was with her when we were waiting for the ambulance that took her to the hospital. I spent hours with her during the death watch. She gradually got worse as her major organs shut down. Judy was sick from the same thing that almost killed her two years ago—septic shock. In the last two years Judy lived her remaining days like she wanted. She went to plays with friends and got drunk when she wanted to. Her children and grandchildren visited frequently. The doctors used morphine to ease her pain as she went from this world to the next.

The wake and funeral were well attended. Friends and relatives came from all over. I got up and said a few words during the service. Mostly I spoke of how long I've known her and some of the good memories we shared. The feast after the graveside service was large. I counted six different kinds of wild rice dishes. I thought it was fitting because Judy really liked to clean wild rice. The wake and funeral brought members of the extended family together again. I like to think she is on the other side playing cribbage or Scrabble with the relatives who have gone on before. We will miss you, Judy.

The recent Reservation Business Committee meeting was well attended. The word got out that a decision must be made about the $5 million profit from Fond-du-Luth. There is a group that thinks most of it should be spent on a new school for the students on the reservation. Another group thinks that land acquisition should be a priority. Others think the money should be spent on programs for the elders or the young ones.

It has been quite a while since Fonjalackers have had to make this kind of a decision. In the past, decisions like this were made by the Bureau of —— Affairs or the Reservation Business Committee. The decisions would be made and we would find out about them later. Personally, I think 51 percent should go directly to the people of Fond du Lac in a per capita payment. The other 49 percent can then be spent for the almost endless list of worthy projects. There might even be enough to contribute to that slush fund called economic development.

After all, it is the Fond du Lac people and their sovereign powers that make the profits possible. The ideal solution would be to let the people decide in a referendum in the next election in June. The different groups could use the time to convince the rest of the voters of the soundness of their plans. Let the people decide in the voter's booth. This would be a true example of self-determination.

Fond du Lac Follies motored to Minny. We went to a protest and a Super Bowl broke out. I don't think naming sports teams after the original people is an honor. In Minny we met with Shinnobs and others at the Peacemaker Center on Cedar Avenue. We listened to speeches from leaders of the American —— Movement. Senator Paul Wellstone was there to add his words and support to the cause. It was a typical Minnesota January. There was wind, windchill, and snow. Someone in the crowd was passing out chemical hand warmers. I heard one Shinnob tell another one, "Don't eat that candy. It tastes funny." Shinnob people, just being true to form, finding something to joke about whatever the situation.

We didn't march. We just met the Protest Against Racism gathering at the Hubert H. Humphrey Metrodome. The sound of the drum drew us close to the tipi. There was more speech making and sign waving. People shared ideas, dreams, and hand warmers. The Buffalo and Washington fans streamed by the protest gathering. The fans couldn't help reading the signs carried by the protesters. For some, the signs were a reminder of the emptiness of the ritual called the Super Bowl. Most of the fans looked and then mentally looked away. We could almost see their eyes glaze over.

The fans put on their invisible blinders as they came near the protesters. Cameras and camcorders were everywhere. The blue-clad Minneapolis police formed a line to separate the protesters from the fans. The police line faced the antiracist signs carried by the protesters. Brown-clad deputies were facing the fans. Isn't the word *fan* derived from the word *fanatic*?

The public-address system inside the Metrodome clashed with the public-address system used by the protesters. After listening to more speeches, the protesters marched around the dome. That was a wise move on the part of the protest organizers. It was just too cold to stand around listening to speeches. It was a good feeling to take part in something that was striking a small blow against racism. I guess they played a football game inside after we left.

*News from —— Country* reports the arrival of three replica ships called the *Nina, Pinta,* and *Santa Maria.* Didn't this already happen once? To misquote Casey Stengel, the famous baseball coach, "Here comes that old deja vu feeling again." What would Chris Columbus discover if he came to this rez? He would discover some of us lining up for military commods. There would be a lot of us sitting at the bingo hall waiting for the caller to call the right numbers. He would find some of us at the casino listening to the *slap* of blackjack cards or the *boing, boing* of the slots.

If Columbus filled out the forms correctly, he could join us in classes at the Fond du Lac Tribal and Community College. He would have to go to Las Vegas to find casino leadership attending yet another training session. Columbus could sit at the clinic and wait for medical treatment. He'd blend right in with the light-skinned patients. He would find some Anishinaabeg in the woods getting ready to boil sap like their ancestors did. Mostly he would find us still here living life, raising children, working, and just basically surviving.

My son has a combat cornet. Let me tell you how it happened. Joseph has wanted to be a musician since he was banging on pots and pans as a toddler. He got his chance when his school announced that band was now available for fifth graders. Joseph thought about it and had trouble deciding what to play. He first decided on the saxophone. I asked his reasons and one of them turned out to be because that girl plays one on the TV program called *The Simpsons.* He later decided to try the cornet.

It was a long week to wait after we signed the papers. Finally Tuesday came and he could pick up his instrument. He jumped off the bus and skipped home with the black case that held the cornet. He unsnapped it and showed us the shiny horn nestled inside the velvet-lined case. He identified the different parts, the mouthpiece, the water valve, the valves that control the sound. He even tried to get some music out of the instrument. At the risk of stunting his growth as a musician, I suggested he go next door and show the neighbors how it sounded.

The folks next door were impressed with the instrument and gave him a lot of encouragement to continue playing. Their son, a stocky seventy-pound ball of fire, didn't know what was happening. All he knew was Joseph was visiting with a new toy. He came running out of the bedroom and jumped in Joseph's lap. The cornet was already in his lap. The cornet was crushed between the two boys. The bell part of the horn was bent at a ninety-degree angle. It looked like the cornet was looking over its right shoulder.

Joseph showed me the damaged horn. I tried to make him feel better by telling him he could now play it around corners. I told him he had the only combat cornet in town. I also told Joseph I was glad that I wasn't standing in his Nikes. I told him I wouldn't want to face the music dude with a bent horn. Joseph's music career remains on hold until we hear what happens in school the next time they have band practice.

I know a Shinnob who recently had some dealings with a bureaucracy. He compared the experience to a fly learning about flypaper. It started off innocently enough. A neighboring county, let's call it Spruce County, called and asked the Shinnob if he would come down and speak to the staff. The director of the welfare office said they would pay him for his knowledge, mileage, and time. He thought about it and decided that he could do the job. It was a two-hour gig plus a little trip down the interstate. Easy money, he thought. Do a little workshop for them and they send a check. One foot stuck to the flypaper.

He got there early so he could demolish another stereotype about Natives and time. The social workers were just getting ready to sit down for a feast. He accepted their invitation to eat. It was a typical white-guy feast, no deer meat, moose meat, or beaver. No fry bread or wild rice. Just your standard grocery-store feast. He ate good and doubled up at the dessert table. Another foot stuck to the flypaper.

After the meal, a burp, and a smoke, it was time for the Shinnob to sing for his supper. He gave them a view of life on the rez. For two hours the Shinnob told them rez stories. He took them hunting, ricing, and berry picking. The Shinnob told them drunk and jail stories. The Native people in the stories were not clients anymore.

They were humans with a history and some great stories. When the Shinnob finished, he was asked to sign a form so he could get his check. He signed and two more feet stuck to the paper.

He went home and waited for his check. Every day when the mail-man drove by, the Shinnob checked for his check. After twenty-six trips out to the mailbox, he began to suspect something was wrong. He thought he might have to sign up for welfare until his check got there.

The Shinnob called the welfare office. He was able to call them on their toll-free line. One foot came loose from the flypaper. The welfare people said they were sorry, but their records showed the check was already mailed. The Shinnob said he was sorry, too, but he didn't get the check. He offered to drive down and get a new check. They told him he would have to wait for seven working days. He thought, why seven days? According to the white man's Bible, the world was created in six days.

After seven working days, the Shinnob called the welfare office again. He was told that his case was turned over to the fraud squad investigator. In three working days, the Shinnob got a letter from the ex-cop that runs the investigations. The letter summoned him to appear in the office and swear under oath that he did not get the check. One wing stuck to the flypaper. The Shinnob jumped the chain of command and called the director of the welfare office. A meeting was arranged in the county building. The director apolo-gized for the mix-up. He was feeling so bad about the situation that he gave the Shinnob and his wife a tour of the welfare office.

The director freed the Shinnob from the flypaper and gave him a new check. Of course this was after the Shinnob signed a notarized form saying he didn't get the original check. The Shinnob buzzed across the street and turned the check into green frog skins. As he was driving home, he thought about the month-long experience. He scratched his head over why they call it red tape. It should be called white tape.

*QUESTION: What's the difference between*
*a gambler and a compulsive gambler?*

*ANSWER: Like drunks and alcoholics,*
*one of them has to go to meetings.*

Bud Grant—congratulations. You have earned yourself a place in
the Follies. Grant is the former head coach of the Minnesota Vi-
kings football team. It was your posturing on the state capitol steps
that did it. Protesting against the treaty rights of the Anishinaabe
people. I am a spearfisher and I have to tell you what I think. We have
faced two-faced people before. We know from the old stories that the
treaties will always be under attack. You are the latest in a long line
of treaty haters. Your brothers who protest on the boat landings are
just the same. Racists going under the banner of equal rights.

It's kind of ironic, but I was walking through the mall in Bemidji
the other day. I entered a bookstore there and found a book with
you in it called *Homeless Dreams.* It was on the discount table and
you were wearing beadwork. I thought the paint on your face was a
bit much. Inside the book on page twenty-seven there was a larger
picture of you. I'll quote what you said:

> Now that I am retired from coaching, I have the opportunity to
> spend more time doing what I like to do outdoors, such as hunting,
> fishing, camping, etc. . . . As a boy growing up, I would have liked to
> have lived with the I\_\_\_\_s and experienced their way of life. It al-
> ways bothered me that in the movies they were always the bad guys
> and always lost the fights they were in. I wanted to help them win. I
> feel that way now about the homeless.
> *Homeless Dreams: Dream Portraits of Minnesota*
> *Celebrities to Aid the Homeless,* compiled and published in 1991
> by Matt Blair and Mike Blumberg

Now, exactly when was it you were lying? Was it when you were
on the capitol steps protesting or was it in the book when you wanted the people to win? Do you still want to experience life with the
Anishinaabeg people? Maybe we can arrange a visit up here on the
reservation. I can probably show you what our life is really like.
Maybe I can tell you some of the old stories where we did win the
fights. So, c'mon Bud Grant, come to the rez and experience life.

*QUESTION: Do "you people" get a government check every month?*
*ANSWER: No, we're still waiting for the first one*
*for what is now called America.*

*QUESTION: What is an overused cliché?*
*ANSWER: "You people . . ."*

Thank you, Christopher Columbus. The quincentennial celebrations have meant more work for me. All the thanks should not go to you alone. The tomahawk chop and the Super Bowl mascot issue have all helped. I also have to thank Larry Peterson, Dean Crist, and the rest of the PARR clowns for keeping treaty rights in the public eye. This is the way it works. A school, church, or university wishes to be politically correct, so they tap into the moccasin telegraph to find an Anishinaabe. The Anishinaabe is brought in to give a view of —— lives and lifestyles. Sometimes I get picked to lead the charge for cultural diversity. Once in a while we call it cultural pluralism. Whatever it is called, I get paid to preach the gospel. A title like cultural missionary seems to fit.

Because the institutions pay mileage also, I've got a new-to-me rez car. In case you didn't know, I will tell you what a rez car is. A rez car is one that is on its next-to-the-last stop before the junkyard. My latest model is not quite a teenager yet. It is only eleven years young. The odometer says it is on its second hundred-thousand miles. It's got a sunroof for looking at the birds flying over. We can also see the stars and moon through the ceiling.

The four-cylinder Pontiac sips gasoline like it doesn't really trust the Arabs and their oil fields. Remember those big old V-8s? The 327s, the 350s, the 383s, and 390s? The ones that had to have a half pail of gas poured down their throats so they would fire up? This Pontiac is not like that. I get thirty miles to the gallon as I earn twenty-five cents a mile.

The travel checks also pay for repairs. So far we have a new radiator and a new starter, brakes, and tires. It sometimes feels like we are trying to rebuild the car one part at a time. The rumble from underneath lets me know that a meeting with Mr. Midas is coming up. Up until now the car has started every time I turned the key. What else could it be but a Pontiac? A skin driving a car named after a skin. Sometimes, to control our own names, we call ourselves skins. Once again, I'd like to thank Christopher Columbus from the bottom of my bottom.

QUESTION: *Can Shinnobs move through the woods silently?*
ANSWER: *Only if they pump up their Nikes.*

The following may or may not have happened. While the lights from the Grand Casino were shining up in the air, other Shinnobs were shining lights down in the water at an unnamed lake in the ceded territory in Minnesota. The reason this may or may not have happened is because of the negative vote about spearfishing by the Fond du Lac RBC. The Follies motored to the lake carrying a canoe, some Shinnobs, and a couple of spears. We used the same car we bought with travel checks when we were cultural missionaries. We traveled in a convoy with a pickup truck that had Fond du Lac license plates. The truck carried a small boat that was powered by an electric motor. The canoe was powered by a Shinnob with a paddle.

The unnamed lake was one that was selected by the conservation committee. It was chosen because it had enough walleyes for spearers and anglers. We offered tobacco before we started. It was a quiet night on the lake. The moon was playing hide-and-seek behind the clouds as we played hide-and-seek with the people who didn't want us out spearing. Using the spear my cousin calls Mr. Death, we gathered fish for food. We had to stop a couple of times to sharpen the spear. The rocks in the bottom of the lake curled the tines back. We stopped when we reached the limits set by the conservation committee. We could have stayed and got more, but we wanted to save some for next year. The rez car got us safely back home again. After we cleaned the fish, we ate some and gave the rest away.

We heard that the Anishinaabeg spearers in Wisconsin didn't have much trouble with the protesters this year. I am happy to report we didn't have much trouble with tribal government as we gathered fish like our ancestors did. This fishing trip may or may not have happened. It may or may not happen again next year.

*QUESTION: If you are a Shinnob, how come your skin is so light?*
*ANSWER: Melanin Deficit Disorder*

FDL Follies motored to Duluth for the dedication of the Northland Vietnam Veterans Memorial. I was curious to see if Anishinaabe were represented at the ceremony. I could see the WHITE monument as I approached the proceedings. There were approximately a thousand people there for the doings. Most of the participants were WHITE although there were a couple of brown faces sprinkled around. It was a typical WHITE guy ceremony. There were prayers, guitars, and a flyover by jets from the Duluth air base. Two Huey choppers went by at the end of the doings.

The huge WHITE concrete structure was built by volunteers from the veteran and construction community. The WHITE monument is in the shape of a half shell. There were openings in the bunker-like monument that overlooked Lake Superior. The names of those who were killed or didn't return from the Vietnam War were etched on a black wall. There were a lot of flags, and honor guards wearing WHITE shirts were standing on the WHITE concrete sidewalks. WHITE seagulls surrounded the crowd. Big puffy WHITE clouds drifted over as the ceremony progressed.

We saw two WHITE people keel over from the heat, or maybe the emotion of the moment. They were assisted by WHITE soldiers from the local National Guard. Former mayor John Fedo made some remarks as part of the doings. I don't think he is a veteran. Anishinaabe people were ignored in the WHITE guy ceremony. I thought it was real WHITE of them to forget our contributions. The Duluth television stations reported that the monument was vandalized some time after the ceremony. We fought the war together but live in peace separately.

The election is over on the Fond du Lac Reservation. In their wisdom, the voters returned all of the incumbents to the Reservation

Business Committee. There was a protest filed by Sandi Savage, a candidate from the Cloquet precinct. The protest is bogged down in a bureaucratic swamp over the interpretation of the constitution. Maybe the issue will be resolved before the next regularly scheduled meeting of the RBC in July. Time will tell if the voters were wisdom-ful in selecting our leaders for the next four years.

I think the whole question of absentee voters must be addressed. It is very common for candidates to lose on the reservation and be swept into office on the absentee ballots. It might sound radical, but I think most absentee ballots should be outlawed. I wouldn't want to deprive anyone of the right to vote, but the current system is full of alleged and real corruption. If an off-reservation voter wants to participate in an election, they could make the drive to the rez to vote. Absentee ballots should be allowed for those who are unable to travel. People confined to hospitals or who are in the military should be allowed to use an absentee ballot. If a person cares enough about the reservation and the election, they could show up to vote.

Another alternative would be to set up polling places in the major metropolitan areas where there are a significant number of Fond du Lac voters. We need to remove the taint of absentee ballot corruption. In the meantime, we will struggle along with the constitution written sixty years ago. Are we ever going to change that darn thing?

What is it with these TV people? Do they think we are so slow that we can't read the temperature numbers on the screen? On each program they dutifully read the numbers as if we had never seen numbers before. Surely there must be other weather information they could be presenting. If I ever meet one of those people, I will ask that question.

The case against two Fonjalackers charged with aiding and abetting another Fonjalacker in the taking of an illegal deer was dismissed by tribal court last week. The rez prosecutor failed to prove the two individuals were involved in the taking of the deer. Judge Dee Fairbanks ruled for the defense in the motion to dismiss the charges.

I saw the two Fonjalackers after the ruling. They somberly walked out of court. Once they got around the corner and out of sight, both of them jumped up in the air, clicked their heels, and came down with smiles on their faces.

Some people believe justice can be found in tribal court. I talked with a deputy sheriff from Carlton County after court. He was a witness in the case and was surprised by the differences between county court and tribal court. At Fond du Lac, nonlawyers are allowed to practice if they meet the court's criteria. We explained that this was our court and we make the rules.

*QUESTION: Do you have big mosquitoes on your rez?*
*ANSWER: Well, our mosquitoes have full-sized wood ticks.*

In July, Fond du Lac Follies motored to Norman, Oklahoma, for the North American Native Writers' Festival. It was an easy ride. We got on Interstate 35 and got off when we got to the Norman exit. Along the way we went through Iowa, Missouri, and Kansas. Iowa was its usual uneventful self. Missouri was hardly remembered. In Kansas, we began watching the sky for storms. After gallons of coffee and gasoline, we got to the red dirt of Oklahoma. Oil wells nodded to us as we drove along. It was hot. The thermometer read a hundred degrees and the humidity was the same. It was uncomfortably warm, wet, and windy. The weather reminded us why we live in cool Minnesota.

We set up camp in an air-conditioned motel and went to the university. Right away we began seeing familiar faces. Roberta Hill was there from back home. Joe Bruchac was the chair of the steering committee that put the festival together. The days were taken up with meetings and workshops. The workshops were about short-story writing, poetry, essay writing, novels, and Native literature in the classrooms. It was difficult to choose because there were so many good ones.

It was a good feeling to see Simon Ortiz again. It has been a couple of years since he brought his words to Minnesota. The winners of the Native Writers' Circle First Book Awards were honored at a banquet. N. Scott Momaday was presented with a lifetime achievement award. For us, the best part was meeting and talking with the two-hundred-some Native writers. We sat together at lunch, we met over coffee, and just talked writing. In the evenings we had our choice of hearing over thirty different writers read. There were some tough choices. Do we go hear Leslie Marmon Silko or Lance Henson? We had to choose between hearing Maurice Kenny and Simon Ortiz. Next, we had to choose between Basil Johnston and Diane Glancy. The schedule had us running between locations to hear the ones we wanted. For us, it was worth the nine-hundred-mile drive.

On the way home, a tornado chased us through Kansas. After that it was a challenge to stay awake on the interstate. The memories of the storytelling with Basil Johnston around the coffee pot and the connections made with other writers all contributed to the good feelings we had about this festival. Just hanging out with the Native writers sort of made up for all the hours spent on the road, all the hours spent alone in front of a computer or typewriter.

The election on the reservation is still unresolved. Sandi "Sandman" Savage is waiting for her day in court. The way it stands now she will be going to a different court. After getting a favorable ruling on whether a hearing should be held in tribal court, the powers that be decided her case should be presented to the appellate court. The as yet unnamed members of the appellate court will decide if she gets a hearing or not.

Because of the favorable ruling by Judge Fairbanks, we wonder how long she will be the judge at the Fond du Lac tribal court. Remember what happened to the last judge we had at Fond du Lac who dared to take a stand? We no longer see Judge Pat O'Brian on the Fond du Lac Reservation. Justice did not prevail here at Fond du Lac. Sandi Savage cannot get a hearing to present her evidence about the election irregularities here in our election. As someone once said, "There's law and order and just us."

Aaron and I have been picking agates. It is the kind of thing we do here in Sawyer when Fond du Lac Follies is not out on the road motoring somewhere. The gravel roads of Sawyer are blessed with agates. I don't know what geological age formed the stones, but I do know a pretty rock when I see one. It is easy for my grandson Aaron to find the rocks, because at two-and-a-half years of age, he is built close to the ground. Air and Water (as we sometimes call him) is becoming quite the rock picker. He knows the difference between agates, quartz, and flint. He finds the smallest agates. Some of the agates are as tiny as a pinhead. He waits patiently while I examine the rocks and finally declare them to be agates. He laughs and takes them to the container where we store our treasure. He sometimes drops them on the way and has to find them again a second time.

I remember my mother and grandmother walking down the roads looking for pretty agates. While walking with them, I couldn't understand what agates had to do with the trip. I always wanted to get to where we were going. Now that I am older, I realize that the journey is as much a part of the trip as the destination. I remember the praise I used to get when I found a good agate.

Aaron brings agates into the house that he finds when he is outside playing. We know the best time to look is after the road grader has gone by. I don't know what we are going to do with our pile of pretty rocks. For now, we just take them out and look at them when it is too dark or rainy to find more. The translucent red rocks with the stripes and bands of color are fascinating for a little boy and his grandfather. Who knows? Maybe we are finding good memories along with the pretty rocks.

Does anyone besides me think it is time to end the use of the image *End of the Trail?* I see that Native slumped over his horse everywhere. The one example I saw recently looks like he is from a western tribe. The background looks like mountains. What would he look like if he was Chippewa? Would he be shown draped over his wild rice parching kettle? Would he be lying in a sinking birchbark canoe? Go to any powwow and you can find the tired Native represented on paintings, beaded belt buckles, posters, earrings, or clocks. He and his horse are everywhere.

The Native looks like he is suffering from a severe calcium deficiency or his backbone is made from rubber. The horse looks pretty bad, too. What is the rest of the story, as radio commentator Paul Harvey asks? How did he get so beat-up looking? Was he in a war? Was it a really long hunting trip? Were he and his horse on a dirty drunk? I wonder why Native people embrace this image. Do we think he represents our finest memories of the old days? Like most things that are overdone, *The End of the Trail* has outlived its time. Just once I'd like to see what that Native looked like at the beginning of the trail. Better yet, I would like to see that tired Native with the international symbol of a red circle with a slash through it.

*QUESTION: Why did he go to the casino every night?*
*ANSWER: To prove he wasn't a compulsive gambler, I bet.*

"Justice delayed is justice denied" is how Sandra Savage opened her news conference. The meeting with the media was held in the back room of the Knight Club, a bar across from the rez bingo hall. The meeting was held there because the tribal court building was locked up. Representatives from radio, TV, and the Duluth newspaper were there to hear her story. A scheduled court hearing had been canceled because the Reservation Business Committee fired Judge Dee Fairbanks because she wanted to hear the Savage case. Let's see if we can follow the twisted logic used by tribal government in their fight to protest the protest of the recent election:

June 9, 1992: An election is held on the Fond du Lac Reservation.

June 17, 1992: Sandra Savage files an election protest.

August 14, 1992: Judge Fairbanks schedules a hearing for August 24, 1992.

August 24, 1992: Judge Fairbanks is fired by the Reservation Business Committee. The Savage hearing is canceled.

In a press release about the firing, the RBC said that Judge Fairbanks's actions posed a "threat to the integrity of the electoral process and the rule of law on the Fond du Lac Reservation." Judge Fairbanks replied by saying the RBC threatens tribal integrity. "They're jeopardizing sovereignty by doing this," Fairbanks wrote in a public letter to the RBC. "When we violate due process and when tribal governments start stomping on the rights of individuals whose rights they should be protecting, I get very worried. I wouldn't be very proud of myself right now if I were a Fond du Lac elected official." The RBC has "made a mockery of our Tribal Courts System," Fairbanks wrote. "It is clear that you will allow only a puppet court to work for you. I can only hope that you will seriously consider the repercussions beyond your own self-interests and allow your court system and your laws to work."

Meanwhile, Sandra Savage continues to explore her options. The RBC is finding it very hard to push these two women around. [Author's note: At the time of this publication, over fifteen years later, Sandi Sandman Savage's case is still unresolved.]


Ricing is a bittersweet time of the year. The preparations remind me of seasons of the past. The different parts of ricing evoke memories and stories of relatives that have passed on. My uncle showed me the best place to get diamond willow for the crutch of the rice pole. The cedar knockers remind me of the trouble I used to get in when I was a kid. It didn't take me long to learn that rice knockers were not made to be used as swords. My grampa made the best knockers. Some of them are still in use today.

As I dragged my canoe to the car, I thought about the rice boats we used to use. Only the people with jobs could afford canoes. The rest of us had to make do with rice boats. The flat-bottom boats were heavy, tippy, and easy to make. The boat I remember the best was called the *Yellow Bird.* It was made from pine boards, tongue-and-groove pine for the floor, and oakum for the seams. We only had yellow paint, so it became the *Yellow Bird.* The *Yellow Bird* served many seasons after I grew up and joined the military. When I came back, people were still telling stories about that rice boat. In those days, rice boats could be found at any boat landing. Someone originally owned them, but they were left for anyone to use.

As I tied the canoe to the top of the car, I used the knots I learned from my dad. I recalled stories of people who didn't tie the boats and canoes on properly. The thought of a canoe blowing off the car at fifty-five miles an hour made me cinch the knots a little tighter. Deciding which lake or river to rice brought more memories. I knew which lakes my uncles preferred. The stories of three-mile portages to hidden lakes made me smile. I remembered to tell my family these stories as we were getting ready for ricing. I thought of ricers who once lived and were now memories. I remembered who riced with whom, who were the best knockers. I knew which lakes were best for long-grain rice, which rivers were easy to pole through. Ricing is full of remembered places and relatives.

Getting on the water felt like a handshake from an old friend. I thought how lucky I was to be able to make rice again. Putting tobacco in the water made me feel close to the Creator. The water, the wind, and the rice are unchanging. The ducks and coots reminded me that other creatures depend on the rice. While knocking the rice, I kept myself amused with stories of who tipped over and where. Parching rice in the old black kettle brought smells that reminded me of my relatives. Nothing else smells like parching rice and wood smoke. I felt sorry for the people who have to eat paddy rice.

Actually, making rice is just hard work. I paddled many miles in my parching kettle. Keeping the rice moving so it doesn't burn brings sweat to my face. Watching the rice turn from green to brown lets me know we will have homemade food for the coming winter. Dancing on the rice reminds me that most people used to do it that way. We still do it that way because it lets us stay close to the food. We also think it is important to show the young ones the old ways. Fanning wild rice makes you realize how important the wind is in the process of making food. I also recognized the genius of the person who first designed the birchbark fanning basket. Watching the brown rice hulls disappear, leaving green rice, makes me hungry.

My grandson Aaron is using his agate picking skills to help clean the rice. Last night after we were done parching, we just sat around the fire telling ricing stories. My sister Doris contributed some funny stories she remembered. Her story involving a beaver dam, a boatload of rice, and an old lady made us laugh. We tried to top her with our best stories. We stayed there until the moon came up over the trees.

Today we get to make rice again.


Joy Harjo, a nationally known Creek poet, came to Sawyer to read her poetry to the community. Sixty-five people came to hear her words and music. She brought her band, called Poetic Justice. After the reading, the people ate together from a feast that was prepared by the community women. Everyone was there who was supposed to be there. Some people drove from Minneapolis to hear Joy Harjo. The poet communicated with the people of Sawyer. It was a good evening.

The Atlanta Braves management and fans were shown on TV doing the tomahawk chop in the recent World Series. How stupid. I guess it is a visible reminder that racism is part of the great American pastime and of America. I am glad the Atlanta team lost the series. Chop this, Ted Turner.

QUESTION: *What is the new Ojibwemowin word for casino?*
ANSWER: *Jer pa win?*


Well, it has been a year since I gave up the word Indian. It has been an interesting experience. It wasn't too hard to avoid the word in my writing. In speaking is where I made my mistakes. The mistakes were costly for me because I foolishly promised my twelve-year-old son Joseph a dollar every time I messed up. In the last year I have given him almost four hundred dollars. My son has learned the power of words. Now when he has to describe the Native people, he uses tribal names. *Indian* is no longer part of his vocabulary. When I took the vow to quit using the word *Indian,* it affected others. People would stumble around trying to find a less offensive word to describe the original people. The game is over now. My son is no longer monitoring my speech to see if I use the word *Indian.* He wants me to banish another word from my vocabulary. He likes making money from my mistakes. He suggested banning the traditional use of the word "traditional."

Our moose repellent worked. We didn't see one moose during the legal shooting hours. There were eight eyeballs scanning the cedar swamps. The only time we saw moose was after sundown, when the Reservation Conservation Code says we can't shoot them. We'd still be out there looking if it wasn't for that federal judge. He shortened the season and saved us from many miserable miles of walking. We went to an area that was good for us last year, but the moose were not there. My cousin said the moose were staying deep in the woods because they saw so many orange and black Fond du Lac license plates. He said he saw one moose peeking through the willows at our license plate.

The Reservation Business Committee took the state of Minnesota to federal court to protect us. Earlier, the state had threatened to arrest us for hunting moose. The threat didn't work because getting arrested in a treaty rights case would make the hunters heroes on the rez. Privately, we were hoping our actions would inspire the other two 1854 reservations to rethink their treaty sale. So far, Grand Portage and Bois Forte have been silent.

It felt good to have tribal government behind us as we used the rights our elders reserved 138 years ago. I am glad the federal judge said our treaty rights do exist and that they should be federally protected. We will use the treaty rights again next spring when we go spearfishing in the ceded territory. In the meantime, I will have to trade wild rice for moose meat with the hunters who were successful (the ones who didn't wear moose repellent).

It is good to know that treaty rights are used and not sold on the Fond du Lac Reservation.

Stones and Bones—that is what the display was called. The bones were glued to a piece of plywood along with some stones. Ballpoint-pen lettering identified the objects on the two-foot-by-three-foot stained plywood sheet. The stones were identified as petrified wood, iron ore, a meteorite, and an agate. Stone arrowheads were also glued to the wood. The bones were labeled "Human Bones (Indian)." I am not a doctor, but the piece of bone looked like a leg with one joint showing. There were several smaller fragments that looked like it in color and texture.

I was shocked. I asked if they had any more. Don Hayes, curator of the Todd County Museum, dug under a table and found two yellow shoeboxes that held other bones. He opened one box and unwrapped a skull. I didn't want to see any more. We looked in his files to see where the bones came from. The piece of plywood identified the donor of the stones and bones exhibit as Leonard Markfelder of Staples, Minnesota. The files showed that Leonard Markfelder donated other items between 1973 and 1978, including a rifle, a groundhog, a gopher, a snow owl, a civet cat, a falcon, an osprey, and a snapping turtle.

In talking with the two curators, I learned that the museum was thinking about returning the bones to the earth. They didn't know who to contact but did talk about reburial in Itasca State Park. The next day I gave them the phone number of the Minnesota Indian Affairs Council. The day after that I stopped in to see if the museum had contacted anyone about reburial. They said they hadn't.

Curator Wilma Finseth met me the following day with some information she had found in the files about the skull. The paper said the skull was found in Long Prairie when a garage was being built. The skull was believed to be part of a bundle burial and further states it was studied at St. Cloud State University. I saw that the leg bone was chipped off the plywood. It was now wrapped in a paper towel. I talked with a relative who was living in the house when the skull was found. He said it was found in 1957 or 1958. On my last day in Long Prairie, I learned that the museum was still unable to contact anyone. The two sets of human bones (Indian) remain locked in the dry museum. I left the museum knowing I would be back.

Fond du Lac Follies motored to D and C again. The BIA called and wanted to hear some Questions from my columns and other writings. The reading was part of the American Indian Heritage Month celebrations. I was kind of worried at first. Oh-oh, summoned to

Washington by the Bureau of Indian Affairs. We were greeted with warmth. It was a little before Veterans Day, so the places we wanted to see were not crowded. We went to the Wall and honored those who had died in the Vietnam War. We walked to the Washington Monument, where we eyeballed the city. The elevator operator stopped and showed us a piece of pipestone that was mounted inside the monument. The pipestone was from Minnesota. He asked us what tribe we were from. My wife Patricia said Dakota. My son Joseph said Chippewa. My sister Doris said Ojibwe. I said Anishinaabe.

We walked to the Smithsonian. We walked to the Lincoln Memorial. We walked back to the Air and Space Museum. We walked and walked. We walked around Arlington. We walked so much my son renamed the city. He calls it Walkington, DC.

We drove across the Potomac to see Princess Pale Moon. Princess Pale Moon is a woman who got into trouble in Spain because she couldn't prove she was Indian. It was reported in *News from Indian Country* a few issues ago. With this in mind, we went to visit her at the American Indian Heritage Foundation, which she founded in 1973. The foundation claims to be the largest privately supported nonprofit American Indian organization in the country. In her literature she says she is Cherokee-Ojibwe. The foundation sponsors the National Miss Indian USA pageant every year.

Princess Pale Moon is the president of the foundation and her husband, Dr. Wil Rose, is the chief executive officer. Her two sons also work for the foundation. We met with Dr. Rose, who gave us some background on Princess Pale Moon and the foundation. We learned that Princess sings the national anthem for the Washington football team. I won't mention the name of the team. When she sings, she dresses in some sort of tribal regalia.

I didn't know what to call her. Is her first name Princess or is it Pale? Whatever, after talking with her husband and hearing of the grand plans for the foundation, I met the woman. She was wearing turquoise and what looked like makeup that made her skin look dark. She was stylishly dressed in regular white people clothes. She was charming and smiled a lot as she talked with the Shinnobs from Minnesota. She gave me a book about her life and background. After reading the book, I failed to see the connection she had with the Ojibwe people. I suppose a person can claim to be any tribe they want to be. There was no mention in the book of how she came to be a Princess.

I left the foundation feeling like this was just another rip-off of Native people. It was hard to dislike the people because they were so friendly, but what they are doing is wrong—pretending to be Indian when they are not. Princess or Pale did buy some wild rice from us. She paid the standard white guy price. I guess after she reads this she will not buy any more rice from us. Too bad. If she really is a Princess, she can command one of her subjects to grow her some. She is as real an Indian as paddy rice is real wild rice.

# 5.
# Iron Legs

# 1993

The Todd County Museum is going to return the bones to the earth. D. Hayes told me he contacted Earl Sargeant and Hamline University. To paraphrase Spike Lee, thank you Todd County Museum for doing the right thing.

Welcome to the world to James Warren Northrup IV, recently born in Pierre, South Dakota.

Yup, they put the pork to us. In a burst of Christmas cheer, the RBC gave everyone a ham. Casino workers, rez employees, and Fonjalackers all got part of that pig. The Reservation Business Committee didn't actually handle the gift. They caused paper to be printed. Each piece was worth exactly one ham at B & B Market in Cloquet. There were quite a few cars lined up when I picked up my pork. The word *Somalia* popped into my head. At the risk of looking a gift pig in the snout, my ham was mostly fat. After I cut away the artery-clogging fat, I didn't have much left. There was enough meat for two sandwiches. The reservation gave out fifteen hundred hams, I heard. There was enough fat on those hams to waterproof all the boots in the Chinese army.

My cousin says the RBC is taking care of us. Instead of giving out dirty old gambling per capita money like the other reservations, they give us the food directly. With this much good luck, we wonder if something bad is going to happen. We're hoping the new casino is a success. Maybe next year we'll get a dozen eggs with the ham.

*QUESTION: What does the Shinnob Santa say?*
*ANSWER: Ho Ho Ho-wah.*

Fond du Lac Follies motored to Hinckles to learn about the pending 1837 treaty sale. It was an informational meeting held at a school gym for all parties to the sale. The Minnesota Department of Natural Resources was there. The state attorney general's office sent two staff members. Mille Lacs Reservation was represented by Don Wedll. The Save Lake Mille Lacs Association had a table loaded with information about their cause. Great Lakes Indian Fish and Wildlife had an interesting display. We learned that the agreement between the tribe and the state would sell two treaties. The 1837 Treaty was signed by Anishinaabeg from two states. It wasn't just Mille Lacs. The treaty contains the specific language reserving hunting, fishing, and gathering rights in the ceded territory.

The 1855 Treaty established the Mille Lacs Reservation. I learned that the agreement was permanent. I thought the treaty itself was supposed to be permanent. There is no provision for past damages. Anishinaabeg who have had their treaty rights violated for the past sixty to seventy years now give up their right to sue or collect damages. The proposed agreement ties gambling to treaty rights. The Mille Lacs people give up the right to build casinos on their 7,500 acres.

Members of the political right ate DNR cookies with the political left-out. Cliff Skinaway from Sandy Lake was there. Rod Sando, new DNR commissioner of natural resources, walked around smiling. After listening to people talk about the agreement, I wondered if the state of Minnesota thinks they are buying our 1837 treaty rights. By our, I mean the Anishinaabeg from Leech Lake, St. Croix, La Pointe, Lac Courte Oreilles, Lac du Flambeau, Sandy Lake, Snake River, Red Cedar Lake, Red Lake, Gull Lake and Swan River, and Fond du Lac. In Hinckles, it was said the treaty sale only involved the Mille Lacs people's rights.

The whole situation reminds me of the 1854 treaty sale here at Fond du Lac in 1988. That treaty sale involved the state of Minnesota, a federal court, Anishinaabeg treaty rights, and a settlement before the case went to court. The people here voted that sale down twice. At Fond du Lac we still have our treaty rights.

While thinking about the agreement to sell the 1837 treaty rights, I wondered why the U.S. government wasn't a party to the sale. The

Anishinaabeg signed the treaty with them. The state of Minnesota didn't exist when the document was signed. The state of Minnesota is willing to spend $10 million in this time of budget deficits. They must think they are going to make out on this deal. As I drove home from Hinckles, I thought about my children and grandchildren fighting for treaty rights forty to fifty years from now.

I learned at a Reservation Business Committee meeting that the new $7 million casino will cost $14 million. When it was first announced, we were given the lower number. The place hasn't even opened or earned one dime and already the price has doubled. The money for the new casino is coming from the existing gambling operations. Boy, talk about putting all your eggs in one basket. Maybe the Reservation Business Committee should change their name to the Reservation Gambling Committee.

By the time this is read, the voters from Mille Lacs will have voted on the 1837 treaty sale. I don't understand why Mille Lacs gave up spearfishing and netting. One paranoid part of me thinks that there is more at stake here than the walleye in the lake. If the treaty is sold, Anishinaabeg will be removed as an influence in the ceded territory. If that happens, can uranium mining be far behind? I saw a DNR map that showed most of the ceded territory is "most favorable" for digging up that radioactive ore. I also wondered if the two Grand Casinos are being held hostage over the treaty sale. Would the state refuse to sign a gambling compact if Mille Lacs didn't sell their treaty rights? On the other hand, I did see some Mille Lacs people wearing buttons that said they didn't want to sell treaties.

Just in case we forget,
gambling is not mentioned in the 1854 Treaty.

We are in the shank of winter. It is the time of the year when dogs are congregating on the roads. The cold is dangerous, but we seem to adapt to it every year. We take the usual precautions and before we know it, the mosquitoes and deerflies are back. I am glad to see the occasional snowstorm. When it falls, it covers the old, used-up snow. When I was a kid, I used to think snow only came in one color—white. Now as an adult I look around and see snow in a lot of different colors. The brown snow and slush where it has been sanded, the almost blue snow when it's fresh. I see the grey snow as night approaches. I am glad we live where we have changing seasons.

Fond du Lac Follies has been motoring a lot lately. It must be the nomad in me. We shared the trail with Senators Inouye, Wellstone, and Nighthorse Campbell. Three out of eighteen senators who make up the Select Committee on Indian Affairs were in Minneapolis to conduct hearings. It was about proposed amendments to the American Indian Religious Freedom Act. The senators were traveling around the country taking testimony. It looked like your standard Senate hearing: lights, still and video cameras, tape recorders, senators and witnesses facing each other behind banks of microphones. There were some differences, however. First time I ever seen an eagle staff at a Senate hearing.

Another difference was the audience. It was mostly Indian people listening to the testimony. Pete Catches was outstanding as a witness. The Lakota man's wisdom was respected by the senators. I could tell by the way they introduced him and asked questions. He reminded the senators that the Black Hills were not for sale. His testimony was interrupted by applause several times and he got a standing ovation when he was done. The hearing went on until the end. It was more interesting out in the halls where Native people gathered to drink coffee and gossip. Old friends greeted each other. On the way home from the hearing one question kept nagging at me. Why do we need federal legislation to codify our beliefs?

*QUESTION: Why do Indian men make better lovers?*
*ANSWER: A lot of them don't have to get up to go to work.*

The moccasin telegraph reports that an RBC man is continuing his string of luck at the casino. Keno gave him $1,700. Lucky guy, he wins the election and then at the casino. More gossip from the moccasin telegraph, which may or may not be true, involves one of the leaders from another Minnesota tribal council that has gambling. This is the version we have so far:

The leader was feeling the burdens of public office and was drinking alcohol to relieve the tensions. The leader drank for several hours in a liquor store just off the rez. After a while the leader got a call from nature and answered it. While sitting on the throne in the bathroom, the leader fell asleep and tipped over. One never knows when a nap will sneak up when alcohol is involved. The leader was lying there in public view, pants at half mast. It was said the leader was either showing he has nothing to hide or demonstrating what happens if you drink too much. Two rez residents helped cover the situation as they helped their leader get upright and presentable. This leader is responsible for decisions affecting hundreds of people and millions of dollars. The voters could do themselves a favor and flush this one out of office.

*QUESTION: When you were young, did you have a town drunk?*
*ANSWER: No, we all took turns.*

Fond du Lac Follies went spearing in Mille Lacs. Now I've got a piece of paper that says a judge wants to talk to me. I have to report to Milaca along with the other Anishinaabeg who were cited for breaking a Minnesota law. We were using our 1837 treaty rights when we went out looking for fish. Shinnobs from Michigan, Wisconsin, and Minnesota were stopped and cited. The memorable parts of the experience were the drum that brought people together, the sky that cleared up just before the spearers went out, the feast held at the East Lake Community Center, the witnesses who gave of their time and gas money to join the Shinnobs, the news media pushing each other to get the story, the police and game wardens acting professional, the feeling of being out on the lake, and the sense of relief when it was over for the night.

Dave Aubid from the Rice Lake Band welcomed everyone to the East Lake Community Center. He brought out his drum and invited people to sing with him. The drum pulled a circle of people inside to listen. The heartbeat of the drum and the power of the songs helped us forget the media. At one point there were five big satellite-TV trucks parked on the old dirt road in front of the community center. One Shinnob came out of the building and looked around. He asked if they were going to launch a shuttle or something. I think there were more microphones than spears at the gathering.

Anybody could have been a media darling at those doings. I saw two Minneapolis TV people standing shoulder to shoulder as they gave their live report. I think they both wanted the community center doorway in the background of the shot. The center kitchen was used to feed those who came to talk treaty. It was a good feed. The witnesses brought their food. It was a culturally diverse meal. Spinach-wrapped rice met fry bread and deer meat. No one was saying where the fresh walleye came from. We all just ate it. After the feast, the spearers gathered in an old school bus to talk strategy and tactics. There were microphones and lenses stuck in all the windows. When we told the media to leave because we wanted to talk privately, they looked like sad-eyed puppies. We waited for dark and watched the sky clear. It had been half-raining all day. We offered tobacco.

The spearers met in Malmo to rally. The sound of the drum was heard in the dark. The singers' voices carried through the quiet evening. Fred Benjamin of Mille Lacs used his four-footed walker to get to the drum. I heard the elder's voice join the song. Sure enough, the media charged. It was like they were looking for something to focus on. Satellite trucks were lined up, ready to transmit the happenings live. The singers used TV lights to see the drum. After we had our convoy of fifty cars and trucks together, we went to the planned primary site to spear. My son Jim and a witness named Chris were in my car. I had a canoe, a light, and a spear. We had personal flotation devices along because we didn't want to break that particular state law. We followed Dave Aubid to Agate Bay on the east shore of Mille Lacs.

Our two cars pulled off the road to wait for the rest of the convoy. Just after we got out of the cars, a shot was fired. I demonstrated my turtle reflex when I heard the gunfire. It sounded like a shotgun, maybe a .20 gauge. We didn't hear any rounds going by, but some of us drifted over behind engine blocks. The game wardens notified the Aitken County sheriff, who came to the scene. It became a law enforcement matter so the spearers decided to go to the alternate site.

We drove south to Cedar Creek where there was a public access. Dave and I drove right up to the water because he knew the roads. My son Jim and I quickly got the canoe off the car, loaded up, and got out on the lake. Chris began to witness as we were leaving. After we got out a ways, we looked back in time to see the media lights arrive. Other boats and canoes were being put in the water and a crowd was forming. We paddled along the shore. The bottom of the lake was full of trash. I saw beer cans, a padlock, paper and plastic bags, and some things I couldn't identify. We also began to see fish. I stood up and began fishing.

The DNR wardens caught up to us and said we were under arrest for possessing a spear before May 1. They confiscated the spear, a light, and a spearing permit issued by the Sandy Lake Reservation. They were courteous and acted like professionals. The game wardens were playing catch and release with the Anishinaabeg spearers. One Shinnob went back for seconds. He got two tickets. We went back to shore to watch the rest of the arrests. The media was there waiting to catch any kind of news. After everyone was arrested, we went back to the East Lake Community Center to eat and tell fish stories. Some Anishinaabeg are willing to stand up for treaty rights.

Aaron and I are together a lot. Just the other day we motored to the Red Cliff Reservation. We were on our way to visit friends. The three-year-old boy was going to see some new sights with his grampa. The trip reminded me that my gramma raised me when I was that age. Before we left we packed some rations. Chips and cookies were in there. We had a jug of Sawyer water, a thermos of coffee, and a Hershey bar that rounded out our supplies. It was a warm, bright day with a slight breeze. I guess we could call it sweatshirt weather, not quite jacket weather but too cool for T-shirts. We went along the south shore of Lake Superior on Highway 13. The leaves were just beginning to come out. The poplars were the prettiest shade of green I've seen this side of money. The roadside grass was finally long enough to move with the wind. The new green was growing past the brown of last year. Aaron pointed at the birds. Sometimes he used his lips but mostly his little brown arm.

Grampa and grandson walked down the beach. The soft sand slowed us down, so we looked at everything closer. We saw an orange and black ladybug resting above the high-water mark. We carried driftwood with us for awhile. Aaron was walking slow on the way back to the car. He was asleep before I got the seat belt buckled. When he woke up, I gave him a drink of our home water. Aaron went back to his job of pointing out cows, birds, and orange school buses. I drank coffee with friends while Aaron explored a new backyard. We drove home on Highway 2, making a small circle through life together.

Fond du Lac's newest is open. The Black Bear Casino is now accepting nickels, quarters, and dollars. The $15 to $18 million casino located at Highway 210 and I-35 had what chairman Sonny Peacock called a soft opening. It's a pretty building. The big round structure looks like someone spent a lot of money there. The free valet parking makes it easy to get inside to spend money. There are a few problems to be solved before the Bear is officially open and functioning. The lack of drinking water, the roof leak, and the bingo game. Some people are saying they will take their bingo dollar to Duluth if the format doesn't change.

I hope they have the $80,000 sign up pretty soon. The Bear is invisible when approaching from the south. Maybe there is some marketing strategy there. If you build it, they will come, if they can find it.

We went to the white tent that is temporarily being used to feed the gamblers. The prices charged for the food were a little steep. Too steep for us, so we gambled hungry. I also began to wonder if the casino has a policy for dealing with bomb threats and other forms of sabotage. Would someone be mean enough to try to plug up the toilets?

The good part is that the casino is providing jobs. I have sisters, nieces, and cousins working there. The steady paychecks let them pay their bills, maybe gamble at another casino. When the thanks and congratulations are passed out at the grand opening, I hope they don't forget the workers: the change vendors, the slot supervisors, the technicians, the maintenance workers, the dealers and pit bosses, and the rest of the staff. They are the ones who have the most contact with the gambling public.

What are they going to do with the profits? When are the Fond du Lac people going to get a slice of that gambling pie? We have been patiently waiting for over ten years for some direct benefit from the gambling. It is past time to give the people a per capita payment. When we hear about a sign that costs $80,000, blacktopping on Highway 210 that costs $60,000, we are wondering when we get just a little chunk of that money. A smart politician would start promising per capita payments right now. The Reservation Business Committee is betting millions the customers will come and gamble millions.

At first, we read about him in the paper. Then a friend called and told us about Jim Weaver's walk to Washington, DC. Iron Legs, as he is called on the powwow circuit, is walking to Washington with a message for Hillary or Bill Clinton. We found him just west of Warba, Minnesota. He was sitting alongside Highway 2. His black Nikes with the swoosh stripes were off and he was taking a break. Cars and trucks went by. My grandson Aaron and I walked over and sat next to him on the shoulder of the road. Pretty soon we were lying back just like him. Aaron wandered off to find a good stick to play with but then found strawberries. At first, he ate them one at a time, then began sharing his find.

Iron Legs was wearing faded blue jeans and a white sweatshirt. The blue jeans had holes in the legs that looked like they were actually worn out from work, unlike those fashionable ones people buy that are pre-ripped. The sweatshirt had a picture of Chip Wadena, the president of the Minnesota Chippewa tribe. Chip was wearing a beret and looked like Saddam. The lettering on the sweatshirt said, "One on Every Rez." The shoulder boards in the picture had dollar signs on them.

Iron Legs had a blue headband and his white hair was in a po-nytail. His soft brown canvas pack was lying in the grass next to his legs. He showed us a license plate he found near Cass Lake. It read, "I owe, I owe, so off to work I go." The pack held juice and extra clothing. A strip of fluorescent orange tape was tied to the back of the pack. He carried a stick that he had carved. On the top end was an eagle head. Underneath the head were tied nine eagle feathers. The bottom end was sharpened so he could stick it in the ground. He said he carries it as a reminder of his forty-nine day fast. His eyes crinkled as he told us about overhearing some white people talking about "that old man out on the highway carrying a chicken on a stick."

Iron Legs sat up and put on his Nikes. He stood up and picked up his pack, grabbed his stick, faced east, and got ready to walk to Washington. He stepped off with a brisk pace and we ran to catch him. The feathers fluttered behind as they caught the wind. Iron Legs walks on the edge of the road, off the blacktop. He says the earth cushions his feet. We walked with him for a while. Cars and trucks went by. He seemed oblivious to the passing vehicles. He was more interested in the birds and animals he saw. Iron Legs pointed out plants and told how they were used by the people. He is seventy-two but walks like he was fifty years younger. He is on a walk to Washington but stops to admire the trees, the clouds.

A Shinnob went by and then stopped. He turned around and came back and asked us if we wanted a ride. His name was Robinson and he was from Cass Lake. We thanked him and told him about Iron Leg's walk. He left with a smile all over his face. We walked along Highway 2 until the support vehicle arrived. We shared some wa-ter and laughs and agreed to meet again. My grandson and I went home and slept like we were clubbed.

There is another big gathering planned for August 5, 1993. It is called a border-crossing rally. The event is coordinated by the Min-nesota Chippewa Tribe (MCT) and Canadian Chippewa tribes. The MCT is hoping that a thousand American Indians from the United States will show up in International Falls, Minnesota, for the rally and demonstration. The rally and march across the border will commemorate the Jay Treaty of 1794.

In a July 13 letter, White Earth president Darrell "Chip" Wadena said, "It is important that we show support to enforce and uphold the treaties recognizing the rights that indigenous people have in respect to international borders, freedom of movement, exemptions from Customs, and other rights."

Both groups will meet at the border and exchange spiritual and traditional gifts. The gifts to be exchanged include wild rice, smoked fish, tobacco pouches, sweetgrass braids, and sage. Canadian and U.S. Customs will be presented with a declaration of rights by participating tribes.

I remember our experience at U.S. Customs a few years ago and the feeling of being suspected of a crime just because we wanted to cross the border. We were worried that a full body search would be made after they finished with our car, pockets, and shoes. They didn't look where the sun don't shine, but we fully expected them to.

"Now what do them Indians want?" a white person asked recently. The person was a Black Bear Casino employee and was reading a news article about the Jay Treaty Rally in International Falls. I will tell that person who is slopping at the casino trough what we want.

We want respect. If you can't stand or understand Indians, maybe you should find another job. The casino is where you will see Indians every day. Some of the Indians might even be the boss. It's hard to look down on someone while kissing up.

Actually, we Indians want the same thing the white people want. We are humans and share the same basic needs, such as air, water, and food. We work so we don't have to depend on welfare, so our children can have a better life than we did.

Another thing we want is a recognition of our rights—the usual human rights and the rights guaranteed in the U.S. Constitution and treaties. As original inhabitants of this continent, we have dual citizenship. We are citizens of our tribal groups and the United States of America. Each kind of citizenship carries certain rights and responsibilities. They are mostly the same, but different in one important area. That area is treaty rights. Treaty rights were not granted by the United States, rather they were reserved by the Anishinaabeg people. We are not a conquered people.

I frequently hear treaties called nineteenth-century documents as if implying they are no longer valid because we are living in the twentieth, almost twenty-first century. Is the Bill of Rights an eighteenth-century document? The treaties are the law of the land today. Do you want to understand Indians? Simple, read the treaties—we do. But then again, I can hear Mitch Walking Elk singing, "And when they want what we got, they just change the laws."

We want solutions to the social problems that plague us. Racism, alcoholism, and poverty are but a few. We could quote statistics about infant mortality, teen suicide, and dysfunctional families.

In spite of the social problems, I suspect there are a lot of white people who want to be an Indian. I think so because of all those who say they are part Indian. Whenever I hear that, I wonder which part is Indian? The right hand or the whole arm? The lungs and the spleen? The top, middle, or bottom half? Hearing that someone is part Indian is a never-ending source of humor for me. Some of us are part white, but we don't brag about it or tell every white person we meet.

Perhaps it is our spirituality that people are seeking. Poet Robert Bly and the drums. The rent-a-shamans who peddle ceremonies and false hopes. The Rainbow who offered to teach me a pipe ceremony. I see people searching for something to believe in. On the other hand, I have met many who don't claim to be Indian. They just live our values and respect our traditions. Those who respect our ways, our history, get my respect. That's what it boils down to—respect, mutual respect.

So casino employee, come and learn about us. Find a fellow employee who is similar in age, family size, and habits. Hang out with that Indian person and their family. It would be a gamble, but you might win. After a while, you won't have to ask what them Indians want.

Fond du Lac Follies motored to International Falls for the Jay Treaty Rally. We followed the signs to Smokey Bear Park. We started seeing Indians on the street and gathering at the park. We knew we were at the right park when we saw the statue of Smokey. The smell from the paper mill was already there when we got out of the car. Hundreds, some say a thousand, First Nation people were there. Shinnobs from both sides of the line. We met friends and talked. After a while, I noticed we were walking and talking. Our walk took us across the imaginary line into Canada. Air and Water, our three-year-old grandson, almost made the entire walk. He wanted to be carried when we got into Canada. In Canada we ate, heard the drum, and listened to the leaders talk. It felt good to be an Anishinaabe that day. We straggled back over the border. When we got to the car, we quickly drove away from the paper-mill smell. We gathered material for family stories. Our grandson will be able to brag that he was fighting for treaty rights when he was three.

Ricing has come and gone again. Once again we were able to get out on the lakes for the Creator's gift. Despite the doom and gloom predictions, we were able to get enough rice for our needs. For me, this was the best year of ricing in a long time. My thirteen-year-old son Joseph went with me. It was his first time out on the lake as a ricer. It was a rez rite of passage. He started off by learning how to pole the canoe from the front. It was a bit awkward for him, but his natural athletic ability helped. At one point when we were just starting off, he wanted to quit. We were out in the lake, so he couldn't walk away. Eventually he got the hang of it and was soon moving the canoe through the water like an experienced poler.

After he felt good about being able to move the canoe, I decided to let him try knocking the rice. He was tentative at first but did show potential. We brought the rice home, and Joseph got the fire built under the parching kettle. When it was hot enough, he learned how to parch rice. He needed help at first, but by the fourth batch he knew how long to parch, how to turn the rice, what to look for while parching. As a proud parent, I let him have the entire day's harvest. Next he will dance and fan. After he cleans it, he should have twenty pounds of hand-finished rice. And he will have something to teach his children.

This year ricing was once again of interest to the media. *Martha Stewart Living* magazine sent out an art director and a photographer from New York. Anne Johnson and Stewart Ferebee had never been to northern Minnesota before and had never seen rice harvested. I guess the whole family will be in the magazine next year. The *Martha Stewart Living* readers will see how Shinnobs make rice without machines. The two New York people took some green wild rice home with them. I hope Martha likes it.

I feel sorry for all the Shinnobs who know it is ricing but were not able to get out on the lakes. The constraints of jobs, kids, school, or jail kept them from taking part in the annual harvest. I think I would be out of sync for the whole year if I couldn't make rice.

Fond du Lac Follies motored to Milaca for another court appearance over the spearfishing issue in Mille Lacs. The Shinnobs were there to face the judge. The lawyers for both sides of the case laid down some ground rules for the jury trial that is now scheduled for February. While waiting for the lawyers, we talked about a benefit at the Seward Cafe in Minneapolis. The purpose is to raise money for the Anishinaabe Liberation Front Legal Defense Fund. More details will follow as they become available.

While hanging around the courthouse in Milaca we talked with some Native people from Brazil. They were traveling with some Shinnobs from White Earth. They came to Mille Lacs County to see how justice is administered. While they were there, we learned that Milaca means something else in Portuguese. The word means something like blowing your nose or maybe some reference to snot. It loses something in the translation. Maybe there is a Portuguese speaker out there who can illuminate this for us.

All in all, it was a good day to go to court. The drive down and back was pleasant. The sun was shining hard as heck. Maples were exploding into red, the birch edging toward yellow. The sumac covered the slopes with an orangish red blanket. Only five months before the wheels of justice begin to grind on this again. We hope the case is settled before next spearing season. Until then, Shinnobs are free.

The Fond du Lac moose hunt is scheduled for October 1. Apparently the state and Fond du Lac have been talking about the seasons. When FDL refused to change its moose season, the state had to change theirs. Now the Shinnobs will be out hunting a day before the white hunters begin. Last year the issue of public safety kept the rez hunters from enjoying a full season of moose hunting. This year the state has tacitly acknowledged the 1854 treaty rights. At least this year they are not threatening to arrest Fond du Lac hunters who are out taking moose.

We are making some progress in the area of treaty rights. In the past the state would have just arrested hunters who were not following the state conservation laws. Now we are at the point where the state is negotiating with Fond du Lac about the seasons. This is an indication that the state recognizes the reservation's ability to monitor its hunters. The treaty rights are still valid. We just have to constantly remind people that the rights in the 1854 Treaty are not granted by the U.S. government but were reserved by the Anishinaabe. The state is learning that we have treaty rights and we will use and protect those rights for the future generations.

The Duluth newspaper reported that the National Indian Gaming Commission has ruled in favor of Fond du Lac. The way the profits are split now is in violation of the Indian Gaming Regulatory Act of 1988. The original 1984 agreement with the City of Duluth splits the profits with the rez getting 25.5 percent, the city 24.5 percent, and the jointly owned Fond-du-Luth Economic Development Commission 50 percent. According to the IGRA, Indians must get no less than 70 percent of the profits. The Fond-du-Luth Casino reported making over $7 million in profits last year. Now that the decision is made, the rez should be getting millions of dollars.

That brings up the question of what to do with the money. As a Fonjalacker, I have an idea of what to do with it. Give some of it to the Fond du Lac people. Make the Fonjalackers a priority instead of the grandiose dreams. For too many years we have been on the outside watching everyone else make money on gambling. Let us have a turn.

There are many good ideas out there from other Fond du Lac people. A new Ojibwe school building is one good idea, another is buying land. Others feel that the money should be spent on the elders and the young ones. Seed money for small business ventures is also a worthy idea. The health-care system could always use money to expand their services. There are many good ideas on how to best use the money.

I have a somewhat radical idea. Let's have a referendum and let the people decide. A couple years ago we voted in a non-election year on the 1854 treaty sale. We could vote on this important decision, too. After all, it is our money. Is there a rez politician daring enough to call for a referendum? Is there a Fonjalacker who would carry a petition for the referendum? It was the RBC and the lawyers who got us into the Fond-du-Luth fiasco in the first place. It was a different RBC but the same system. I think we should let the people decide.

We took *Walking the Rez Road* on a book tour. It was Patricia, Aaron, Pea, and me. Pea is my horseshoe partner. He signed on as an assistant driver. We left from Sawyer on the rez. Of course, we started with a rez car. The tired Mercury ran fine for the first two hundred miles, then it died. We were ten feet from our first stop on the book tour. We pushed the car into the parking space at the American Indian student house in Madison. We were there to meet and eat with the students at the university. We prayed and then ate together. After the last burp, we went outside to stare at the dead car. Everyone became a mechanic. Some suggestions were the timing chain, the carb, the coil. Pretty soon there were ten of us out there offering suggestions.

As we tried to get the car started, the dead car stories began to surface. For a while there we were stuck in Wyoming with a broken heater core. Then we were in California at 3 AM with two flat tires. At that point we were trying to outdo each other with dead car stories. The skins told stories for three hours before we quit trying to start the car. We went to bed wondering about cars and book tours. A tow truck dragged the rez car to the Ford dealer. The dealer began planning his trip to the Bahamas when he saw the car. The mechanic's machine said the car was brain dead. The module or the computer was fried. We became transportationally challenged.

The next day we borrowed a car to make it to the first two gigs. In Milwaukee we missed our exit and passed through a tough neighborhood. The windows in the brick buildings were either missing or boarded up. Graffiti was on all the flat surfaces. I was wearing my red headband and didn't know if I was a Crip or a Blood. I took off my headband until we got back on the freeway. After the gigs we tried to solve our car problem. The rez car was in the Ford garage while the dealer was adding up mechanic's hours times dollars. He was smiling. A friend came through town and took us to the car rental place at the Chicago airport. After that we were motoring in a rented Chrysler.

We did the radio, bookstore, and college campus gigs. We were mobile again. We went to the beach and threw a rock in for my nephew. After experiencing the lake we motored to the freeway. While we were at the lake, the interstate had converted into a long, skinny parking lot. We waited there quite a while with the people who usually park there every day. It wasn't too much fun in rush hour Chicago traffic. Good music, though. We scanned the dial and listened to a lot of good music. We stayed at Lola Hill's house in Joliet. Pea and I took a side trip to look at the riverboat casino, but we missed the boat. No gambling for us.

The next morning we talked on the radio with Kevin Mathews about the book. The producer later said we were talking to the 700,000 people who were just beginning to park on the freeways. Since we were already in the Loop in Chicago, we went to the Sears Tower and became tourists. We shoehorned in with the other tourists and rode to the top. The elevator lifted us 110 floors to the observation deck in seventy seconds. I know I left my guts and other internal organs back on the first floor. We looked around and came back down. The elevator does the seventy-second drop from up there. They almost got a squeal out of me that time. We went back to the rental car and got out of town fast.

The book tour brought us to Michigan. It was more of the usual—bookstore, college campus, radio, and TV gigs. We quickly learned the people in Michigan drive fast. One time we were driving ten over the limit to avoid getting run over. The cars and trucks were still passing us. The readings and book signings developed into a pattern. At each one, I would introduce Pea to the crowd. I told them that Pea led the standing ovations at the end of the reading. Pea would give the crowd a Sawyer wave. I also told the listeners that some of what they were going to hear would be understandable if they lived on the rez. I told them to watch Pea to see if he was laughing. If they saw his shoulders shaking, they would know it is the politically correct time to laugh.

We met many people on the book tour. For the most part it was a good experience, except for the rez-car part. When I first heard about book tours, I read about limousines, great hotels, and jetting from city to city. No one ever mentioned a rez car. On the way home we stopped in Madison to rescue the rez car from the Ford dealer. He was still totaling the bill a week later. It cost us hundreds of dollars to find out we were driving a rez car. We already knew that. We came sliding in to Sawyer. When I stepped out of the rez car, I made the umpire's hand gesture for safe. We were home.

# 6.
# seLf-sanding Roads

## 1994

Christmas—what a bummer. My earliest memories of Christmas were formed at the federal boarding school at Pipestone. We were given presents of ribbon candy and fruit. All it meant to me was some big guy was going to beat me up and take my presents. When I was in the Christian boarding school I was older so no one beat me up, but the season was still a disappointment. I learned about that time that there was no such thing as goodwill toward man.

When my son was in the first grade, he told the teacher that we didn't celebrate Christmas. She went out of her way and bought him a fake tree. We thanked her but left it in the box and later gave it to someone who does Christmas. In Vietnam Bob Hope came to help us celebrate Christmas. I couldn't figure out the link between peace on earth and a rice-paddy firefight. Today there is no tree inside my house. We just leave them outside where they continue to grow. No tinsel, angels, stars, or cute manger scenes. My light bill stays the same because we don't outline the house in colored lights. I could never make the connection between lights and the birth of the Christ child. The only real connection I can figure out is that the power companies sponsor lighting contests every year.

We went to Prairie Island for a bingo game. On the way down there, we saw many, many Christmas lights. When we got there we could see the red lights at the nuclear power plant. It looked like they were all decorated up for Christmas, too. Maybe if we didn't use as many lights, we wouldn't have to worry about above-ground storage for nuclear waste, especially in a flood plain.

No frenzied shopping at the mall for us. When we want to give a gift, we just do it regardless of the time of the year. For us, gift-giving is a year-round activity. We usually wait until after Christmas when the prices come down in the clearance sales. I am proud to be called a Scrooge. I am not the Grinch that stole Christmas. I just ignore it and it goes away on its own.

I am still confused—who are we supposed to honor at this time of the year? Is it Christ or Santa Claus? I was raised to respect other people's beliefs, but this doesn't mean I have to buy into the white guy's holiday. I just sit back and watch people go nuts. Call me un-American, but I don't believe in Christmas. I hope it works for those who do believe. As I was writing this, my grandson Aaron came walking by singing, "Jingle bells, jingle bells, jingle all the way."

Fond du Lac Follies rode the dog, the greyhound bus, to the Cities. It was the usual winter dead-car story. All my relatives who could give me a ride were either working or their cars weren't. I had to get to the Cities. The bus pulled into Cloquet and the driver said, "Standing room only until Hinckley. Otherwise, you can wait for the next bus six hours from now." I had to use the bathroom, so I got on first. Five others decided to stand in the bus aisle. After standing for a few miles, swaying around the corners, I decided the whole idea was silly. Stand on a bus all the way to the Cities? There must be a better way, I thought. I knew where there was an open seat. I went back in the bathroom. I closed the lid on the blue-water tank and had a seat. The plastic was kind of hard, but compared to standing—this was great. I had more elbow room than the other fifty-two passengers.

I opened my newspaper full width and read. There was a little window in there that I could open. I couldn't see much besides snowbanks and ditches but felt like I could control my environment. Fresh air when I wanted it. I propped the door open so the other passengers would know I was a social animal. I used a Greyhound moist towelette to wedge the light on. The vibrations from the motor were coming through the plastic seat. I stood for a while because I was beginning to enjoy the buzz. I thought of those vibrating motel beds that cost a quarter.

After Hinckles, more people got on. They began to use the bathroom. My private sitting room wasn't so private anymore. I was careful to air the place out after each visitor. I could see the strangers' butts rubbing as they squeezed up and down the aisle. I took a little power nap draped over the sink. My private sitting room got to the Cities the same time as the rest of the bus. I got off that bus, walked away, and never looked back. My butt quit tingling after about an hour.

Fond du Lac's "newspaper" came out. We got a copy of volume 1, number 1. The reason given for not using a Fonjalacker's print shop to print the publication is because he couldn't print in color. I looked and looked. There is no color but black and white used in the publication. They will have to come up with a new reason for not using the small business owned by the Fond du Lac band member.

The new effort is called *Nah-Gah-Chi-Wah-Nong, Di-Bah-Ji-Mo-Win-Nan*. It's funny. When I hear those words spoken in our language, I don't hear the dashes in between parts of the words. If you say it using the dashes, it sounds artificial; sort of what Hollywood thinks we sound like using our language.

The mission statement for the publication says, "It is not our intention to be a vehicle of divisiveness. To that end, we do not plan to publish editorials, letters to the editor or opinion/editorial pieces. There is an abundance of opportunity for the publishing, airing and dissemination of material of personal opinion in other communication vehicles available throughout the area, region and state." In other words, if it ain't good news for the RBC, they won't print it.

In some places the editor, Mike Legarde, calls his effort a newspaper, in a couple of other places, he calls it a newsletter. Let's hope he finds its identity before too much money is spent on this public-relations device. I would bet a dollar to a donut that the Fond du Lac Follies will not appear in *Nah-Gah-Chi-Wah-Nong, Di-Bah-Ji-Mo-Win-Nan*. Let's see what it would sound like: Fond-du-Lac-Follies. Nope, doesn't work for me.

QUESTION: *What's the difference between praying*
*in a ceremony and praying at the casino?*

*ANSWER: At the casino, you really mean it.*

The Follies motored to St. Paul, Red Lake, and Duluth in Minnesota and to Wisconsin and Illinois to share my book. We learned something from the last road trip. This time we used a rental car and left the rez car home. It was too easy. The hired car just ate up the interstate miles. Gone was the tension of waiting for something to break. We only had to stop for gas—how boring. It seemed unnatural. The rental car effortlessly got us to Beloit College. We spent time in a classroom talking about *Walking the Rez Road.* Later that evening there was a reading for the college community. Sure enough, we met another Fonjalacker in Beloit. John Sharlow and his wife came to hear the words from home. We played the "Do you know _____?" game with the Shinnobs.

The next morning the rental car purred to Galesburg, Illinois, to Knox College. On the way we drove past Ronald Reagan's boyhood home. We didn't stop, just speeded up a bit to get away from that place. I noticed the dirt blowing across the road. The white man continues to amaze me. They went ahead and invented self-sanding roads. I never would have thought of it. Here's the way it works. They plow the cornfields bare of vegetation, then the wind comes along and blows the topsoil across the roads. Self-sanding roads. What will that white man think of next?

When we arrived at Knox College, Dave Williams showed us where we would eat, sleep, and teach. We met another Indian at the college. She was a Diné from the Southwest. I think she was homesick. At one point she said she wanted to speak her language to me because I looked like people from home. We ate together and talked about white people. She had never heard of self-sanding roads either. I invited her to visit Fond du Lac and meet the family.

While we were visiting, Dave Williams offered to show us a building that was used in the Lincoln-Douglas debates. We didn't feel like arguing, so we went on the tour. Lincoln? Wasn't he the president that hung thirty-eight Dakota at Mankato? We looked, but it just looked like an old building.

I think the students at Knox learned that the Anishinaabe are alive and well. We watched the sun come up three times before we could point the rental car north. Along the way home, we stopped in Madison, Wisconsin, to hear Fred Ackley talk. He is the Mole Lake Sokaogon Chippewa tribal judge. He spoke eloquently about the reasons why Exxon should not mine in northern Wisconsin. Yes, Exxon, the same folks who brought us the *Exxon Valdez* oil spill, want to mine in Forest County. There was a video that showed the alliance between Indians and environmentalists. My favorite part was when Walt Bressette counted coup on the mining machines. It had a Chinese feel to it—humans against tanks.

We gassed up and glided north in the rental car. We had spent so much time in the car we wanted to name it. My wife wanted four lines of the Follies to say hello to her friends. I told her we couldn't use my newspaper column for personal messages to Mary Jane Stillday, Lou Losh, Shirley Larsen Wilson, Renee Senogles, Toyo Conito, or Doris Smith.

We tapped into the cycle of seasons once again. It was a family affair to go to the sugar bush. Anishinaabeg have been making maple syrup for hundreds of generations. We are just one of them. The sun says it is sugar bush time. Aaron, our three-year-old grandson, went to be in the woods. His grandmother told him we were in the deer's house and should be quiet. When we walked on the deer trail, he could see the tracks. He also saw the deer's leavings. Aaron was quiet. The cool wind was a reminder of winter. The warm sun was a promise of spring. The feeling of family made us warm inside.

We were looking for trees to tap. Actually, Aaron's sugar bush began when he watched his grampa make taps for the trees. Instead of Barney and Big Bird, his eyes followed the maple sticks that were drilled, carved, and turned into taps. He practiced his counting when he put the completed taps in a coffee can. The numbers he used didn't match the taps he was counting, but that didn't matter. He was counting. Aaron was learning sugar bush and math. His grandparents picked out a good spot to begin tapping. The trees were the right size and close together. There were no hills to climb. The sun had melted the snow at the bottom of the trees. The maple trees had a little brown collar of last fall. The leaves that looked like a flag from Canada were inside the collar. Aaron already knew about making an offering of tobacco. He had done that before. The holes his grampa drilled were at just the right height for Aaron to get a close look. He watched for a while and then handed his grampa a small twig to clean out the shavings.

Aaron put a milk jug on the tap. He used a hole his grandmother had cut into the white plastic container. After a few trees, he was telling his grampa to hurry because he had a jug ready. Aaron watched the sap drip from the taps. He looked at a couple of trees before he tried tasting it. Aaron caught the drips of sap on his tongue. His smile was like a warm sun to his grandparents. He soon noticed that he could walk on top of the snow while his grandparents were breaking through. While we were trudging through the snow, Aaron was dancing from tree to tree. He wanted to tap more trees, but his grandmother told him we were out of taps and jugs. He took a jug off a tree and had a final taste. The three-year-old was still looking for good trees while walking on the deer trail out of the woods.

The next day we went back to see how much sap we had collected. On the way to the woods, we pointed out a bald eagle to our grandson. He didn't say anything as his eyes followed the flight of the brown and white bird. The milk jugs were half full. Aaron was a big help in gathering the sap. It was easy for him to run on top of the snow. He emptied the milk jugs into the five-gallon pails we carried. We brought the sap home. We sometimes boil sap out in the woods, but we didn't this year. We had firewood at home and it didn't make sense to haul the wood to the woods. As soon as *Barney* was over on TV, Aaron came outside to watch the boiling of the sap. He recognized the big black kettle from our last wild rice season. We had a hot fire and Aaron learned to stay away from it. He also learned to stay upwind of the smoke when he was playing in the yard.

The fire burned on for seven hours. As the sap boiled down, we added more. We knew that sitting around a fire was a good place to tell stories and hold a grandson in your lap. We boiled until we had syrup. Aaron got to taste it as it got sweeter and sweeter. He stood back as we lifted the kettle off the fire. We took the syrup inside, where we filtered it. The golden brown syrup was warm as we poured it over pancakes. Aaron wants to go to the woods again. He is learning something that he can teach his grandchildren.

QUESTION: *Why is some of your syrup dark and some light colored?*
ANSWER: *Some of it we boil at night.*

Now my TV tells me I need to buy a new kind of food for the cat. It is designed for the cat's urinary tract. I didn't even know I was supposed to worry about cat pee. The ever-vigilant manufacturers and ad agencies have enlightened me and I now realize the error of my ways. Jeez, another addition to the list of things I have to worry about. Let's see now: Prairie Island nuclear waste, acid rain, clear-cutting Minnesota, Wisconsin mining, unsafe drinking water, ravaged rainforests, and ozone holes. Also war, racism, poverty, injustices, cultural genocide, ignorance, rent-a-shamans, treaty rights, crime, and a rez car that won't start. I'll have to drop one worry from the list to make room for the cat pee problem. I also have another worry—we don't have a cat. Now I suppose I'll have to get one so I can buy urinary-tract food.

QUESTION: *(Asked at a restaurant.) Do you have a reservation?*
ANSWER: *Yes, Fond du Lac.*

It was a nice Indian Spring day. The sun was shining all over the place. Fond du Lac Follies motored to the Upper Peninsula of Michigan. We went to Northern Michigan University at Marquette. We were invited to read poems and stories for the Indian studies department. We set up camp in the local Ramada. We had a great view out the window. I looked and thought gee, they have parking lots just like we do back home. We met the Shinnob students and ate together. I learned that we were still in the ceded territory after a five-hour drive. The imaginary line was about ten miles east of town.

The Follies has been motoring around the Midwest. In the early part of the month, we went to Marshall, Minnesota, to talk to the students at Southwest Minnesota State University. The countryside around Marshall is flat. For a woods Shinnob it felt kind of strange. No trees and you could see for miles in every direction except down. It reminded me of that old story about running away from home. Couldn't do it there because they can see you for three days.

Cruised down there in the rez car. Surprisingly, nothing broke, didn't have to stop for repairs anywhere. Just when I think I understand that car, it does something different. It just politely drank gas and sipped oil.

Once we got there we finally got to meet Bill Holm, the Icelandic storyteller. He's a big guy, kinda looks like the stereotypical Santa Claus image except this Saint Nick smokes Camel straights. His office is delightfully cluttered with books. The books looked like they had been well used. Bill Holm wrote some of the books on the shelves. My favorite is called *Coming Home Crazy.* It's a story about a Minneota, Minnesota, college teacher who goes to China for a while. We see culture shock from a white guy's point of view.

Due to a misread schedule, I arrived five minutes and twenty-four hours early. Once I found out, I tried to pretend it was all planned that way. Okay now what? Since Pipestone was just forty miles away, I decided to go there.

It's been years since I have been to the Pipestone boarding school. I looked for familiar buildings that I first saw as a young Shinnob in the late 1940s. All I saw was the gym, the superintendent's house, and the hospital. The shop building, the boys' dorm, the administration building, the school building, and the girls' dorm were all gone. Those old red Sioux quartzite buildings were torn down to make room for a technical college. It looked like part of the grounds was being used for a nursing home. The two big stone pillars by the road to town are still there.

I went to town to the Pipestone County Museum. I toured the exhibits. They had pipes made of Pipestone on display. Out of respect, the stems and the bowls of the pipes were not joined together, which is the way the old people say it should be. I met Joe Agar, the director of the museum. He showed me some old pictures that were taken when the boarding school was still in operation. I didn't find anyone I knew in the pictures, but the buildings looked familiar. I even found the dorm window I used to use to look for home. Joe told me that the farmers around Pipestone were paid a bounty for reporting runaway Indians. He said the townsfolk would like to forget that part of their history.

Joe is interested in collecting oral histories of students who went to school there. Boy, I could tell him stories about that place. I went back to the school grounds and walked around. The wind that was constantly blowing was familiar. The black soil of the cornfields reminded me of my early childhood days. The cottonwood trees near the creeks reminded me how naive I was then. My older sister Judy told me we get cotton from the cottonwood tree. I believed her and would spend hours looking for a new shirt, pants, or socks on the trees.

It made me feel a little sad to be there. I remember the nights. One kid would be homesick and would start crying. That would get everyone else started and pretty soon the whole boys' dorm was bawling. I suppose we were crying so we wouldn't explode; maybe it was the only thing we could do in that situation. It didn't feel too good to be back there. I escaped like I used to do when I was a student. I walked past where the girls' dorm used to be. I snuck behind the superintendent's house and made it to the brush. I walked to the falls and just sat there soaking up the positive ions from the moving water. The sound was relaxing and I forgot about the crying in the boys' dorm.

I looked at the rock formation we called the Great Stone Face, also called Leaping Rock. I walked behind it and jumped out to it. The leap across wasn't as scary as when I was a kid. Howah, this fifty-one-year-old Shinnob can still do it, I thought. Just being in that place reminded me of how much I have survived. Not just me, but all the lonely, homesick Indians who went to Pipestone. I picked up a couple of pieces of Sioux quartzite. It looked like part of the original buildings. I brought the rocks home for my cousins and friends who had also survived the boarding-school experience.

*QUESTION: Why did you think he hitchhiked a lot?*
*ANSWER: He used a suitcase made from a five-gallon gas can.*

I went to the monthly open Reservation Business Committee meeting at the old casino building. I felt grateful that we are still having open meetings. I hear some other tribal governments still don't meet with their people. There was a brisk question-and-answer period. I learned that we have $17 million in the bank—profits from two casinos. The results of the election are in. The people said no—gaawiin—to using casino profits to build a new school because the federal government is obligated to build schools as a part of our treaty rights. The people won.

We motored to Mole Lake for some environmental doings. My son Jim and I went to a conference to see what was what. We brought a tent, air mattresses, and some Sawyer water. The festivities were set up in a large grassy field next to the pallet-making plant at Mole Lake. At the registration booth I learned that we were a little late because some four hundred people had already signed up before we got there. We joined right in. We found a place to pitch our tent and listened to the talent show. There were people singing, reciting poems, and playing music.

We began to have a feeling of community right away because we began running into old friends. I snuck up on Joe Campbell from Prairie Island. For the past several years we have been playing a game of sneaking up on each other. Sort of reliving the old Dakota-Ojibwe wars. This is a friendly game we play. The one who wins is the one who can say hello before the other person knows who is there. I won this time because I saw Joe coming across the field. I hid behind an elder and before Joe saw me, I stood up and said, "Hello." Joe staggered back and said, "You got me." He then reminded me of the time he was able to sneak up on me. It was at the Black Bear Casino and I was so intent on the nickel slots I didn't see him until he tapped me on the shoulder and said, "Hello." It was good to see him again, but it was better to see him before he saw me.

There were Native people from all over the place there in Mole

Lake. I met some folks from Alaska, Washington State, and New York. It was not surprising that we were all of the same mind about the proposed mine. No—we don't want a mine. Stop right now. If you mine you'll ruin the environment. We took part in a march to the proposed Crandon mine site. It was a good feeling to be a part of the hundreds of people who were walking together. I heard a five-mile-long AIM song. The drum and singers kept the people synchronized. When we arrived, I took a look at the proposed Exxon mine site. The birch trees there are some of the best I have seen in many years. The birch are dying all over northern Minnesota, but the ones there were in great shape. It would be a shame to cut down those beautiful trees so they can make a hole in the ground that will pollute the water.

While we were at the mine site, the law arrived. Captain Gibson, that's G-I-B-S-O-N, said he was there to protect the mine site from the people who want to protect the earth. He told us we had to leave but was decent enough to wait until the ceremony was over. He asked me how long it would last. The only answer I could give to him was from the beginning to the end. I later heard someone put a bumper sticker on his squad car that said "No to Mining."

Will Exxon win this one? They must need the money after paying billions for the massive oil spill in Alaska. The answer may be found on the state seal of Wisconsin. It shows a miner.

We went to the powwow at Mole Lake. I especially liked the maple and cedar arch they use for grand entry. I was also glad to see that Jim "Iron Legs" Weaver is still walking around the powwow circuit. He and his wife had their shirt stand set up at Mole Lake. I wonder what powwow I will see him at next?

Bob Holman from the PBS series *United States of Poetry* invited me to take part in his project. He and Washington Square Films are filming poets all over the United States. It was an honor to be asked to take part. They picked about seventy poets from around the country. To be in the film, we had to meet them in Milwaukee. They flew us down there from St. Paul. It was a little bitty plane. It was so small that it looked like it could take off and land on the wing of a regular-sized plane. My wife Pat and grandson Aaron went with me. Pat has flown before, but that didn't stop her from squeezing my hand until it went numb. This was Aaron's first time in a plane. We watched him to see his reaction to his first official airplane ride. He stared out the window as we were taking off. Once we were up a couple of hundred feet, he went to sleep. He slept all the way to Milwaukee.

Once we got there, our part of the filming took several hours. After each take, the director would say, "Beautiful, beautiful. Now, let's take it from the top again." It took at least twelve takes before the director was satisfied. Aaron watched the filming. The next morning we were eating breakfast. When the waitress brought Aaron his pancakes, he told her, "Beautiful, beautiful." We got back on the plane and Aaron went to sleep. The film came out the next spring.

QUESTION: Didja hear any new snagging lines
at the Prairie Island powwow?
ANSWER: Yes: "I get a gambling per capita check, too."

The Follies has been on the road again, just trying to get every last mile out of that rez car. Our travels took us to the Lac du Flambeau Reservation. Once we got there, we went to Nick and Charlotte Hockings's Ojibwe village. They have constructed wigwams and an educational walking tour. During the tour, people learn about the seasonal life of the Anishinaabeg. I saw a sugar bush and a rice camp. There was a birchbark canoe. The tour is conducted by the Hockings or one of their volunteers. I like what Nick and his wife are doing. I think they are preserving parts of our traditional life-style. They are becoming a cultural resource bank. Nick said Anishinaabeg people stop by and share what they know. I added some little bits I knew about basswood and birch bark. Another reason I like it is because it educates people about us. Since racism is fueled by ignorance, Nick and Charlotte's educational programs help by teaching people about us. Maybe if people knew more about us, we could get along better.

Fond du Lac Follies motored to Cloquet to take part in their First Annual Traditional Veterans Powwow. It was a baby powwow. They had an entry. It was a pretty good entry, but I don't think it was grand. Maybe next year they'll have a grand entry. Joe Martineau did a good job of pulling the whole thing together. He was on hand to answer questions and solve problems that came up. The vendors really liked this baby powwow because there was no charge to set up a food stand. No three-hundred-dollar food-stand fee like other powwows around here. If there is going to be a second annual veterans powwow, there could be more advertising. In spite of the small size, it felt good to be there. There was an intimate feel to the dance. Not crowded like some, where people raise dust just walking around.

Next we motored to the annual Mashkawisen powwow. The Follies didn't have to motor to this one because it is always held just down the road, but we did anyway. My sister Nita and I did a quick powwow checklist:

Eagle flying over—check
Bone-whistle lecture—check
Lost kids at the emcee's stand—check
Dropped feather—check
Honor songs—check
Tape recorders around the drum—check
Meeting old and new friends—check
Pull-tabs—check
Three-hundred-dollar food-stand fee—check
Powwow buttons—check
Long-winded emcee—check

The powwow seemed smaller this year compared to a few years ago. The buttons were free this year and we ate good at the feast. I guess we'll go again next year just because it is down the road from the house. Not long after the Follies reported on the garbage at the last Mashkawisen powwow, the organizers started hiring ten or fifteen young people to pick up the garbage and secure it in bags throughout the day. If Iron Eyes Cody (a non-Indian actor) rode his horse around this powwow he'd have no reason for tears.

While motoring on Interstate 35, I saw a rez car on the side of the road. The car was headed north. I knew it was a rez car right away because I have driven so many of them. The hood was up and one Shinnob was staring at the engine. The other Shinnob was gathering sage. It was as if they were illustrating that old saying, "If the good Lord gives you lemons, gather sage." A couple miles past the first car there was another carload of Shinnobs also gathering sage. Of course, we know it is dangerous to stop alongside of the interstate. It is also illegal unless you have an emergency. Would being without sage constitute an emergency?

QUESTION: *How did you know he was a rookie ricer?*
ANSWER: *He was using a kayak.*

Once again, the annual gift of wild rice was given to the Anishinaabe people. Compared to previous years, this year we had a good crop. There also seem to be more and more ricers nowadays. A few years ago we would be the only canoes on some lakes. There were a lot of people working on preserving and enhancing the wild rice crop. The Rice Committee should be thanked for their efforts. Sonny Greensky and his crew worked all spring and summer to make sure the water moved through the reservation watershed. It is hard work to clear the ditches of trees and brush. I know because I got tired just watching them. They must have fed a lot of mosquitoes, too. Reggie Defoe was out monitoring the crop. I would run into him way out in the woods as he went about his duties.

My family took part in the wild rice harvest. This year we just stayed on the reservation and riced the committee lakes. My fourteen-year-old son Joseph was out on the lake poling again this year. He is getting better at it. He didn't even scare me once with a tippy canoe. Joseph and my oldest son, Jim, went out together. When I saw that, I started thinking and got very profound. When they went out to gather rice, I realized that I had seen four generations of Anishinaabe ricing. My grandparents, my parents, myself, and now the next generation have all been ricers. We are lucky.

This year moved our rice camp from the backyard to the side of the house. At the original location we couldn't see who was going by or coming to visit. We moved the rice camp just because we were nosy. It made it easier to parch the rice when there were others to help. As usual, Pat danced on the rice while I fanned it. The whole family gathered together to clean it. There were heads bent over plates on the kitchen table as we told stories and cleaned rice.

Fond du Lac Follies motored to the Chicago area to read a poem. The event was a reception following a concert by Bonnie Raitt. It was held in a large tent on the grounds of Poplar Creek Music Theater where Bonnie Raitt performed. She sang and then came to the tent to meet the fans. Bonnie Raitt is a gracious woman who helps Native causes. At the doings they wanted me to read one poem. I told them that I drove five hundred miles to get there and I would recite two poems. Nobody stopped me, so I did. After the reading, I gave Bonnie Raitt my autograph in a book. She thanked me and hugged me. I hugged back. My wife later told me I looked like I was hugging too enthusiastically.

Up close, Bonnie Raitt has crinkly blue, blue eyes that seem to look deep inside you. She's slender; my cousin would say she is as skinny as a turn signal. She has big hair. She came by again and told Pat that she has a "cool husband." Pat said, "I know." I agreed with both of those women.

We motored to Mille Lacs for the second annual Native Arts Circle gathering. We camped right on the shore of the lake. What a setting. I felt just artsy. It felt good to sit there and sew on a birchbark basket. A lot of time was spent just walking around and saying, "Hi, how are ya? Hi, how are ya?" to the assembled artists. We began meeting old friends right away. I said hello to Ellen Olson from Portage. She said she is working on a bandolier bag for the new American Indian museum in Washington D and C. Howah, someone we know will be a part of that new museum.

It was a pleasure to see Baptiste Sam again. I always get a warm feeling inside me when she smiles at me with those eyes. She was demonstrating one of the many arts she has mastered. A couple of eagles circled the grounds for a while. They looked like they were pretty serious about hunting. Maybe they were just checking out the doings. There was a powwow, too. Part of the powwow was a fry bread contest. Naturally, my wife Pat won. Is that bragging? Nah, it's fattening.

FDL Follies jetted to New York to attend a water conference. We drove one of our rez cars to the airport in Duluth. We were hoping the airlines were not using a rez jet. At the airport, I learned that my suspender buckles set off alarms. I took them off and then quickly became worried that the pants would fall off my skinny Ojibwe butt. I sat in my assigned seat and hoped we wouldn't be like that plane in Pennsylvania that tried to fly underground.

It sure doesn't take long for a plane to get to the Cities. It was an uneventful landing. It takes about two and a half hours to fly to New York. That is a long time to go without a cigarette, especially when you are scared to fly in the first place. New York, the Big Apple. I immediately began seeing thousands of people that I didn't know. The city looks just like the pictures I have seen of the place. We got a room at the Washington Square Hotel and learned that Bob Dylan and Joan Baez used to live there.

The hotel was just across the street from Washington Square Park. While I was sitting there, I noticed that the police were sur-rounding and sealing the park. I wasn't worried. I knew I had paid that parking ticket from 1976, the last time I was in the city. Turns out they weren't looking for me. They were after drug dealers that they had been watching all day. A man tried to run and was thrown to the ground right in front of me. The cop took out his gun and told the guy, "Don't move, don't move!" as he stuck his gun against the man's head. The man said, "I'm not moving, I'm not moving." I said, "I am, I am!" as I got out of the line of fire. I had been in New York for five hours before I saw my first gun. After the arrests were made, the cops unsealed the park. While all this was going on, the drug dealers just moved across the street to carry on their trade and wait for the cops to leave.

New York is busy, almost like everyone had two pots of coffee before they hit the streets. I was invited to meet some people at a fancy restaurant on Fifth Avenue. Being a Shinnob, I ordered a rabbit dish. Fifteen bucks for a little bitty bowl of something that could have been rabbit. Just a couple of pieces, about as much meat as on one hindquarter. I wanted to show them how to really cook rabbit, but they didn't look interested. I was going to leave a snare as a tip but didn't have one with me, so I just left money.

The Smithsonian Institution had just purchased the George Heye collection to create a branch of the National Museum of the American Indian near Battery Park. They were remodeling the building for the grand opening. I found a little piece of the building and kept it for good luck. We went to an art show in Soho. I was carrying one of my birchbark fanning baskets. I set it down while I found a bathroom. When I came back, the people were surrounding it and oohing and aahing over the basket. I let them admire it for a while, then picked it up again.

While in New York I hung out with Bob Holman, the guru of poetry. He reported that the project we worked on together will be out in the spring. It is called *United States of Poetry.* He showed me his digs at the Nuyorican Poets Cafe. I stood up on my hind legs and recited poems to the East Village crowd. The people listening laughed at the right times and were silent at the right times. There was some kind of a satellite hookup with Santa Monica, California, and Toronto, Canada. I ran into Anishinaabe poet Diane Burns at the Poets Cafe. It felt like home when she said "boozhoo" to me. I gave her some wild rice because I don't know what kind of ricing season they had in New York City.

QUESTION: *Is that really a poem or did you just make it up?*
ANSWER: *Yes.*

Fond du Lac Follies motored to the ceded territory to hunt moose under the provisions of the 1854 Treaty. On the way, my cousins and

I were discussing what kind of moose we wanted. We were not after a trophy, we were after meat. We decided that a two- or three-year-old dry cow would be best for us. Next year we'll try for a trophy rack. This year we just wanted to eat moose meat.

We drove to our reservation-assigned zone and proceeded to look for a moose. It didn't take too long to spot one and shoot it. It was a dry cow. We learned the last few times we went hunting how to move that much meat. We were prepared with a bone saw, knives, and a come-a-long. It was a simple matter to winch the dead moose up into the pickup truck. Skinning the moose took longer than the actual hunt. It was a family affair to skin the animal. Cousins and nephews all got a turn at learning how to skin the moose. After removing the hide, we salted it down. I can already picture moccasins made by my wife Pat from the hide. I can almost taste the moose steak now. Here at Fond du Lac, we are using our treaty rights.

The 49ers scalped the Redskins according to a sports reporter on one of the local TV stations. My fourteen-year-old son Joseph, a sports jock, reacted quite quickly. He said, "Hey, that's a racist thing to say." He called the TV station and was given the brush-off. I called the next morning and went upstairs. I talked with the news director of the station. We had a long and meaningful discussion. He said the reporter was new and he was surprised it had happened. The news director said he is a thousand percent against things like that and promised to work closer with the Indian community. He assured us it would not happen again. As one way of making amends, he invited my son to the studio to see how the sports reports are put together.

Fond du Lac Follies motored to Minny to talk at a Christian church. The name of the church was St. Joan of Arc. At first I thought it had some connection with welding but later learned that it is a Catholic church. We had a great time singing with the Catholics. This church was unlike any other Catholic church I have ever visited. I brought one of my fanning baskets to show them I was prepared for the collection part of the worship. It didn't hurt a bit to go to church with these Catholics. They were just people having a good time together. The Catholics invited us back and we might just take them up on it. I'll think about it for the next twenty-five years or so, then decide.

## 7.
# FuLL-BLooded white PeopLe

## 1995

Hell just froze over because Fonjalackers got a per capita gambling payment. After almost fifteen years of high-stakes bingo and gambling casinos, we got a check for $1,500 each. That comes out to a little over a hundred dollars a year. I'm glad we got the money. Now Mom can get that operation and I can send my kids to Harvard. I can also get that Ferrari I've always wanted. I'll decide on the color after my round-the-world vacation.

What is it about this gambling? It has taken over our lives. If we're not actually gambling, we're talking about it. If we have or don't have a job at the casino, we're talking about it. We're always talking about gambling. Now the latest subject is the per capita payment. We're all talking about the $1,500 payment. Wall-to-wall Shinnobs at Wal-Mart. Everyone is just cashy now. What a boast to the local economy. The cash registers are singing around the rez. At any gathering of Shinnobs, the subject of gambling always comes up. You hear things like:

"I hit the white sevens on the single-line machine last night."

Or, "There's been a change in the casino's personnel policy manual. Now you can get a day off for a funeral—if it is your own."

Or, "I had an out on the G-ball game. If they would have called my number, I'd have $12,000 to spend."

Or, "Gramma, are you going to bingo again?"

Or, "Split those nines."

Or, "We just had a jackpot on the quarter Double Diamonds. That winner got $1,250."

Or, "What is the RBC doing with all that money?"
Or, "I hope I break even. I can use the money."

Gambling is starting to get me worried. I can't think of anything in the past forty years that has come into our lives with such an impact. This must be what it was like when Christianity first came to the Anishinaabeg. I must confess, I was one of the first gambling workers here on the rez. I worked as a bingo board vendor. It was when Fond du Lac first started with high-stakes bingo. We were using chips in those days and selling boards for a dime. We had carpenter's aprons to hold our change as we walked around the bingo players. The game was held at the Ojibwe School and the spillover crowd sat in the Elderly Nutrition Program dining room. Back then I didn't know it would grow into the monster that so dominates our lives here at Fond du Lac.

Fond du Lac gambling is buying us a hotel. The RBC and other dignitaries will be breaking ground for a multimillion-dollar hotel adjacent to the Black Bear Casino. That's a good business move because of the shortage of quality hotel rooms in the Twin Ports area. When I was growing up on the rez, tar-paper shacks were common. Now the talk is of skywalks connecting the atrium to the casino. What a change in just a few years.

I read in the newspapers that when people are arrested for stealing from their employers, they blame the Indian casinos. A new legal defense is born: Blame the Indians.

When will the gambling mania end? More importantly, what is going on while we are all so busy talking about gambling? Is someone trying to sneak off with our water or the uranium under the rez? Other than Walt Bressette, who is protecting the treaty rights?

QUESTION: *What's a new snagging line at Fond du Lac?*
ANSWER: *"I didn't cash my per capita check yet."*

Winter is here and my grandson "Aaron Ezigaa" and I went out in the woods to see if we could choke some rabbits. We were tired of TV.

Ayaa biboon omaa ninoozhishe "Aaron Ezigaa" bimose waabi

giishpin giinetwindgii daa-giibinewen aanind waboozoog. Gii-daa ayekozi ganawaabaam mazinaateshiigan.

Snaring is an old and honorable profession among the Shinnobs of northern Minnesota. I told my wife that this is the time of the year when Shinnobs check their trap lines. She shook her Dakota head and said, "A one-snare trap line?"

Miish nagwaaganan gete-mino anokii megwe. Anishinaabeg ondaadad Minnesota giiwedinang. Aajind nindekwem azhigwa memwech apii Anishinaabeg naadaasoonaagane. Wiwewebikwetaw bwaanikwe idash ikido, "Nagwaagan dasoonaaganan bezhig?"

We're already starting to hear Sawyer Shinnob snaring stories. One guy said he got one rabbit and an owl got the other. The owl did leave the empty snare and certain internal parts. We went out in the woods to snare our own stories.

Giimawindemin madwe Gwaaba'igan Anishinaabeg agood-waagan. Bezhig inini aajind dadibaajimo bezhig waabooz miisa gookooko'oo giiwiisin bezhig waabooz.

Gookooko'oo nagad agoodwaagan idash nagizhy. Giinawind jekaakwa'am agoodwaagan maamigin aajim.

Aaron was about to join the ranks of the rabbit-chokers. He has been on the planet for almost five years and has never set a snare. His education was lacking until today.

Ezigaa wii izhaamagad niapiitendaagozi waabooz agoodwaa-ganan. Gii bimaadizi aki gegaa naanobiboonagizi gaawiin bagidi-nagoodoo. Gii gikendaaso gaamashi biinish noongom.

We began by studying the tracks. Aaron learned the difference between rabbit and dog tracks. He also could tell which tracks were new and which were old. While looking at the tracks, Aaron showed me how the rabbits leave those marks. He crouched down and did a fair imitation of a rabbit hopping through the snow.

Niinawind maajii nandagikend okawitoon. Ezigaa nandagikend bakaan nisawayi'ii waabooz idash animosh nandokew.' Ganawaa-band gikend giishpin gete oshkinaagwad. Eshkwaa nandokawe' Ezigaa gikinoowaaband'iwe waaboozoog nagad ozhitaw beshibii. Izhichige mino-ayaa gwaashkwani zhaabwayi'ii goon.

Just being in the woods with the little boy brought back memories. First, of course, was the cold. It was ten below zero with a wind-chill of fifty below. We were layered up for the cold, so no problem. Then there was the snow. My grandson is tall enough now to walk in the woods without tripping all the time. It makes it easier. I could see he was learning how to walk through the brush and snow. I remembered walking behind as grampa or some older relative broke trail for me. It felt good to be breaking trail for my grandson.

Enda-ninawind megweyaakong wiiji gwiiwizens biigiigaazo gizikanend. Wayeshkwad gisinaa. Wendaniikaadad! Michaa gisinaa. Ninawind okosidoo biizik aanish inange. Imaa goonikaa. Noozishe ginoozi minose megwayaakong nano-bizogeshin apape. Niinawind babimose wendad. Nidaamisaaband ginandagikend ginitaa bimose zhaabaayi'ii zazaagaa miinawaa goonong megwekob. Ni mikwend nibabimose aazhawayii'ii eshkaa nimishoomis inawemaagan izhichigaade miikana niminochige. Ni mino giziigad izhichigaade miikana ninoozhishe.

We waded through the snow until we began seeing rabbit trails. I showed Aaron how I like to hang a snare. We picked a rabbit freeway.

Niinawind zanagad zhaabaayii' ishpaagoon binish niinawind maajii daanooji waaboozoog miikana. Ni gikoowaaband'iwe Ezigaa nizaagitoo agoode nagwaaganeyaab. Niinawind onaaband waaboozoog gichi mangademo.

The snare is made from picture-hanging wire. It has a noose fashioned at one end. The other end is wrapped around a heavy stick, heavy enough so the rabbit can't drag it home.

Nagwaagan izhichigaade onji mazinaakizon agoode biiwaabik. Nagwaagan ay didibininjibiizon izhichigaade bezhigoishkwe-ayi'ii. Bezhigo ishkweagi'ii wiiwegin giiwitaa-ayi'ii gichi mitig memwech waabooz gaawesa odaabaad giiwebatoo.

We used dry branches from the nearest balsam tree to close the exits on the rabbit freeway. Aaron caught on right away to what I was doing. He helped build the fence that would channel the rabbits through the snare. The snare was set.

Niinawind inaabajitoo basso mitig onji beshowad maanazaadi gibaakwa' bagone agijayi'ii wabooz nangaademo. Nisidotam aapiji daatabii ni waabanda. Ni wiidookaa ozhitoo minjikanaakobijigan daa agaasadayaa miikana waabooz zhkaabwayi'ii nagwaagan. Ba-gidin nagwaagan.

Then the hard part came. We ran around in the woods trying to chase a rabbit through the snare.

Miiwapii zanagad iw apii. Ingii babaamibatoo megweyaakong ingii biminizha'w waabooz zhaabwayi'ii nagwaagan.

Naw, I was just kidding about that part; instead we went home and warmed up.

Gaawin, Ni anishaa babaa-i'iw, niinawind giiwe awazo.

My grandson asks every morning if it is time to check the snare. I think he likes the walk in the woods with his grampa. I can hardly wait to see the look on his face when we actually catch a rabbit. Another rabbit-choker is born.

Ninoozhishe gagwedwe moozhag gigizheb giishpin apii naada-goodoo. Ni gikend zaagitoo ingii bimose megweyaakong wiidosem nimishoo. Ni gaawesa bii'o ni waabam onishkiizhig apii giina-tawind debibin waboozoog. Bezhig nawaj waaboozoog giiyasewi-nini ondadizi.

Now, if that Energizer Bunny ever comes around here . . .

Zhigwa giishpin wa'aw Inigaazid Waabooz wiikaa zaagewe omaa . . .

We're kind of tough on dogs around here. We go through them like some casinos go through managers. Some stay a day, and others are around for a year or more. We have tried different sizes, different breeds. Most were mixed breeds, but their end was the same. They died so we could get to know a new dog.

Concrete was the product of a broken home. Neither one want-ed custody of the dog when the marriage failed. The big golden retriever came north to live with us on the rez. Since he was a city dog, he preferred sleeping on the front steps made of concrete. Thus, he named himself. In the coldest weather, he slept on the concrete. He refused offers of a dog house, a sheltered spot under the canoe, or even inside. Concrete just laid on the concrete and protected the house.

When not on duty, Concrete liked to ride in the car. It didn't matter where it was going. He'd stick his head out the window, a goofy
look on his face as he sampled the passing odors. His ears were
windblown as he smelled all of Carlton County. One day, I had to go
somewhere. "Get in," I told the tail-wagging dog. Concrete jumped
in and took up his place in the back seat. I stopped a couple of miles
from home because I recognized my brother's car. I parked and
asked if he needed help. I let the dog out of the car to run around
while we jump-started my brother's car. When his car was running,
I yelled, "Get in." A big golden blur jumped into the car. When we got
home, I opened the back door and said, "Get out." The dog jumped
out and went tail-wagging toward the house.

I looked closer at the dog. He didn't look right. I said, "Concrete, where did you get that collar?" He didn't have one on before
we started our little trip. "Who put it on you?" I knew he couldn't
have done it himself. "Concrete, you gained weight and who put that
blond streak in your fur?"

This wasn't Concrete. It was some other golden retriever, an im-
poster. I asked him what he did to my dog. He didn't answer. I opened
the back door and said, "Get in." The strange dog jumped into the
car. I drove back to the scene of the crime. There was Concrete, sitting patiently on the side of the road. When he saw the familiar car,
he started wagging his tail. He was squealing with excitement. I
stopped the car, opened the back door, and said, "Get out." The fake
Concrete leaped out. "Get in," I told Concrete, who was now licking
my hand. We drove home. When we got there, I said, "Get out." Concrete walked up the sidewalk and laid down on the concrete.

Concrete died one winter when he and a snowplow tried to be
in the same place at the same time. Another one of our dogs was
a cute little pup we named Bingo. I think he died of loneliness the
first night away from his ma. He never got past the brown fluffy
puppy stage. His dauber dried up real quick. There was another one
named Frybread, who was just the right size for an owl Happy Meal.
Then there was Speedbump. I forget what we first called him when
he came to live with us. His name changed after an accident on the
gravel road. We were just coming home from somewhere. He was so

happy to see us that he ran under the car. I hit the brakes and slid. The front wheel of the heavy Buick rode up and over him. I thought I had killed my dog. Then I could hear him thumping under the car. He was still alive. I cut the wheels sharp and slowly backed up. The front wheel passed over him again. When he was finally clear of the car, he took off howling for the woods. He didn't come home for three days, but when he did, he had a new name—Speedbump.

The current dog is named Outside. Our grandson Aaron named him. Now we can stand at the front door and say "Inside, Outside," or "Outside, Outside." Outside is a Sawyer dog—that is, he doesn't care where he eats. He makes his rounds, sampling a pork chop here, deer bones there. Outside is the same color as dirty snow, and we are worried that he might become a pancake because he likes to run on the roads. We are hard on dogs, but we always seem to have one.

*GAGWEDAWIN: Aaniish anishinaabebiigeyin ina?*
*NKWETAAN: Nanda-giikinawaabam miinawaa ishkonamaw*

*QUESTION: Why are you writing in Ojibwe?*
*ANSWER: I want to learn and save something for someone.*

Fond du Lac Follies motored to Minny, jetted to London, and then trained to Aberdeen, Scotland. It was a long trip. Once we arrived in London we bought a pass that gave us unlimited rides on the red double-decker buses or the subway (tube). The big red bus took us near Buckingham Palace. We got off and went to the front gate. The empty flagpole above the palace told us the Queen wasn't home. We saw the guards with the big bearskin hats protecting the Queen's palace. We took pictures of the tourists. The changing of the guard ceremony was cancelled for some unknown reason. I don't think it had anything to do with us. We didn't even let the old girl know we were going to be in town. I doubt She would have seen us even if She knew.

We heard Big Ben bong as we walked around that part of London. There were a lot of people of color walking around the streets. We didn't stand out too much. What was unusual about being there was we didn't see any other Indians from America. We usually run into at least one when we travel.

It took all day to ride the train from London to Aberdeen. Along the way we noticed the conductor sounded like a British movie as he announced the towns. We also noticed the trees in the English countryside looked kind of scrawny compared to northern Minnesota. Robin Hood would have had a hell of a time hiding from the Sheriff in those woods.

We finally got to Aberdeen, where we met the people who had asked us to come to Scotland. The International North American Indian Association is a group of Shinnobs and white people. They spend a lot of time educating Scottish people about Native issues. Debbie Picotte lives there but has relatives in Minnesota and Nebraska. Rose Porter is from the Fond du Lac Reservation and lives in Aberdeen with her husband, Dave. The members made us feel welcome. When we got off the train, I noticed they have dark over there just like we do at home. It was damp and cold because the North Sea is just at the end of the street. My moose-hide mitts from home kept my hands warm. Two of the club members gave us a ride to the flat (apartment) we would be using while in town.

The ride was in a little car through narrow wet streets. I was sitting in the front seat with the driver to my right. We drove with the cars and trucks (lorries) coming at me on the wrong side of the street. I didn't have a steering wheel, horn, or brakes. It was kind of scary until I got used to the traffic pattern. Just when I got over that, they threw another worry at me. They don't have intersections as we know them. They have roundabouts, which have four or five roads converging at a circle. The cars get on the circle and then get off on the road they want. Somehow it all works and we got to the flat with fenders intact.

The rooms were small in that large stone apartment building. The hall floor had a squeak that at first was romantic until it got annoying. We had car, jet, and train lag. The next day we crawled out of bed to crawl around a castle with our new friends. We toured Dunnottar Castle, which is built on a cliff on the North Sea. There was a damp rain falling sideways in the wind as we explored the castle. It was a genuine castle, complete with a dungeon. The dungeon was once used to hold 140 prisoners. The castle felt dead, hundreds of years dead. We admired the stonework but were happy to leave. It was an interesting place to visit, but I wouldn't want to live in a dungeon there.

While eating out with the group members one evening, I had to use the bathroom (loo, water closet). I asked a civilian for directions and found the two bathrooms. The international symbols for men and women were on the doors. One was wearing a skirt. I was in Scotland, land of the kilt. I couldn't decide which was which. Finally, my bladder seized control and I picked one that turned out to be the correct choice. That's when I noticed the toilet-flushing handles are also on the other side.

We sampled the local foods. I had seconds on haggis. It tasted something like corned-beef hash with a lot of pepper. It used to be cooked in a sheep's stomach, but I don't think they do that anymore. There was a whitish looking food that I thought tasted like potatoes. Our hosts told me it was mashed potatoes with butter. The bacon is real lean, couldn't get a decent bit of bacon grease for our morning porridge (oatmeal).

We went to the Glenfiddich Distillery, where we learned a little about whiskey making. Single-malt Scotch is distilled and bottled there. Whiskey making goes on day and night. The warehouses have barrels full of Scotch whiskey just waiting to be old enough. We saw some that were fifty years old and cost D5,000 ($7,500) a liter. This place was a chemical dependency counselor's nightmare, didn't look like a good place to hold an AA meeting. I had a wee dram (water glass full) of Glenfiddich.

We stayed at a croft (small farm) on the Black Isle before we went to Loch Ness. Of course, we had to go look for Nessie. Our first stop was at the Official Loch Ness Monster Exhibition Centre, where we got an overview of the history of Nessie. Locals have been telling stories about the animal that lives in the cold, dark, deep loch (lake). Some of the oldest stories are from AD 600, almost 1,400 years ago.

Loch Ness is a long skinny lake. We watched a rainstorm coming up the loch. The colors were changing in the sunlight. There were shades of red, orange, yellow, green, blue, indigo, and violet, and some I can't name. Then we stood on the shore and waited for Nessie. The camcorder battery was fully charged and we had a fresh cassette. The still camera was loaded with a roll of thirty-six. We waited, then we saw Nessie. The animal was traveling incognito up the loch about five hundred yards offshore. The animal had cleverly fashioned a disguise that looked like a fishing boat. We watched, took pictures, and marveled at the realism of the disguise. What a piece of work. It looked exactly like a fishing boat, right down to the motor *putt-putting* along. We weren't fooled, though. We took pictures of the Loch Ness Monster.

There are rent-a-shamans stalking the land in Scotland. One called himself Pretty Painted Arrow. He was peddling sweats, vision quests, and pipe ceremonies in Aberdeen. Pretty Painted Arrow was in the newspaper because he left town with another man's wife. She must have liked the color of his arrow, I surmised. Our trails didn't cross.

We are tapping maple trees again as we do every year. As I travel around Indian country, I see more and more Indian people going to the sugar bush.

Niinawind ozhiga'ige miinawa niinawind gwayakochige akina gikinoonowin. Amanj'igo apii niin babaamaadizi giiwitaaayi'ii Anishinaabewaki, niin waabi eshkam Anishinaabeg izhaa iskigamizigan.

The crows told us it was time for making maple syrup. Two bald eagles flew over the fire when we were boiling the water out of the sap.

Aandegwag biidaajimo maajitoon zhiiwaagamizige. Niizh migiziwag babaamibide ishpayi'ii giiwitaashkode aanapii niinawind ishkwaagamizige.

We have a small sugar bush, barely over a hundred taps. We take only what we need for feasts and funerals, gifts and pancakes.

Niinawind ayaan agaasaa iskigamizigan, agaawaa ishpayi'ii ingodwaak ozhiga'ige. Niinawind onjiwiidoon minik niinawind manezi wiikondiwag dash bagidenjige, debaa'ooki dash gwekiwebinigan.

Once again it was a learning experience for our grandchildren. They helped us gather the sap from the trees. They are too young to help with the boiling, so they just watched, and listened when we told sugar bush stories.

Aabiding minawaa gikinowaabi noozhishenhyag. Wiinawaa wiidokaazo naadoobi onjiwidoon aninaatigoog. Wiinawaa gaye oshka'aawi naadamaage iskigamizige ji-ganawaabandan dash biz-indaw aanapii niinawind aadodan iskigamizigan.

We watched winter turn into spring. The sun was warm and reminded us of summer. The wind was cold and was a reminder of the winter that just left.

Niinawind ganawaabandan biboonong aanjitoon ziigwan. Giizis abaaso nanda-mikwendan niibin. Dakaanimad nanda-mikwendan biboonoog endanagadan.

Making syrup is just a lot of work. Sometimes it is hard work, but most of the time is spent just staring at the fire, watching the sap so it doesn't burn. We spend hours cutting firewood.

Zhiiwaagamiziganike indigo ondamanokii. Ayaangodinong miish zanagendan anokii aanawi awashime daso-diba'iganed ganawaa-bandan ishkode, naanaagadawaabandan wiishkobaaboo ji-gaawiin agwaabikizan. Niinawind dazhitaa daso-diba'igan manisaadan.

I remember how my grampa used to keep the sap from boiling over. He hung a piece of salt pork over the hot sap. When it came to boil over, it would get as far as the salt pork and go back down. It was easier than using a balsam branch.

Niin mikwendan nimishoomis nagajitoon nagaashkaatoon wi-ishkobaaboo ziigigamide. Wiin inagoodoon bakwezhan zhiiwita-gani-gookoosh ishpayi'ii gizhizo wiishkobaaboo. Aanapii wiishko-baaboo ziigigamide, miish zhiiwitagani gookoosh daamaajitoon azheshkaa. Miish wenipanad indawaaj inasabajitoon zhingob wadikwan.

I feel happy when I am using my black kettle to boil sap. Just knowing that Indians all over northern Minnesota were making syrup like I was felt good.

Niin inendam minawaanigozi aanapii miwaabajitoon makade-waa okaadakik ishkwaagamizige. Enda-gikenjige Anishinaabeg miziwe giiwedin Minnesota zhiiwaagamiziganike dibishkoo niin minwamanji'o.

When we say we are of the earth, it is true. I think there is something in the maple syrup that I need. It makes sense. Countless generations of my ancestors depended on the syrup for food. I will continue to make syrup every spring.

Amanj igo apii niinawind ikido niinawind odaadad aki, miish debwe. Niin naanaagadawenim ayi'ii memwech megwe-ayi'ii zhii-waagamizigan manwezi. Mino-inendan, gaawin agim aanikoobi-jiganag apenimo zhiiwaagamizigan miijiim. Nin wii-zhiiwaagam-iziganike akina ziigwan.

We are thankful for the gift of syrup from the Creator.

Niinawind miigwechiwendan debi'zhiiwaagamiziganike onjibaa Gichi-manidoo.

On a related note, I once read a book about the way the white guys do it. I don't have the book title anymore, but I recall that they had 7,000 taps connected with eight miles of plastic tubing, sucking the sap from the trees using vacuum pumps. They expected to collect 70,000 gallons of sap to make 1,700 gallons of syrup, which could be sold for a huge profit. The book used the phrase "Native Americans" only once while telling the story of making maple syrup.

As part of my work as a writer, I do quite a bit of traveling. One day the Follies went to Mankato to talk to some librarians about Native American literature. Since I was the only writer there, I talked about myself and my work. The librarians catalogued my comments about literature and then I went home.

It felt good to be in the woods again. My grandson Aaron and I went out to gather willow for the birchbark baskets we make. He watched me offer tobacco, so he wanted to do it, too. His part of the mission was to carry the knife we use to cut the willow. He can now recognize the kind of willow we use for the baskets. When we are out trotting in the bogs, it is easy to forget that places like Minneapolis exist. I need to spend more time with my grandson and the woods.

I felt lucky to share a concert stage with Jorma Kaukonen Jr. and Larry Long Song. The doings were held at St. Scholastica college in Duluth. Here's the way the evening went. Larry Long came out and sang and played. Once again we got misty when he sang "Anna Mae, Anna Mae, Anna Mae." It is always a pleasure to hear America's troubadour singing. Larry, with tongue in cheek, calls himself Larry Long Song.

Next, I came out and read some poems and prose pieces for about forty-five minutes. Then there was an intermission, after which Jorma started playing. This was the highlight of the evening for me because I had never heard Jorma play before. I was amazed at what he could do with that simple instrument of wood and wire. It felt good to just close my eyes and listen.

Jorma is a guitar god. In talking with him, I learned that he once opened a concert for Bo Diddley and performed with Janis Joplin. His early years were spent with Jefferson Airplane and he is now in a band called Hot Tuna. He played the acoustic guitar and sang. I have never heard a guitar played like that.

For the finale, Larry and Jorma made music while I recited one of my favorite poems, which is about John Wayne. I almost caught the beat there a couple of times. I got close enough to the beat to see it disappear around the corner. After the concert was over, I asked Jorma if I could see his hands. I counted and he had five fingers on each hand. He was doing so many things with that guitar, I thought he had ten fingers on each hand.

*QUESTION: What do you say to people leaving the casino?*
*ANSWER: Miigwetch, ambe giiwe endahyin chi-nagi*
*bahtwadamin nawaj zhooniyaa.*

There is a brand-new Shinnob staying at our house. I forget what his birth name is. We just call him Lug. He is eight months old and is beginning to crawl. The Lugger has been cutting some new teeth.

He likes chewing on strips of basswood bark. It is clean and he can scratch his gums with it as he chews. He is now the proud owner of four teeth.

Luggy, as his maw calls him, is still on a bottle and wears the latest Pampers. Luggish is learning about this brand-new-to-him world. It makes me laugh when he laughs. The Lugster is reminding all the big people in the house about baby stuff, about the baby's view of things. He has us all trained. When he cries, we all stop what we're doing to see what he wants. Lugnuts has a big smile for anyone that he recognizes. There is something warm about being greeted by a big baby smile when you walk into the house.

We jetted to New York City in August. In keeping with the myth of beads for land, I took along twenty-four-dollars' worth of beads to see if I could buy the island back. I read in the history books that is what the white man paid for Manhattan. Our camcorder jetted to Baltimore with someone else's luggage. Northwest Airlines did a great job of tracking us down and getting the camcorder back to us. I'm going to get a T-shirt made that says, "My camcorder went to Baltimore and all I got was this lousy baggage claim check."

My wife Pat and I were invited to the National Museum of the American Indian to demonstrate how we make birchbark fanning baskets. We felt honored to be asked. The museum is a part of the Smithsonian Institution and is located in the George Gustav Heye Center near the southern end of Manhattan. We met a lot of museum employees. One of the employees was Clinton Eliot, a Shinnob who has relatives in Wisconsin.

Clint and I went outside to have a smoke and throw Ojibwe words back and forth. While standing on the front steps, we noticed a film crew shooting in the park in front of us. Pretty soon a young production assistant came up and asked us to move because we were in the background of their shot. While walking over to the side of the steps, I told Clinton, "This has happened before. Shinnobs have to move out of the way for the white man." We laughed and continued visiting. Then another film crew member came up and told us we didn't move far enough. We told him we were not moving anymore. He told us they paid $1,500 a day to film there. Clinton said, "That is the way of the white man. It always comes down to money." We smoked and spoke more Ojibwe until we were good and ready to move.

At the museum our work was to do the same thing we would be doing if we were home, that is, making baskets. In addition, we explained what we were doing to the visitors. We answered their questions. Sometimes the questions would go beyond baskets and into racism, gambling, treaty rights, or life on the reservation.

We rode the Staten Island Ferry and I don't know why. I don't think we know anyone there. Maybe it was just the boat ride. I do know it was cooler on the water than in the concrete canyons of Manhattan. We saw Ellis Island, where so many immigrants came through. It looked like a prison or boarding school. The Statue of Liberty was standing there, holding up the torch and law books. She looks a lot slimmer since they took the scaffolding off. Miss Liberty was looking toward Europe and had her back turned toward the original people. Her teeth and the rest of her are still green. She gets lit up every night.

One afternoon we took a smoke break in Bowling Green Park, just outside the museum. While sitting there we saw a man grazing in the garbage cans. When he found a half-eaten sandwich in the can, he would shovel it into his mouth. He was talking to himself as he went from can to can. There was another man rummaging through the cans looking for aluminum. We and the can collector stayed out of the way as the man continued to look for food. I was going to get him a meal, but he didn't look like he was in the same world we were in.

It was a good experience demonstrating in the museum. I think the visitors learned that the Anishinaabe people are still here, still living our lives with the seasons. I think the museum staff learned, also. The museum decided to add one of our baskets to their collection.

QUESTION: *Why do you write the Fond du Lac Follies?*
ANSWER: *Because I'm not from Mille Lacs, White Earth,*
*Red Lake, Leech Lake, Nett Lake, or Grand Portage.*

# Anishinaabe syndicated

*GAGWEDWIN: Aaniin dina ozhibii'igeyin*
*Nagaajiwanaang Follies?*
*TKWETAAN: Gaawiin onjibaasiin Misi-zaaga'iganing,*
*Gaa-waabaabiganikaaning, Miskwaagamiiwi-zaaga'iganing,*
*Gaa-zagaskwaajimekaag, Asabikone-zaaga'iganing,*
*gemaa Gichi-onigaming.*

It took two sleeps to go back thirty years. Fond du Lac Follies motored to Washington, DC, for a Vietnam veterans' reunion. Grunts from India Company, 3rd Battalion, 9th Marines got together again. The patrol base was a plush Arlington, Virginia, hotel. The perimeter was set up in the hospitality suite. The veterans drank whatever they wanted. Some had mineral water, others had coffee or beer. The hospitality suite had a sign-in sheet. The grunts looked through the list for familiar names as they signed in with their names.

We looked at helmets, slides, pictures, maps, flags, the company guidon, flak jackets, and jungle boots. But mostly, we looked at each other's eyes. The feeling of being with a brother again. I saw three grunts pushing each other so they could push another vet's wheelchair. While I was there, I learned why we were called the Flaming I. When someone asked where India Company was operating, the first part of the directions went like this: "Do you see all that smoke over there? That is India Company."

India Company went everywhere together. We went to the Wall. Names, so many names of our friends. Another part of our patrol was to the Iwo Jima monument. I looked up at the statue and thought of Ira Hayes. "Jeez, another Shinnob marine," I thought. India Company used to ride on tanks and amtracs. This time we were riding in an air-conditioned cushy bus. The patrol stopped at Marine Barracks, Washington, DC. Every marine knows what the address "8th and Eye" means. It is at the top of the chain of command. The commandant sleeps here.

The Silent Drill Platoon was impressive. Twenty-four marines doing the same thing at the same time. The old grunts sat up a little straighter when the marines marched by. The music from the band stirred us. When they played "The Marines' Hymn" we all jumped to our feet. We left with the sound of taps ringing in our ears. The bus ride back to the motel was quiet.

The last patrol was at the banquet. The grunts ate together just like twenty-five or thirty years ago. We told war stories again. At each table, members of India Company promised to see each other again. Some grunts got up and thanked everyone for what was done to make the reunion happen. It was kind of funny when the DJ suddenly made a loud noise with his sound equipment. Every grunt in the room ducked . . . some more than others. The DJ played oldies music from our time in the war. While some danced with their wives, others continued to tell stories. We knew we were helping each other heal from the Vietnam War. The hospitality suite was full of grenade pins and empty C-ration cans by the time we were done.

On the drive back to Sawyer, I had plenty of time to reflect on what happened in the past five days. All in all it was a good time, but there were some bad parts also. It was good seeing the faces of the guys I knew, but I couldn't help but wonder about the marines who were not at the reunion. Were they dead? I could also see that some of the reunion vets were still troubled by the Vietnam War. As for me, the nightmares have returned. At first it was scary, but after three months I could sleep through the night without them. I think that is the price we pay for being veterans. It takes more than honor songs at powwows to heal that hurt. Hug the next vet you see.

For me, it's Veterans Day, the Fourth of July, Christmas, New Year's, and my birthday all rolled into one. Ricing is here and we were glad to take our share of the Creator's gift. After about a twenty-year decline, I see more and more people making rice. Some of the people I saw on the lake were from the Ojibwe School here on the reservation. My neighbor said he helped rescue two students who tipped over. He said they were cold and were really worried when they saw the school bus leave. The adults with the students also tipped over on their way to rescue the students. Maybe the school should have a class in canoe safety before they turn the students loose out on the lake. We are lucky no one was hurt. The students were lucky that my neighbor was there to assist in the rescue.

I like the idea that the Ojibwe School is teaching the students about wild rice. It is such a big part of our history and current life. We took our grandson Aaron to the lake to play while we were out harvesting rice. We also took an elder from the community to watch him as he played. This creates a circle in my life because one of my earliest memories is playing on the lakeshore while my parents were out on the lake harvesting wild rice.

Students from Ain Dah Yung, an emergency shelter for American Indian youth, came to our home to learn how we turn the plants into food. Most of them were city Indians. They were a great help in gathering the firewood we use for the parching kettle. Some of them took turns parching rice. One of the adults with the group took a turn in the dancing pit. She learned how to grind the hulls off with her feet. I'm glad the kids from the Cities got to learn what ricing is like on the reservation.

My family has enough green rice for the year. We don't get involved in the competitive part of ricing. Whenever anyone asks how much rice we make, we always say we are satisfied with the Creator's gift.

QUESTION: *What do fry bread and Indian men have in common?*
ANSWER: *They're both round, brown, and greasy.*

QUESTION: *Do you know that person well?*
ANSWER: *I knew them before they were Indian.*

Fond du Lac Follies has a new computer. It has been an interesting trip. Like most folks, I started off by drawing pictures in the sand with my finger. In school I graduated to chalk and a blackboard. Later I mastered pencils and a Big Chief pad of paper. Eventually I learned to type on a manual typewriter. Then I was turned on to electric typewriters. I entered the computer age when a friend gave me an Apple IIe. I learned how to write on it and then print something. I once even saved something on another disk. But I noticed one small drawback. Like me, it had a problem with memory. I can't remember anything, and the Apple couldn't remember enough.

I no longer have that excuse. This new machine has plenty of memory. I just have to learn how to drive this hard drive. The new machine almost got me scared. It has started every time I turned the key. My kids have taken a spin through the games programs, but I haven't taken it out of the driveway. The motor makes a whirring sound, lets me know it is ready to do some thinking as we sit here, alone, together. Just for fun, I ran the spell check. The machine and I agree that the words are spelled correctly so far. It also tells me exactly how many words I have used. I don't really know if I need that information just yet.

The Apple was a good introduction to computers, but now I have to learn about the real world of big machines with big programs. My kids tell me there is a fax modem on here, whatever that means. They also said I can surf the net. I will try it once I find out what it means. In the meantime, I will return to the regularly scheduled columns.

We have a visitor from Scotland here at our house on the Fond du Lac Reservation. Marlene Forsythe is here to learn about life on the rez. So far we have taken her to the bingo hall and made a few jaunts into the woods. She was suffering from jet lag for the first few days but is now adjusted. We met Marlene, M as we call her, last February when we jetted to Scotland. M made us feel welcome when we were in Scotland and now we are able to return the gift. She took us to her homeland on the Black Isle where we met her mum. We have had discussions about rez English and proper English. I think by the time she leaves, she will be sounding like a rez Shinnob. She already knows what "hai" means, although I haven't heard her use it in a sentence.

M has seen the Sawyer Mall: Larry's store in downtown Sawyer. Her visit is complete. She can go back to Aberdeen, Scotland, and tell her son Lowell that she has seen it all, the best America has to offer. I wish I could be in Aberdeen when she begins telling her rez stories.

QUESTION: *How do you say "moccasin" in Ojibwe?*
ANSWER: *"Makizin."*

Sometimes I have to brag about my grandson Aaron. He is in kinder-garten. Ezigaa likes school and reports that his teacher is nice. He sometimes leaves ten minutes early to wait for the bus. For show-and-tell he brings things like sugar bush taps and fry bread. But that is not why I am bragging. Aaron got his first check for being featured in a story in *Scholastic News,* the classroom newspaper. He scrawled his name on the back and cashed it at the Sawyer Mall. I helped invest some of his money at the bingo hall. In the story, he is pictured making wild rice with his family. In the article, only Aaron is mentioned by name. Students all over the country will see Aaron and his family making wild rice.

# 8.
# Indian-Looking Indians

## 1996

*QUESTION: How many Shinnobs does it take to change a light bulb?*
*ANSWER: One, but the time must be right for it to happen.*

Fond du Lac Follies has been motoring nowhere. That's right. After months of having to be somewhere, now I just sit at home and work. How radical. A writer who writes? Like a lot of people, I have to commute to work. Nowadays, my commute is measured in feet. The computer is just a few steps across the bedroom. I really appreciate that when I think of how I used to commute. A job down near Chicago required a forty-five minute drive one way. To add to the fun, it was rush-hour traffic. Thousands of people I didn't know were trying to crash me up on the way to work, then on the way home. Another long commute was one where I drove 106 miles one way. No rush-hour traffic? I just had to weave in and out of the deer herd that lived alongside the road. I was glad when that job ended. It was putting a strain on my rez car with all those miles.

One drawback to working at home is I can't call in sick. First of all, there is no one to call. Second of all, I wouldn't believe any of my excuses anyway. One more drawback is I don't look like I am working when I'm staring out the window trying to put my thoughts in order. My wife will say something like, "Well, as long as you're not typing anything, dump the dog, walk the garbage, change the oil, get oatmeal from the store, babysit, shovel the grass, cut the snow, or something." I have to convince her that I must think before I write.

There is another drawback. I can think of the dumbest reasons to leave the keyboard. Wait, is that a dog? I thought I heard a dog somewhere . . . is one of them. I know the mailman gets here sooner if I stand outside and watch for him. Any reason to leave the typo-machine is a good one. I really like it when relatives stop by to visit. Getting caught up on the latest gossip is always a good reason to leave the writing.

There is no way around it. Writing is hard work. I used to think working construction was hard. There, all I had to do was move heavy stuff from here to there. Writing is much more complex than that. I have to move heavy thoughts from here to there. But in spite of the drawbacks, I would rather be doing this than anything else. We Shinnobs need to make our voices heard because the main-stream press seems stuck on subjects like the O. J. Simpson murder trial, the Tonya Harding Olympic assault (where is she now?), and the conflict in Bosnia. The more I watch TV and read newspapers, the more I realize that we need our own media, something that lets the world know that we are still here. I get tired of watching and reading about other people all the time.

I have found a way to cut my bingo costs in half. Easy beans, my wife went to work at the bingo hall and she can't play bingo there anymore.

I'm glad the weather has been cold. It gives the weather people on TV something to talk about. But I keep hearing the same thing over and over. "Last night was the coldest one we ever had." Here we go again with the cultural arrogance. Does that white man think they invented weather or something? Do you suppose it ever got colder here on Turtle Island before the white man came? The records are just over a hundred years old. What about the glaciers? I think it might have been colder here when the ice in what is now called Minnesota was a mile high. I don't think it was balmy or even cool. It was cold. I know because I have heard parts of the old stories that told of the people moving out of this area because of the glaciers.

It could be that I am looking at it all wrong. The weather people on TV are not serious. They're a comedy show in disguise. The anchor on the news turns to the weather person and seriously asks, "What kind of day are you going to give us tomorrow?" as if the weather fluff has something to do with creating weather. In my house, we know who creates the weather. I can hardly wait for next summer when the weather fluff will say, "Today has been the hottest it has ever been."

Fond du Lac Follies got a letter from Joe Ager of the Pipestone County Historical Society. He is looking for former students to provide information about Pipestone Indian Training School. He writes,

> Most of the former buildings are gone, but that doesn't make it any less a part of Pipestone's rich history. Almost all that is left of the school are the memories of the students. The Pipestone Indian School is a chapter in our history that should not be forgotten . . .
>
> I would like you to write down a few of your experiences and thoughts about the school. It doesn't have to be a grammatically correct essay or thesis, just a long or short collection of random thoughts about your experiences at the Pipestone Indian School. It is virtually impossible to obtain information about the Indian School. The Pipestone Museum does have a large collection of photos of the Indian School and students, but there is no information accompanying the photos. The museum recently purchased copies of the 1912 through 1939 Indian School census records from the National Archives. Even though we have photos and census records, we still can't tell the true history of the school without first-hand information. It is vital that this information be recorded before there is no one left that remembers.
>
> My reason for doing this is I would like the Pipestone Museum to put this accumulated information together in a small journal about Pipestone Indian School. I have enclosed several sample questions that might help jog one's memory.

Here are Joe's questions and how I would answer them.

**1. When did you attend? How old were you?**
1949 to 1952, first grade through the fourth grade, skipped one year. I was six, almost seven years old when I first went.

**2. Why were you sent to Pipestone?**
Times were hard, my father was absent from the home and my mother had four children and was living in a three-room house. She had just buried a baby and was undergoing a series of operations for a tumor and infections. My grandmother could only take two of the children so my older sister Judy and I went to Pipestone. It was her way of keeping the family together while she was in the hospital.

**3. What are your favorite memories of Pipestone?**
Getting on that yellow school bus at the end of the school year because I knew I would see my mother soon. My grandmother would send my sister and me a maple sugar cake. We would take tiny bites and make that sugar cake last until the next one came. Just that little taste kept us connected to the family and life on the rez. Today I make maple sugar cakes every spring.

**4. What are your worst memories?**
Being homesick all the time. The first meal was a brutal learning experience. While I was eating a big guy reached across and took most of my food. After that I would eat with one arm around my tray and my fork in a stabbing position. Marching on sidewalks everywhere. Imagine, a six-year-old being forced to march. Fighting, constant fighting almost every day. I quickly learned how to fight back because crying didn't stop the beatings. When I first got to the school the house matron twisted my ear because I had used an Ojibwe expression. She told me we don't use that language here. I asked her what language was. I didn't like having my head washed with kerosene and being force-fed a tablespoon of cod-liver oil.

**5. What kind of food did you get at meal time?**
I don't remember anything specifically but I suppose it was normal institutional food. I remember seeing a pyramid nutrition chart on the dining room wall. The school had gardens that grew a lot of our food. At Christmastime we would get an apple or an orange.

**6. Did you get to go to town? If so, when?**
We could walk to town on Saturday. I couldn't go to the movies because I didn't have the necessary dime. We would play at the Pipestone National Monument.

**7. What type of punishments were you given and for what?**
I was slapped in the face and whipped on my ass and legs with a leather belt when I ran away from the school. I was punched and kicked many times by the older boys, mainly because I was smaller than them.

**8. How did attending the Indian School affect your relationships with family?**
At the end of the school year I couldn't remember what my parents' faces looked like. I couldn't picture them. At first I couldn't write so an older girl, Pauline Moose, would write my "Dear Maw—How are you?—I am fine" letters home. She also explained the mystery of envelopes and stamps and where to mail them. My mother always used the Ojibwe language with me but when I returned home after nine months at the school she used only English. When I'd try to speak Ojibwe with older people they would laugh and tell me I sounded like a white man.

**9. Did you have any unusual experiences?**
Running away from the boarding school after being there a couple of months was unusual. I told Judy what I was going to do; she tried to talk me out of it but couldn't. She walked me to the rear gate of the school and pointed out Highway 23 to me. She said if I just followed the signs north I would get close to home. As she was saying good-bye she gave me the rest of the maple sugar cake and told me to tell Maw to send her some candy. I began walking right after breakfast. The thought of seeing my mother's face kept me putting one foot in front of the other. About noon I found a hawk's foot on the side of the road. No one else I knew had a hawk's foot so I picked it up to show my mother what came with me on the long walk home. It smelled a little ripe but I didn't mind because now I had company.

Just about dark I heard the sound of a car sliding to a stop behind me. I turned and looked and saw two big white people running toward me. I turned and ran into the cornfield. They chased me up and down the rows of corn. I used my fall-down-and-ball-up trick to trip one of them. They caught me and while walking back to the car they told me I had made it nine miles. That is when they noticed my smell. One of them dug into my pocket and threw my hawk foot back in the ditch. I don't remember the slaps and the belt but do remember feeling bad about that hawk foot. As an adult I found out area farmers were paid a bounty for catching or reporting runaway Indian children.

**10. Was there ever an outbreak of diseases or illnesses?**
There were outbreaks of measles and mumps. We were warned to stay away from one particular building because that is where the sick kids were kept. We heard some of them died there.

**11. Describe a typical day from beginning to end.**
Someone woke us up in the morning and we went downstairs to wash up and get dressed for the day. After that we went back upstairs to the dormitory to clean up the place. After that we formed into squads and marched to the dining hall for breakfast. After that we marched to school and our individual classrooms. At noon we marched to the dining hall again. After the meal we marched back to school. After school we were allowed to play outside until it was time to march to supper. After supper we marched back to the dormitory and went into the basement to play until bedtime. We made our toys. I remember a crawling type of toy made from a rubber band, a thread spool, a button, and a stick. Pipestone wasn't a toy kind of place.

The nights in the boys' dorm were the worst. I remember hearing one boy begin crying in the dormitory at night. The boys on either side of him would tell him in English and Ojibwe to stop crying. Maybe he was crying because he was homesick or had been abused sexually or physically. The crying began at one end and came traveling bed to bed until the boy in the next bed was crying and then I was sobbing, too. We cried until we got tired and went to sleep. After a night like that we all got up and pretended like it didn't happen.

QUESTION: *Why were the treaties etched on real thin glass?*
ANSWER: *Easier to break, of course.*

It is the middle of winter here on the Fond du Lac Reservation. The dogs are leaving little land mines everywhere. I look out my back window and see the sunlight creating diamonds on the snow when the light hits just right. I am glad I live where we have seasons. I can't picture myself living in an urban setting. I think I would go crazy or something worse.

Winter is a good time to tell stories and my son Jim came home with one. He's a good storyteller and enjoys telling them. When he begins, we shut off the TV and the CD and gather the family around to listen. He is able to act out the parts of all the people in his story. We know immediately when someone else is talking in the story because he changes his voice or the way he stands. He must have been listening and copying the storytellers he had heard when he was growing up on the Fond du Lac Reservation.

It seems Jim was out in South Dakota when his trip lasted longer than his money. He had his family with him and was waiting for money so he could get back home. That's when he heard about a car sale. He was kind of halfway looking for another car because the dashboard oil light on his current car was blinking like a turn signal. He was worried about bringing his family—Lisa, Niiwin, and Noona—across the prairie from South Dakota to Minnesota. It was record-breaking cold and the snow was drifting across the highway.

The car sale was at Wegner Auto of Pierre. It was their Nineteenth Annual Traditional Blizzard Sale. The sale was scheduled to begin at 8:00 AM on Saturday. In years past people would begin lining up days in advance. The price cuts were dramatic. My son had his eyes on a Buick that was marked down from three grand to three hundred. The lowest-priced car for sale was eight bucks.

The father of my grandchildren started the line on Thursday morning. He prepared by putting on twelve layers of clothing, opened up his powwow chair, poured a cup of coffee from his thermos, and settled down to wait for Saturday morning. During business hours people took turns going inside to warm up, look at the cars, and use the bathroom. The car dealer had two powwow toilets outside, but no one used them. Nobody wanted to leave a ring of flesh on the seat. One Indian suggested doing jumping jacks to stay warm. By three in the morning of the first night, all he could manage was one-half a jack. He raised one arm and one leg. My son said he was freezing his nits off.

The Indians were the only ones waiting when the doors opened for business on Friday morning. It had been a long, forty-below-zero night. The car dealer generously parked a big Ford truck near them for a windbreak. On Friday night, others began joining the line. Once again it was a long time to morning, but it was shortened somewhat when one of the Indians shared a pot of chili with the others. They told each other their life stories through the long, dark night. They also played the "Do you know _____?" game. Sometimes people would get out of line and go to their cars and warm up.

Because of problems in years past, a police officer parked and waited with them. My son said shivering for thirty-six hours was kind of tiring. The thought of his family sitting in the new-to-him Buick kept him in front of the line. He was wishing he had put on thirteen or fourteen layers of clothes. By this time there were about a hundred people in line; thirty of them were Indians. The doors opened at 8:00 AM and the Indians scooted inside. The people coming behind them got wedged in the door, and that allowed the Indians a chance to pick the cars they wanted.

Jim got the Buick he was waiting for. But he still had the problem of getting his family home. He used up his relatives in three states and bummed enough money to get back to Minnesota. He said he had the heater on full blast the whole way back to our rez. He left his old oil-light-blinking car out on the prairie. I imagine he will be telling that car story until he has to junk it and get another car and another story.

Oh no. The deer are dying in northern Minnesota because of the severe winter. The legislature leaped to the rescue and spent $750,000 to buy food for the deer. The Department of Natural Resources says it is a wasted effort because they will only be able to reach a small percentage of the total deer herd. What a noble, if not Nobel, effort to save one of God's finest creatures, the Minnesota deer hunter, whose known contributions to the state's budget are measured in thousands of dollars annually. Oh, oh. We should feed the deer so the Minnesota deer hunters have something to shoot at.

The legislators must be walking around with puffed-up chests because they saw a problem and threw money at it. I bet the bloody heart liberals are happy because Bambi will live longer, maybe long enough to wander by someone's deer camp next fall. The deer hunters are happy because they will have a better chance of bagging the big buck. Some Shinnobs are laughing because they see the puny effort to try controlling the way things happen in the woods of northern Minnesota. A food shelf for deer. What will they think of next? Somewhere deep in the woods on the Fond du Lac Reservation, a wolf is thanking the legislature for thinking of the deer.

Noozis Ezigaa giinawind noopiming nandokawechige. Ma'ingan. Giinawind bagakaabandan zkigidan ezhishin. Baanimaa apii bagakaabandan ma'iigan nitoon miish gidaanawe waawaashkeshi. Makedewizi miskozi miskwi ningizan bagwaakidemagad bindemagad goonikaamagad.

My grandson Aaron and I were out in the woods looking for tracks. Wolf. We saw where the wolf marked his territory with urine. Later, we saw where the wolf killed and ate a deer. The dark red arterial blood melted a hole in the snow.

It is a good time to be a Fonjalacker but a bad time to be an American. On this reservation, we are sitting pretty with our two casinos. Both of them are making money for us and we are building up a cash reserve. There is even gossip on the moccasin telegraph that we will be getting another per capita payment soon. I'll believe that one when I endorse and cash the check.

Something happened that is even more important than money. According to Judge Richard Kyle, United States District Court, Fond du Lac continues to possess the right to hunt, fish, and gather in the ceded territory of the 1837 and 1854 treaties. The ruling of March 18, 1996, says the State can regulate the treaty harvest if it is done in a nondiscriminatory manner and where it is reasonably necessary for conservation, public safety, and health purposes. Further, the ruling said the State may not impose its own regulations if the Fond du Lac Band can effectively regulate its members on these issues.

I hate to say I told you so, but damn it, I told you so. I was a member of ALF, the Anishinaabe Liberation Front. We protested the treaty sale in 1988 because we thought the treaty rights belonged to the generations to come and should not be sold. We tried to convince our then leaders, but they were blinded by the almost $2 million annually that the state was offering. ALF members were labeled as dissidents, malcontents, troublemakers, and all-around bad guys because we opposed tribal government.

We believed our treaty rights existed and now we have verification from a federal judge in this judicial district. We also knew our 1837 treaty rights existed and that is why we went spearing in Mille Lacs. At that time, ALF was composed of Anishinaabe from Michigan, Wisconsin, and Minnesota. We thought treaty rights transcended state boundaries. Some Anishinaabe were arrested and had fishing gear confiscated by the state DNR officers. The charges against us were dropped and I am still waiting to get my spear back.

ALF members should be honored for keeping the struggle going. ALF members should also remember that treaty rights will always be under attack from those who covet what we have.

I found another good reason to be a Fond du Lac band member. According to the official rez newspaper, *Nah-Gah-Chi-Wah-Nong, Di-Bah-Ji-Mo-Win-Nan,* we are exempt from the payment of Minnesota motor vehicle excise taxes if certain conditions are met. Those conditions are:

1. The buyer of the motor vehicle must be an enrolled member of the Fond du Lac Band of Lake Superior Chippewa.

2. The Band member must reside on the Fond du Lac Reservation.

3. The sale must occur on the Reservation. A sale is on the Reservation if a) Payment has been made on the Reservation, b) The papers relating to the purchase are signed on the Reservation, c) The vehicle is delivered on the Reservation.

Now I can save money on the purchase of all the rez cars I go through in the course of a year.

Yup, it is a good time to be a Fonjalacker. Being an American is another matter, however. Americans are dying in Bosnia. So far it has been just a few, but I'm sure the families of the dead soldiers think it is a major event in their lives. I support the troops who, as they say, are putting themselves in harm's way, but I do not agree with the idea of putting American troops between the warring people. On the other side of the world, we have sent aircraft carriers to the strait between China and Taiwan. Somebody is going to end up with a bent saber if we keep rattling them.

I wonder where America is headed? I know where we are headed. The crows tell me it is time to go to the woods to make maple syrup. It will be a family affair, almost a community affair, because so many people have offered to help.

I have been watching the crows feed in the backyard. If we have bread that is starting to turn green, we share it with those guys in the black coats. The crows live in a world where almost everyone else is bigger and is a threat. They first see the food as they are flying by. The crows then land in the pines and just watch the food. Occasionally, they fly to another branch to look at things from another angle. After sitting and looking for a while, they glide down to the food. Their wings flare and they settle gently on the snow. The black feathers on the white snow really stand out, looking like one single word on a page. They walk to the food. Some walk while bobbing their head in time to their feet. Others walk straight to the food, eyes fixed on it. Then before pecking at the bread, they look around in all directions. They peck, swallow, peck, swallow, then grab a larger piece and fly off.

Sometimes a large crow flies directly at a smaller one, deciding who is top dog in the crow world. One stopped pecking long enough to crow loudly. He sounded like he was happy to be eating. They live in a simple world, fly, eat, sleep, fly, eat, sleep. Maybe a little time out to make some baby crows, but other than that, fly, eat, sleep. No worries like Bosnia, the Unabomber, and per capita payments. Nothing to worry about but a crow hop.

One Sawyer morning I was looking out the window at the crows. I had the powwow tape on loud and I noticed them dancing. Nah, just kidding about the dancing crows.

QUESTION: *How do you bathe?*
ANSWER: *First, I wash down as far as possible,*
*then I wash up as far as possible, finally, I wash possible.*

Another election is over. We didn't throw any rascals out, so we couldn't throw any new rascals in. The incumbents are celebrating and the challengers are protesting. If I have learned nothing else in watching elections over the last twenty years, I've learned that the protest will be filed and then forgotten. Since the election board is appointed by the RBC and the incumbents get to vote on the protests, I don't see any changes coming.

There is a fine line between cynicism and realism, but I think I am being realistic here. Our voting system is broken and there is no way to fix it. Why do we faithfully troop to the ballot box and vote if nothing ever changes? We need term limits and primary elections. We need to change the absentee voting system because of the threat of corruption. It is getting to the point where I am thinking of quitting this whole voting business. In the most recent election, I liked all the candidates so much, I voted for every one of them.

With the election and leadership problems, I sometimes need to get away. I make my usual escape by going to the woods. You will notice I said woods and not forest. Forest is not the word I use to describe the flora and fauna of northern Minnesota. Forest is just too civilized for me. When I go to the woods, I see the massive stumps of the white pine trees. The large trees were cut and used to help build America in the last hundred years. I'd bet the woods I am seeing is different than the woods my great-grandfather knew.

In spite of the changes, I am still glad. My senses seem to work better when I am in the woods. I can see about fifty different shades of green. I especially like to see the green of the woods and the blue of the sky together, maybe a white cloud or two for contrast. When walking in the woods, I just naturally seem to be quiet. I remember my grandfather telling me I can't learn anything when I am talking, so I keep quiet. If I am silent, I can hear the critters I share the woods with. I like hearing the loons when I am near a lake and the birds singing in trees. I stand and watch in awe as the hawks and eagles circle above me. Last week I saw a bear sunning himself in an open field. Just west of the rez, we saw a bobcat passing through. The drumming of the partridges always reminds me of an old Ford Model A starting up.

There are a few drawbacks, of course. The mosquitoes and deerflies are one, but they are only here for a few months. The one that troubles me the most is the pollution. I see piles of construction debris at the end of some logging roads. I also see green plastic bags full of household trash. I wish I could identify those responsible for leaving their garbage in the woods. I would pick it up and then return it to the litterers. I would make a neat pile on their front steps. If the garbage comes from a business, I would return it to their main office. That action might get me in trouble, but I would be letting people know I don't like what they are doing to the woods.

One other drawback is the machines in the woods. The four-wheel drive ATVs are obnoxious. In the winter we have snowmobiles. It is getting to the point where it is no longer quiet in the woods because of the machines. I might feel different if I owned one of those loud machines, but since I don't, I can complain about them.

I like teaching my grandson the things I have learned from the woods. I do it because someone took the time to show me things about the woods. For me going to the woods is like going to a ceremony, a church, a mosque, a shrine, a temple, a museum, a shrink, and a rummage sale all at the same time.

> QUESTION: *What is the difference between*
> *a Chimook ghost and a Shinnob ghost?*
> ANSWER: *A Chimook ghost says, "Boo!"*
> *and a Shinnob ghost says, "Boo!—aaaay."*

The reservation is planning a huge powwow to honor the veterans of the Vietnam War. It will be held at Mashkawisen on the weekend of July 12. Tickets and other gifts will be presented to the vets. I heard they are going to pay the travel expenses for vets who live off the rez so they can come home for the celebration. I also heard all Vietnam vets, even white guys, will be honored. I am looking forward to the powwow because my wife, Patricia, will be making her award-winning fry bread. Usually the only time I eat it is at a funeral. It will be good to eat fry bread when we are gathered for a happy occasion instead of a sad one. The only other way to get fry bread is to tell my grandson to tell his gramma that he wants fry bread.

> QUESTION: *Didja see all those people running*
> *from Two Harbors to Duluth in the marathon?*
> ANSWER: *Did I see them? They were trying to get away from me.*

My aunt Inez Northrup Turner died. She was born here in 1925, and I remember seeing her when I was a kid. She left the rez to see the world and was gone quite a while. Inez came back home a couple of years ago. She has now joined those family members who have gone on before her. Her middle name, Louise, was my great-grandmother's first name. Once in the early 1970s I heard she was living in Michigan and I happened to be pretty close, so I looked her up. We visited a long time. She told me stories of her early days here in Sawyer. I would name a relative and she would tell me a story about them. Inez spent all afternoon telling me stories and I was glad I found her. The family buried her on July 6, but we will remember her a long time.

The reservation's powwow for Vietnam vets was just good. The living and the dead veterans of that war were honored by the Fond du Lac Reservation and its people. The living vets from Fonjalack were given gifts by the Reservation Business Committee. As a vet, I got an eagle feather, sage wrapped with the colors of the Vietnam campaign ribbon, a knife, a clock, a calculator, a rez flag, two nights at the Black Bear Hotel, a couple of T-shirts, a shiny black jacket with the rez symbol on the back, and the respect of the people. Two Fighting Falcon jets from the 148th Minnesota Air National Guard flew over.

Some people later said they got a lump in their throat as they watched and heard the tribute to all veterans. One woman said she got "welly" and almost cried. This time the entry was grand. The powwow was great. I'd like to thank all those who worked to make this happen. As a Vietnam vet, I felt honored but still think we should quit making veterans.

Mary Goggleye invited us to Cass Lake to try out for a Pequot museum project. The Pequot people were recently federally recognized. After centuries of intermarriage they were looking for real Indian-looking Indians to be models for their museum displays. We filled out the forms. I think everyone lied about their weight. We were then measured repeatedly, top to bottom, front to back. They used a calipers to measure cheekbones and a tape to measure inseam length. The last part of the process was the pictures. It was just like a mug shot except you didn't have to hold that little wooden thingy with the numbers.

For the Shinnobs who are picked, it will mean a casting experience and a hundred bucks. If I am selected, I will hold out for a hundred bucks, a trip to their casino and hotel, a little gambling money, and unlimited buffet privileges.

I bet two hundred Shinnobs showed up to be measured and photographed for the museum project. I hope the Pequots find what they're looking for.

Ricing is once again here and I am ready. I washed out the inside of my canoe, checked my knockers, and even made sure I have a backup pair. I have three poles standing by. I need three in case I break my backup pole. My kettle is still sweet from the last sugar bush season. My woodpile is tall and well seasoned. I am ready. My grandson Ezigaa is still too young to knock or pole. He can't parch or dance on the rice yet, but since he has been watching the process all his life, I know he will be ready when he is big enough. Right now he is a big help around the rice camp. He runs errands and helps clean the rice of stalks and leaves before we adults parch the rice. He also brags to his little chums that he knows about rice.

*QUESTION: What was a Sawyer credit card when you were growing up?*
*ANSWER: A five-gallon gas can and a siphon hose.*

My grandson Ezigaa was selected to take part in the Pequot museum project. This coming weekend we will motor to Cass Lake for the casting. We have been told he will have to breathe through straws for about eight minutes while they put the gel on his face. He will get his hundred-dollar check when they are done. I will try to trade with him—I will give him a handful of shiny quarters for that little piece of paper called a check. Hey, wait a minute—don't they have a bingo hall in Cass Lake?

*QUESTION: How did you know she was happy*
*to get back to the Cities after her rez visit?*
*ANSWER: She hugged the first streetlight she saw.*

*QUESTION: How did you know they liked to play bingo?*
*ANSWER: Their car was named "Odaabaan."*

Another Veterans Day has come and gone. It has been over thirty years since I was in the Vietnam War and I remember it like it happened last week. I am proud to have served with some of the finest men I have ever met. The mud marines of India Company, 3rd Battalion, 9th Marines were in a difficult place to do a difficult job. Six months after I left Vietnam, a platoon leader from my company won the Medal of Honor. Lieutenant John Bobo gave his life for his men and his country. We were young and strong and thought we were bullet-proof. Each dead marine that was loaded into a helicopter took part of that bullet-proof feeling away.

We used to tell ourselves that the bad things always happened to the other guy, but I used to wonder when it would be my turn to take that one-way chopper ride. At the time I was more worried about getting wounded than getting killed. Our attitude then was—if it moves, shoot it; if it doesn't move, burn it. Actually I was more concerned with the mundane matters, like how far do we have to walk today? Will the choppers be able to make it in to deliver ammo, food, or water? When the choppers couldn't come in because of weather or enemy fire, we would get hungry. We'd play little games, like do you remember what mashed potatoes tasted like? What about blueberry pie or ice cream? Can you picture the sound an apple makes when you bite into it?

We were eating nothing but C-rations, and I learned to like the taste of Ham and Lima Beans because most marines wouldn't eat ham. I always had Ham and Motherf—ers to eat when we couldn't get resupplied. I went to Vietnam weighing 180 pounds and when I returned I was 130 pounds of lean, mean fighting machine. My all-time overriding thought was about water. I used to try to imagine a tall cold glass of ice water, beading up on the outside of the glass, ice cubes floating in it. My favorite dream was about drinking a tall glass of ice water. Water was an obsession with me because sometimes all we had to drink was foul-tasting rice-paddy water.

So as another Veterans Day comes and goes, my thoughts are of those brave marines I served with. I know other people had worse experiences than I did in the war, but I will always remember the mud marines of India Company, 3rd Battalion, 9th Marines. On Veterans Day morning, I stood up and saluted all veterans of all wars. After that, I sat down and had a tall glass of cold water.

# 9.
# Treaty Rights Are Not for Sale

## 1997

We are hunkering down for winter on the Fond du Lac Reservation. I have winterized the rez car. I put warm clothing in the back seat for when the car breaks down and I have to walk for help. I don't know what's wrong with that car. It has started on every below-zero day we have had.

Ezigaa reminded me that it is time to snare rabbits. Time to take a walk to our favorite swamp to see if we can choke a rabbit or two. Be warned, Mr. Waabooz, we have snare wire and incredible amounts of patience. Hey Waabooz—want to come to dinner at our house? You can be the guest of honor at the meal. For me, winter means snaring rabbits. For me, winter means sugar bush time is coming soon.

*QUESTION: What is rush hour in the village of Sawyer?*
*ANSWER: Two cars at the stop sign.*

On December 3, an application for a gambling license was received by the Fond du Lac Reservation Business Committee. The application is required under FDL Gaming Ordinance #09/93, as amended. The application was submitted by the board of directors of Fond du Lac Management, Inc. Hey, wait a minute! These are the same guys that sit as members of the Reservation Business Committee. Did they really ask themselves for a license? Want to guess what the vote was?

I wasn't there, so I will have to surmise what happened at the meeting. Did the chairman/chairman ask for the license or was it one of the other voting members? Were they sitting on one side of the table as applicants and then on the other side of the table as voting members? I think Fond du Lac Management should have regular citizens on the board in addition to the RBC members. It has been happening like this since the ordinance was passed by the RBC in 1993. It ain't pretty, but it is what passes for democracy on the Fond du Lac Reservation.

QUESTION: *When do Shinnobs know it is safe to go out on the ice?*
ANSWER: *When the white guys quit falling through.*

I think I am lucky to be living on this reservation. One reason, of course, is that we are ten miles from town. We don't eat fast food very often. Mickey D can go to Moscow, but he doesn't come to Sawyer. Good thing, too—I'd be just round if we had a fast-food place around here. Going to town is big doings in our lives. We usually wear our going-to-town clothes for such occasions.

During the day in Sawyer, it is quiet: a dog barking, an occasional airplane, and if the wind is just right, we hear the highway and railroad. The nights are even quieter. If we hear a siren, it is usually about someone we know. We know most of the people we see as we move around town. This gives me a sense of security. I feel connected to this place when I greet a relative, laugh with a friend, or nod to an acquaintance. I don't feel racism from my relatives.

While sitting here on this part of the rez, I can see the moon come up outside my window. At first it is just a white light in the black of the trees. It gradually rises higher and takes on a round shape. Norway pine branches are silhouetted for a short while as the moon climbs and becomes a white circle with dark smudges across the face. There are no streetlights, so I can enjoy the cycle of the moon without light pollution. The moon is a reminder of all the cycles in life. I'm surprised the white man hasn't figured out a way to make money off looking at it. Until they do, I'll be sitting here beaming at the moon. The pace of life is slower here, and I like that. I can't think of any reason why I would choose to live anywhere else.

The *Duluth News Tribune and Car Ad Company* took an editorial stance in regard to treaty rights. They don't own the rights but think they should tell us what to do with them. Gawd, save us from these protectors. In January of this year, federal judge Michael Davis ruled that the Anishinaabeg have 1837 treaty rights in the ceded territory in Minnesota. Some of that territory includes Mille Lacs, elsewhere described as the premier walleye-fishing lake in the state. I know that lake.

Instead of exercising our treaty rights, the Duluth paper's editorial board thinks we should wait until the state of Minnesota finds another way to take those rights reserved in the 1837 Treaty. The white men and women who wrote the editorial worry about the "hotheads" who might try to interfere with the Anishinaabeg people. It is time to remind them we are citizens and deserve equal protection under the law. If local law enforcement can't keep order among the "hotheads," maybe the feds can. We know the feds have the resources to keep the peace. Witness Bosnia, Kuwait, and Iraq.

There is further talk in the editorial about the ruling's potential effect on gambling. I couldn't see a connection between treaties and gambling, but apparently they can. In all my readings of the treaties, I don't see gambling mentioned at all. Maybe it was a not-so-veiled threat. Treaties or gambling: "you people" can't have both.

I was going to write an angry letter to the editor but decided to write about it in the Follies instead. I'd like to ask the editorial board to read one of the old issues of their own newspaper, particularly the edition that reported that the Fond du Lac people voted the treaty sale down twice. I'll give them a clue. It was sometime between 1987 and 1989. Maybe they think we changed our minds since the last vote. Take notice editorial board: treaties are not for sale. I'll say it again: treaties are not for sale. Jeez, how many times do we have to tell them?

*QUESTION: What did that Indian say when he saw a white man wading ashore?*
*ANSWER: Is that a treaty in your pocket or are you just glad to see me?*

In my never-ending quest to learn more of the Ojibwe language, I just found a good source. Fond du Lac Follies motored to Mipples to talk to Rick Gresczyk's class at Hans Christian Andersen school. The students have been studying a book called *Walking the Rez Road,* so I stopped by to share what I knew about the book. Rick was being generous and gave me an Ojibwe language book and a cassette tape. On the tape Rick is speaking English and Margaret Sayers is speaking Ojibwe. My grandson Ezigaa is learning with me. Here is some of what I've learned from the book.

> Boozhoo.  Hello.
> Aaniin.  Hello.
> Aaniin ezhi-ayaayan?  How are you?
> Nimino-ayaa. Giin dash?  I am fine.
>   And you?
> Nimino-ayaa, gaye niin.  I am fine, too.
> Bi-wiidookawishin!  Come help me!
> Aaniin dina?  What's the matter?
> Nimbakade.  I'm hungry.
> Bi-wiidoopamishin!  Come eat with me!
> Bakwezhiganiketamawishin!  Make some
>   bread for me!
> Ahaw.  OK.
> Wiisinin!  Eat!
> Eya'.  Yes.
> Ambe omaa!  Come here!
> Gaawiin.  No.
> Omaa bi-izhaan!  Come here!
> Ganabaj.  Maybe.
> Booshke giin.  It's up to you.
> Gagwejimishin!  Ask me!
> Boozin imaa odaabaaning!  Get in the car!
> Daga ikodon, miinawa.  Say it again, please.
> Giiwedaa.  Let's go home.
> Ojiimishin!  Kiss me!

The snow is deep on this rez. A person walking in the woods sinks to his hips with each step. Fortunately Shinnobs solved this problem a long time ago. Using just the materials at hand, the Anishinaabe made snowshoes. My grandfather Mike Shabiash used to make his own. A pair he made is being kept in the family, passing from one to another. I remember seeing a black-and-white picture of him from the 1940s. He was dressed for winter and the snowshoes were standing beside him. I haven't seen that picture for years, but when I close my eyes I can still see it. My brother Vern has the snowshoes now.

We thought it would be a good idea to look at the sugar bush, so off we went. I got to wear my grampa's snowshoes for our walk in the woods. When I looked closer at them, I could see where grampa had repaired one with a piece of snare wire. Must have been out snaring rabbits when the shoe broke, I thought. My grandson Aaron came along. He was wearing snowshoes for the first time ever. He learned how to walk and run in the snow. I laughed when he was tipping over frontward. I helped him up while remembering how I used to tip over like that. Aaron was learning something that was not taught in school.

We looked at the tracks to see who else was moving around the snow. Aaron pointed at the deer and rabbit tracks with his lips. We used the snowshoes to make trails at the sugar bush. Actually we were making sidewalks for easier walking. With the snowshoes on, we'd sink down about eight inches in the snow. Without the snowshoes, I would have had to crawl to get around. A couple of days later I went to the sugar bush to look around again. This time I didn't wear snowshoes. Easy beans, our trails were solid, just like walking down a sidewalk in the city. While looking at the maple trees, I am mentally going down a checklist to make sure I am ready for sugar bush. Kettle—check. Taps—check. Firewood—check. I think I am almost ready for the hard work of the woods.

Fond du Lac Follies motored to the store, the Sawyer Store. It was a three-minute road trip to our version of the mall. The store is where we get the mail and the gossip and find out about deaths in the community. On the way I drove by my sister's house, then a first-cousin's house. While making the turn, I saw an uncle's house across the road from a nephew's house. I waved at another nephew who was standing on his porch while I glanced over at a friend's house.

I continued down the road to the store. I passed another first-cousin's house almost kitty-corner from two more cousins. Another cousin lives at the corner. I have aunts and uncles, brothers and cousins to the right of me, aunts and uncles, brothers and cousins to the left of me. Oh yeah, another sister lives on that road over there; more cousins, too. Another brother lives down at the end of that road. Two more sisters live a couple miles away, but I don't wave at them — too far away, they wouldn't see me. I get just tired from nodding and waving to my relatives. I wouldn't have it any other way.

In years past, I used to be an urban Indian. I lived in the big boxes full of strangers and I hated it. The noise, always the noise of the city. Sirens, airplanes landing, traffic — all assaulted my ears. The worst was the feeling of not really knowing anyone. There were always more strangers' faces than those of friends or relatives. So for those who live in the cities: Yes, I feel sorry for you and no, I won't trade places with you.

I am blessed with grandchildren. Our daughter Dolly brought three grandsons for an extended visit. They joined Aaron, age seven, already here at the house. Mato was five years old, Happy was eleven months, and Russell was eleven days old when he first came to visit. For a while there, I didn't know which one to hold, which one to pick up, or which one to hug. Two more, Niiwin and Noonah, joined them and added to the confusion. Six grandchildren in the house at the same time is a new family record.

I remembered my years as a parent and knew which end to keep dry and which end to keep wet. I pulled rank and reminded everyone that as a grampa, I am exempt from diaper duties. I almost got away with it until the night Gramma went to bingo and Dolly escaped, leaving me with Aaron and her three little darlings.

Things were quiet for a while, then the whole house fell apart. The five-year-old little darling had an accident that required a bath and change of clothes. While running the water, I was feeding the youngest little darling while the toddler little darling cried against my leg. The oldest grandson wanted money and a ride to the store. Baby formula, aah! How much do I put in? Watch your step! Happy got into all the pots and pans and scattered them on the floor. Happy, stay away from the steps. Somebody, anybody, close the gate! Hey, is the dog biting the baby or is the baby biting the dog? Okay, everybody go to bed.

I do know I can still outrun them if I really have to. But my Grampa of the Year award might be in jeopardy after my babysitting experiences.


Yup, we made maple syrup again. The cycle of seasons continues and we were able to gather our share of the annual gift. I told my grandson Aaron that the Creator must like us: we were given syrup again. We did a good job making snowshoe trails to walk on, but at the last minute we moved the sugar bush. We went to another place that had hip-deep snow. My cousin Chuck Greensky and our kids made new trails in the new sugar bush. I think the cold outside air makes you sleep more. After breaking trails all day, we went home and slept like Rip Van White Guy.

Barb and Tom came up from the Cities to help tap. They brought a friend, so that means our company had company while at the sugar bush. A van-load of teenagers came from St. Cloud. They wanted to camp out as part of the sugar bush experience. Too bad it was rainy and snowy. We told them about the Black Bear Hotel with the video arcade, swimming pool, and Jacuzzi. The adults didn't want us to think they were city Indians, so they stayed in the woods. We checked on them the next morning; their fire was still smoldering.

Aaron introduced them to his woods and his sugar bush. He was a tour guide for the older children from the city. After he showed them around, he helped gather standing dry wood for their fire. I shouldn't be surprised—he's been going to sugar bush all of his life, all six, almost seven, years of it.

My son Jim built the frame I use for hanging my kettle. It is still good for a few more seasons. We boiled sap into syrup. A lot of people surrounded the fire. My niece Deb, her husband, Greg, and their three daughters put in quite a few hours at our sugar bush—

enough hours that they are talking about where they are going to put their own sugar bush next year. They came to learn and now they can make their own syrup. Jim Denomie, noted Ojibwe artist, stopped in long enough to help gather sap while gathering images of sugar bush. He brought friends and family on a one-day escape from the city.

One day the children from the reservation Head Start program showed up. I guess we're a field trip for them. I wonder how many of those young Shinnobs will be making syrup when they grow up? The children had a taste of real maple syrup before they left. I don't know how many there were; they were moving and it was hard to get a good count.

The visitor who came the farthest has got to be Nadia. She has a last name, but I can't spell it or pronounce it, so I won't even try. She came from Sweden by way of Thunder Bay. She read the Follies when she was a nanny in Chicago some years back and continued to read it in Sweden. We connected and she came to meet the family. I'd never seen so many relatives when they heard we had a visitor from Sweden. It was mostly male relatives when the moccasin tele-graph reported that Nadia was young and single. We discovered that Nadia likes to cook, so we ate European-style for a while. It was a change from our usual oatmeal/wild rice/meat-and-potato diet.

She learned sugar bush real fast. My wife and I wanted to show her how some of the real Indians lived, so we took her to bingo. She had an out but was three numbers behind, so I don't think she knew it. I couldn't tell her since I was the competition. Pat was already playing one of her boards. At halftime Nadia threw four quarters into a slot machine. Reckless people these Swedes, I thought. Pat took Nadia to catch her bus back to Thunder Bay and Sweden. I think we will be seeing her again. I hope she comes during ricing; we can use her help with the parching kettle.

So, President Bill Clinton apologized to the black people for the in-famous study on syphilis done at Tuskegee. People were injected with the disease and were not treated so the scientists could study what happens. Way to go, President Bill Clinton. Say, as long as we got you in an apologizing mood, do you think you could whip out another one for the indigenous people of this place? Let us start with the theft of the continent. Next, we could consider the many forms of genocide committed against the Native people. After that we could go on to the boarding schools and the tribal governments established in 1934 by the Indian Reorganization Act. Then we better quit, since you only have a four-year term.

"The worst mass murder in American history," says the Duluth newspaper. Peter Jennings of ABC news called the Oklahoma City bombing "the worst act of terrorism on American soil." How convenient it must be to be blessed with a short memory. What a relief to forget about the early years in this nation's history, when Indians were dying by the hundreds of thousands while America forged ahead with its manifest destiny policies. Does this mean it is only history when it happens to white people or their institutions? Now, I am sorry that so many innocent people died in the explosion that destroyed the federal building in Oklahoma, but that terrible event shouldn't be used to gloss over American history. I remember. I won't let America forget, either.

QUESTION: *How do you say cordless drill?*
ANSWER: *M'goos (awl).*

Fond du Lac Follies jetted to Taos for the World Poetry Bout Association's Sixteenth Annual Taos Poetry Circus. My old friend Ted Charles met me at the airport and showed me his Navajo Cadillac: a pickup truck. He must know since he is a Navajo from around Gallup. We drove to Taos together, and back in time to when we were young. Ted and I were in the Marine Corps almost a hundred years ago—no, really it was more like thirty-five years ago—the old Corps. We met at Camp Pendleton shortly after boot camp. Ted and I spent the next three years together in the same outfit. We went to Cuba in 1962 and toured a lot of Asia with our Uncle Sam in 1963 and 1964.

Ted went to school after the marines and became a teacher and school principal. He works at a school that has a lot of brown faces near Gallup. Ted and I remembered our history as Indian marines in the early 1960s. We dragged up names and events we thought we had forgotten. It was a couple-hour ride to Taos and I think we stopped for gas once. I didn't see the scenery, Santa Fe, or the gauntlet of casinos because we were reminiscing about our past. After a while, we talked about the present and then the future. It was a good visit.

We went to the Taos Pueblo just to hang around with Indians. We were able to gossip with the folks there because we have many of the same experiences. It felt good to gnaw on a piece of fried bread and tell stories. I saw dream catchers in almost every little shop. Dream catchers used to belong to us; now they belong to everyone. It must be the Shinnob's gift to the world.

I had ringside seats to the World Heavyweight Championship Poetry Bout. It had judges, a referee, a bell ringer, and a tall woman who held up cards announcing the rounds. The poets took turns reciting poetry and the judges scored each round. The two poets recited their best stuff to the crowd that came to this event. The judges scored it a tie and Jimmy Santiago Baca retained his title.

Personally, I wouldn't get into such a fight. Maybe it is the competition part of it that I dislike. I feel it would be better to respect another's vision than try to beat them at reciting poetry. The main purpose of the championship bout was to get people out to hear poetry—and it worked. I heard over five hundred people came to the bout. Getting five hundred people to come and hear poetry is quite an accomplishment.

When I got home, I took off my headband and found I was a lighter shade underneath. That New Mexico sun browned my forehead. When I got back to Sawyer, a cousin asked where I'd been. He said my tan didn't look like I was in jail.

Fond du Lac Follies motored to Cloquet to look at the new building that houses the Reservation Business Committee. The building also is a community center for the Cloquet area. The inside is a maze of halls and walls. It was good that we had a local Indian as a guide, otherwise we would still be wandering around there. When the RBC first considered the building, I was aware we needed a new building to replace the old one. The old one was built in pieces over the years and was called a firetrap.

Some people protested spending that much money for a building without the people being heard on the issue because, after all, it is our money. But the RBC decided for us. It is an impressive building and it looks like millions were spent making it nice.

One highlight for me was the back bar from Molstad's tavern on Big Lake. It was taken from the tavern, refurbished, and made into a centerpiece for the new RBC building. When I saw the back bar this time, it didn't look blurry, as it used to occasionally when it was part of the tavern. I understand it is an antique and now worth hundreds of thousands of dollars. I haven't been there on official business yet but do appreciate that two of my sons helped on the construction. All in all, I would say this is a good use of gambling money.

It was the weekend and we really needed a fix of powwow, so Fond du Lac Follies and family motored to Red Cliff. My wife Patricia and pal Betty Jack were there to feed the multitudes. The two cooks fired up their matching stoves and began heating lard. Both were professional fry bread makers and they were prepared. While the cooks were cooking, I sat in the hot sun and worked on my tan. Nah, not really. I just sat there and worked on birchbark baskets. I'd sew a bit, then get up and eat, sew some more and eat again. The dancers, singers, and drums added to the magic of the gathering. I got the powwow fix I needed. I drove home full of fry bread and new memories.

Fjond du Lac Fjollies fjlew to fjool around the fjords of Norway. What? Norway. You might ask what the heck a skin is going to Norway for. In my case I went to recite some poetry and read some prose at three towns there. I went to see if they were still making and exporting Chimooks. When I got to Copenhagen, I was going to look for snuff cover lids but didn't have time. I was in the airport for two hours between planes and didn't see one jingle dress. You would think that a city named after snuff-can lids would have a few around, but they didn't. It was a short flight from there to Trondheim, Norway. All countries look the same from 25,000 feet. I didn't see one national boundary, although I must have flown over four or five different ones.

There are some six million Norwegians in America; in Norway, there are about four million. Before I started reciting poetry, I asked the audience in Trondheim if they wanted some back. There was a dead silence in the room. I could almost chew on the silence until a voice from the audience said I could keep the Norwegians in America. I was impressed by what I saw and experienced in Norway. What a clean place—I didn't see one highway billboard sign the whole time I was there. Think about it, not one sign littering the landscape.

And what a landscape. Steep mountains with sides that come all the way down to the road. Hundred-foot waterfalls; pine trees climbing to the tree line where the rocks and snow take over. I saw blueberries in the woods as I climbed around some hills. Every curve in the road gave me something new to look at. The steep mountain slopes continued down into the deep blue-green water of the fjords. The blue sky and white clouds made me think I was in a Hollywood movie or something. It was easy to picture a Viking longship coming up a fjord.

The roads followed the edge of the fjords and dipped, twisted, turned, tunneled, climbed, and descended. I asked if the roads were laid out by a snake and was told the road workers were paid by the meter, so they make long, crooked roads. There was a dairy farm in every half-way flat spot in the mountains. When I commented on the manure smell, I was told that I was smelling money. I looked at the cows grazing on the slopes but couldn't tell if they had shorter legs on one side from walking around the mountains.

Kristin Knybrott and her sister, Marian Bruset, worked hard to get the Follies to Norway. They sold raffle tickets, changed Norwegian words into English, arranged the events, and motored us around. Their efforts are appreciated and we talked about what I would show them when they come to America to visit. One day we went to Oslo, or as some say it there, Oooooooooooooslo. That is the only place I saw four-lane roads. We went through Lillehammer where they had the Olympics a few years back. The roadsides were clean, the rushing rivers were clean. I liked how the people of Norway took care of what the Creator gave them. I saw flowers everywhere. I must have come at the right time of the year.

I saw the famous balsa raft that crossed the ocean, built and sailed by Thor Heyerdahl. It was called *Kon-Tiki.* I remembered studying about that ocean trip when I was a young pup in school. At another museum I saw a Viking ship. What a beautiful piece of work. The lines of the ship were graceful even after 1,200 years. A Norwegian friend was walking along showing me the ship. When I asked if it was metal or wooden pegs that held the planks together, he reached out and touched the ship. The security guards descended on him and began talking loudly in Norwegian. I was glad I didn't understand what they were saying and was even gladder I hadn't touched the ship.

Of course, I had to go to bingo in Norway. My friends were amazed that I knew how to play bingo until I explained the bingo halls back home on the rez. They were even more surprised I could understand the Norwegian words for the numbers. I told them I couldn't understand Norwegian but I could see the monitor right behind them and the numbers came up there before they were called. The bingo caller actually sang the numbers and it was a nice sound, as she sang each number twice. Singing or not, she didn't call any of the numbers I needed and I had the same luck as I do at the bingo hall at home.

My time in Norway was over all too soon. The flight across the ocean was uneventful, but I did get a little excited when we landed at Newark and saw the jet that had crashed there the night before. I want to go back to Norway as soon as possible.

*QUESTION: Is that one a Shinnob?*
*ANSWER: Yup, fool-blooded Indian.*

Ran into Rick Gresczyk, Gwayakogaabo, at the Mash powwow and he added to my collection of Ojibwe language books with *Let's Speak Ojibwe,* which contains the following language lesson:

Aapiji go gi'zhawenim'in. I love you very
    much.
Gi wii-ojiim'in, na? Do you want to
    kiss me?
Gaawiin gosha. No way.
Zhigaagawanzhiig in'gii amaawaag.
    I ate onions.
Ojiimishin igo. Kiss me anyway.
Ni'minwenimaag zhigaagawanzhiig. I like
    onions.

Gert Morris died. Another language speaker is no longer here to teach us what she knew. I am one of the people wearing the floral beaded moccasins she made. We will miss her. Like a friend said, it feels like a library burns down every time an elder dies.

I just heard that three federal judges ruled that the Anishinaabeg do have treaty rights in the 1837 ceded territory. Once again, I hate to say it, but I told you so. Nah, not really—I just like saying I told you so to the state of Minnesota. We members of the Anishinaabe Liberation Front were ahead of our time when we were spearing and netting in Mille Lacs a couple years ago. It is nice being right even at the wrong time.

My grampa was correct when he said we had treaty rights; so was my dad. Now I can tell my children and grandchildren they have treaty rights. Before we start celebrating too hard, we have to remember this is just another battle in an ongoing war that has lasted 160 years. We must teach our young ones that the time will come when they will have to use, preserve, and defend treaty rights.

I think the Creator likes us because we were given wild rice again. My family and I gathered rice at both Mud and Perch Lakes here on the rez. We were invited to East Lake, but we got our share of the annual gift around here. Pat and I carried the canoe and ricing gear through a quarter mile of swamp to get to the lake. It sure looked nice when we finally got to the shore. The local gossip said

Mud Lake was full of rice and the gossip was right. The rice covered the entire lake; we didn't see any open water anywhere.

It felt like we were where we were supposed to be. We were so close to nature I felt mystical. A rice grain bouncing off my ear brought me back to reality. We gathered rice all day. We made two trips back through the swamp to get the canoe, ricing gear, and rice loaded on and in the rez car. Once in the car we started the engine, turned on the air conditioning, and leaned the seats back. We laid in state for a while until we caught our second wind.

The next time we went ricing it was easier. Perch Lake had plenty of rice. There were plenty of moose-ear plants, too, but we were able to weave around them with the canoe. We surprised a muskrat. He showed us his pretty brown fur coat as he went from his house to the water. During one of our many breaks, we watched four eagles. They were circling higher and higher until they disappeared from sight. As we were bringing our rice back to the landing, we paused to watch two more eagles doing that circling thing. It didn't look like they were hunting; it looked like they were flying just for the fun of it.

My son Joseph and I spent a day in a canoe on Perch Lake. This was his third year ricing and he is getting pretty good. Before he got too catty in the front of the canoe, I reminded him it took most of his first year to learn how to pole the canoe. We took a break where two other canoes were stopped. We told ricing stories and each of us, in our own way, told how good it felt to be out ricing.

Gathering the rice was just the beginning. We brought it home and built a fire under the big black kettle. We parched the rice, a basketful at a time. Once again this was a family project. Ezigaa cleaned the rice of stalks and leaves while it was drying in the sun. We took turns parching. Pat taught Joseph how to dance on the rice. We all fanned the rice to separate the hulls from the grains. The rice bouncing in the basket turned from the brown of the hulls to the green of the grain as we fanned. We had friends visiting, so they got to help us remove the rice that didn't lose its hulls during the process.

We have rice again. We should have enough to last until next ricing. The reservation was buying rice for seed again this year. The price I heard was $1.50 a pound right at the landing. I mourn the passing of the old days when almost everyone in this village was making rice at this time of the year. Now it seems like there are not many Shinnobs out on the lakes. I wonder where they are and why they are not making rice. I don't want to be the grampa who tells the children that the Anishinaabe used to make rice. In my family, we will continue to make rice even though the work is hard.

President Clinton tells me through the media that we must be prepared to go to war with Saddam Hussein of Iraq (again). It seems that Iraq has weapons that could be used against large groups of people. These would include biological and chemical weapons. Scud has come back into our vocabulary again. In the latest saber rattling, these missiles are now called weapons of mass destruction, a nice buzzword. Someone said Saddam is not supposed to have such WMD. Here is where it breaks down for me. We have WMD, too. A five-hundred-pound bomb is a WMD, as is a cruise missile. So, we use our WMD on his WMD? The smart bombs might be aimed at Saddam, but I wonder, who is the real target? . . . I gotta quit watching the television news.

Fond du Lac Follies motored to Mipples to be a part of the Frederick Weisman Art Museum's exhibit "Indian Humor." I laughed at most of the offerings, but there were some I didn't understand at all. I was gladdened to see Jeff Chapman has some work in the nationally touring exhibit. Local artist Jim Denomie has a couple of paintings representing his version of Indian humor. I saw a commod car made by Anthony White of Red Lake there. Where do these artists get their ideas? Kim Blaeser delivered a lecture on Indian humor. That White Earth woman has a way with words.

Our part of the doings was the performance of a play called *Shinnob Jeopardy*. Dale Roy, a Sawyer Shinnob usually known as Pea, made his acting debut in this production. He played the part of an urban skin named Franklin Lake, who wears long braids, a cowboy hat, mirrored sunglasses, and an AIM T-shirt. Jeanine Standing Bear played Tradish Ikwe, a contestant who lives with the seasons on Fond du Lac Reservation. She wears a ribbon shirt, a ribbon skirt, dream-catcher earrings, and white tennis shoes without laces. Brad Erickson was John Johnson Jr., the contestant who was adopted out. He has an anchor-man haircut, a blue blazer, a gray turtleneck, slacks, and shiny tassel loafers.

I, of course, played the part of Al Treebark, the host of the show, who wears a camouflage coat and a red headband. The play unfolds much like the real game show, with an Anishinaabe twist. The six categories are Ricing, Powwows, Tribal Councils, Higher Education, Casinos & Gambling, and Race Relations. Questions test the contestants' knowledge of life as a Shinnob.

After the surprise (don't give it away) ending, the real audience got to ask questions about what they didn't understand. I would estimate 40 percent of what we said went over their heads because they were not familiar with skins and their humor. They might have been looking for legends when we were looking for laughs. For instance, one question was "When do the dead come to life?" The answer of course is "Just before the election."

It is my hope that the ones who didn't understand the play ask the next skin they see about it. Maybe people will understand us better when they see what makes us laugh. I wonder where we are going to perform it next. It seems like a natural for Shinnob communities around the Midwest.

*QUESTION: What do you say to*
*Anishinaabe actors before they go on stage?*
*ANSWER: Break a legging.*

## 10.
# Blue as a white Guy's Eyes

## 1998

Fond du Lac Follies motored to Minny to catch a jet to Norway. What? Norway again? Yup, they wanted to learn more about Shinnobs, so they invited me back. I was blessed on this trip because I got to meet a genuine rent-a-shaman. There are quite a few fake rent-a-shamans around, but this one was real. He was advertised as Paul the Ojibway. What luck, I thought: Paul the Ojibway was going to be in a little town in rural Norway at the same time I was. The gods were smiling at me. The flyer gave the location and the price for attending the healing circle. I learned that I could get in for half price when I called the number on the flyer (must have been a Shinnob discount or something). I paid twenty bucks; the Norwegians had to pay forty. Half price for a half-ass healing circle, that sounded about right. Lord knows I had twenty bucks to spend so I could meet a genuine rent-a-shaman.

The doings were held in a rented conference center in the center of town. There was a Christmas tree in one corner serving as a backdrop for the event. A single strand of lights coiled around the plastic tree. The fake presents under the tree added to the ambiance of the setting. An electric Christmas star was blinking in disbelief in one window. There were six paying customers at the healing circle, some curious, some seeking spiritual help, and one skeptical Shinnob. I saw some bright yellow plastic shopping bags on a couch. The bags said "BunnPris" on the side ("low price" in Norwegian, I think).

Paul the Ojibway walked in and shook hands all about. He didn't look like any of my relatives. He sat down on the couch and pulled out some moccasins from one of the plastic bags. Paul took off his street shoes and slipped the moccasins on. As he pulled on the calf-high moccasins, I couldn't help thinking—the Doctor is in! He went on duty at that point. He was in charge of this healing circle, by god. There were two cute little bears drawn on the toes of the moccasins. He carried the plastic bags to the table and set up shop. I saw crystals, I smelled sage, and I saw seashells and an eagle feather. There were four cassette tapes standing by on the table.

Paul spoke in English with a Norwegian translator. We sat in the chairs and began to get our money's worth. The lights were dimmed and the healing circle switch was turned on, or the meter began running, I don't know which. In a soft voice, Paul told us to relax and listen to the music he provided on a palm-sized cassette player. The sounds were of tinkling bells, loons, and wolves. Flutes, too. The Doctor began slowly speaking as the pretty New Age music washed over us. I felt silly to be sitting there, but had to see what this guy was all about.

In a soothing voice, Paul told a terrible story about the sexual abuse he had suffered as a child. He asked us to introduce ourselves and share a story of a pain or a pattern of problems. When my turn came, I took a pass like at an AA meeting. Some people in the circle told sad stories, though. I felt sorry for them. Paul continued selling. Private healings were available for another fifty bucks. He was speaking softly as he muttered pop psychology phrases. Paul promised pendulums and crystals and more music for the private healings.

The next morning I went back to where Paul the Ojibway was doing business. I wanted to let him know what I thought of what he was doing. The waiting room had one Norwegian man waiting for his turn to see the Doctor. He asked if I was Paul the Ojibway when I walked in. I told him no, I was Jim the Ojibwe. I opened the door to the room we had used in the healing circle. Paul the Ojibway was crouched over a Norwegian woman. She was flat on her back on the couch and Paul was holding a swinging pendulum over her abdomen. The crystal on the pendulum caught the light from the fake Christmas tree in the corner. The music was floating through. Ooops, barged in on a healing.

I asked Paul if I could talk to him when he was done with her.

Twenty minutes later the woman was healed and Paul came out. I asked him about the eagle feather and sage. It wasn't a ceremony, he claimed; it was aromatherapy. I left thinking there was a horse's ass under his ponytail. Paul the Ojibway wasn't.

QUESTION: *How did you know he was a wanna-be Indian?*
ANSWER: *His Mohawk haircut went from ear to ear.*

After traveling around so much, I like to come home to recharge. One important part of that recharging is watching my grandsons at play. I was lucky over one weekend when two of them were here. I saw them playing mountain climber on the snowbanks and I wanted to be with them. After getting all my warm clothes on, I went outside. I was wearing my grampa hat, so I thought we should go for a walk. I also wanted to show them how to build a fire in the snow.

We went through the trees and into a swamp. Ezigaa, age seven, knew this swamp and wanted to be the trail breaker. Niiwiin, age five, seemed glad someone was breaking trail for him. The snow was knee deep to me. With frequent glances over his shoulder at his grampa, Ezigaa led the way. He just needed a reassuring look to continue leading the expedition into the unknown. The boys didn't know where we were going or why. They were just going somewhere with grampa.

The sky was as blue as a white guy's eyes as we waded through the snow. Along the way we remembered to be quiet as we walked through the familiar swamp. Ezigaa spotted swamp-tea sticking out of the snow. He told Niiwiin about the tea, how Gramma really likes it when he brings tea home from the swamp. Niiwiin wanted to bring some home, but Ezigaa told him to wait until summer. We climbed out of the swamp to a small hill. Looked like a good spot to build a fire to me. The close-knit balsam trees protected us from the wind. Ezigaa showed Niiwiin how to gather the dry branches from the bottom of the balsam trees.

The boys gathered branches while I looked for a birch tree. Once I stripped off enough bark for our fire, I came back and admired the pile of branches the boys had collected. I sent them after more because I know how fast it burns. The three of us stomped on the snow to make a pit. After watching me, the boys collected green balsam branches for the base of the fire. Using a mixture of dry wood and birch bark, we got the fire going on top of the green balsam branches.

The snow slowly melted down and the fire roared on. The warmth of the fire kept us quiet as we turned around to feel the heat all over. Niiwiin's gloves were steaming because they were wet from the snow. I hung his gloves on a stick so the fire would dry them. He watched every move I made. I added larger pieces of dry wood and so did Niiwiin. Ezigaa helped keep the fire going. In the middle of the winter of northern Minnesota, we found warmth around a fire we had made together.

Fond du Lac Follies motored to Cloquet to attend a meeting about spearfishing held at the new tribal center. The Reservation Business Committee called the meeting to explain how we would be getting fish this spring because the latest federal ruling said we can use our treaty rights in the 1837 ceded territory.

As I was driving along, I had time to reflect on spearfishing here on the Fond du Lac Reservation. I have been involved in spearfishing for quite a while, been doing it for at least fifteen to sixteen rez cars now. Back then we were called many different names. Among the ones I can write here are radicals, malcontents, and troublemakers. The other names had swear words attached to the front or back of them. We also had names for ourselves. We were most proud of calling ourselves treaty activists. We also called ourselves ALF, the Anishinaabe Liberation Front.

Ten years ago our tribal leaders were opposed to any use of treaty rights and seemed afraid to take on the state of (what is now called) Minnesota over treaty rights. In fact the leaders were just another entity standing in the way of Fonjalackers using treaty rights. They even told us we should sell our rights to Minnesota. They wanted us to forget our history to accommodate the white man. The leaders signed one agreement before we could fully debate the idea. They later told us the treaty rights were not sold, we just couldn't use them. The money came in but it did not trickle down to the people. At that time, before the gambling gold began to flow, I suppose $1.85 million was a lot of money to a cash-strapped tribal government.

The people of the rez petitioned for a vote on selling any more treaty rights. The idea of selling our rights was opposed by the majority. The RBC even held a second vote in a very unusual off-election year. Once again the vote was to not sell treaties. Meanwhile, the Mille Lacs Reservation was talking about selling their 1837 treaty rights to the state, and that didn't work out either. To show our opposition to these proposals, Anishinaabe throughout Indian country gathered to spear and net fish. About a dozen of us were arrested. We went to court several times before the state dropped the charges against us.

At the meeting in Cloquet I learned it would be legal to spear and net this year and our activities will be monitored by our own game wardens. The reservation's biologist will be taking daily readings so we will know when the water is warm enough for the fish to spawn. I also learned we will be spearing in ten different lakes in the 1837 ceded area. Once again, I have a plan for the spearfishing season. I am going to bring along an extra canoe for the trash I pick up from the lake bottom. Since the reservation will be weighing and measuring my fish, I will insist they weigh and measure the trash I take out of the lake, too.

Fond du Lac Follies motored to Cass Lake for training as a judge in this year's tribal primary and general elections. What? Me as a judge? I have been whining about election boards for twenty years. Now, I am part of one. I don't know why I was selected, but I am going to be able to write about the elections from an insider's point of view. With that in mind, my sister Doris and I got in the rez car and pointed it northwest toward Cass Lake.

The current rez car is a shiny gray Mercury Grand Marquis. It is one of those big old cars that outweighs most of the other ones on the road. I like it because if I get in a crash, I have more weight to throw around. We must have been cashy when we got tires for the car because they are all the same age. The ones in the front are cousins to the ones in back. It is a pretty good car. The original owner ordered cruise, air, electric seats, a tilt steering wheel, the works. The FM radio still sings loud through all four speakers. There is only one minor wound on the car. One time, a certain licensed female driver in this household was backing up with the driver's door open. The door went into the snowbank and was pushed under the front fender. It took just a little tire-iron body work to get the door working again.

To get to the meeting we had to drive on deadly Highway 2. We made it to Cass Lake without rubbing against anything but the wind. Doris and I walked into the tribal building and met Judy Moe of tribal operations. She pointed us in the right direction and we signed in. We were given a packet of information about the elections. Immediately to the left of the sign-in sheet were the tribal rolls. I looked at the row of bismarcks and picked the fattest one, and also a cup of coffee because I think it is traditional with the tribal rolls. I sat with Anishinaabeg from the six member reservations. Judy Moe and Gary Frazer, executive director of the Minnesota Chippewa Tribe, went over the procedure manual with us. They answered questions and told war stories about previous elections. The ballots for the primary election were issued and we all went home.

I have been hanging out on Tuesday nights with people who want to learn how to use the Ojibwe language. We meet and eat at the community center in Cloquet starting around 4:30. Here is what I have learned so far:

> Boozhoo.
> Bangii etago ninitaa Ojbwem.
> Ninga-gagwejitoon ji ojibwemoyaan.
> Jim Northrup niin indizhinikaaz zhaa-
>      ganaashiimong.
> Niin nindoodem makwa.
> Nagaajiwanaang niin indoonjibaa.
> Niminwendam ginkinoo'amaagooyaan ji
>      nitaa-ojibwemoyaan.

Nimino-ayaa gaye niminwendam omaa
 ayaayaan noongom.
Mii o'o minik waa-ikidoyaanh noongom.
Mii gwech bizindawiiyeg.
Giga-waabamin miinawaa.

We share the communal thought, "With the language you are Anishi-naabe. Without it, you are just a descendant of the Anishinaabe."

There is talk about this reservation having its own police depart-ment. On the one hand, I applaud the idea, but (and there is always a "but") law enforcement is just one part of a judicial system. Shiny new police cars with the rez logo on the doors would be nice to see, but we need a court free of the RBC first. We have seen our tribal judges fired by the Reservation Business Committee before. To para-phrase some Chimook, a nightstick is a nightstick is a nightstick.

Anishinaabeg from the Fond du Lac Band of Lake Superior Chip-pewa went spearing in the 1837 Treaty ceded territories. Ferd Mar-tineau reported that it was a very quiet season. The walleye taken from the lakes had nothing to say. Seems like just yesterday we were arrested for spearing at Mille Lacs. Now it's legal for band members to spear and net at that lake. Yeah! Treaty rights!

> QUESTION: *What did the walleye say*
> *when he swam into a concrete wall?*
> ANSWER: *Dam!*

The recent primary election held on Fond du Lac Reservation was fair and free from the taint of voter fraud. Everything I saw was con-trolled by a series of checks and balances.

Election day started early for the precinct judges, clerks, and tellers. I motored to Cloquet to pick up the necessary supplies to conduct an election on the rez. Three of us counted the ballots is-sued by the reservation election board, just to make sure there were no mistakes. At the community center the election was run by

Sawyer voters. I checked the ballot box and it was empty before the first voter came through. Then the voters came in. They identified themselves and after the clerk checked their name on the voter list, they were issued a ballot and shown the polling booths. After voters made their mark, ballots were handed to me and I put them in the ballot box. I was the official putter-inner of the ballots.

One high point of the voting was when a Shinnob we all know came in. He was at the right precinct but on the wrong reservation. The Mille Lacs skin didn't try to vote. We laughed about that one — right precinct, wrong rez. At the appointed time, we closed the box and counted the votes. About fifteen Sawyer Shinnobs gathered to watch the vote counting. After our count was complete we took the election materials and ballots to the election board. Our numbers matched; we had the right number of ballots and the right number of voters. The votes were counted again in Cloquet by the general election board. We worked from 6 AM to 10 PM. The next day we certified the votes. Now on to the general election. Once again I will be there watching with a close eye. I can certify that our part was honest.

QUESTION: *What were you found guilty of in court?*
ANSWER: *DWI: Driving While Indian.*

A new community center is being built in Sawyer. It is one of the many new buildings that have gone up on this reservation. I suppose the old one will be torn down and landscaped out of existence. I have a lot of memories associated with that old building: ceremonies, feasts, treaty meetings, funerals, weddings, poetry readings, elections, and bingo games.

QUESTION: *Didja have a lot of relatives visiting*
*from the Lower Sioux Reservation?*
ANSWER: *Had almost enough to make my own Custer movie.*

Fond du Lac Follies jetted to New York City to attend an event at the National Museum of the American Indian. We were invited because the museum had selected the video *Jim Northrup: With Reserva-*

*tions* to be part of the exhibit "Indian Humor." Media Mike Hazard and Mike Rivard made the video. Before the doings started my son Joe and I stood in line for the ferry to Liberty Island, stood in line to get inside the Statue of Liberty, then aborted the mission inside the old girl because we ran out of time. Of course, we had to stand in line for the ferry to get back to Manhattan. We could see the King Kong towers called the World Trade Center all the way back. The museum is at the George Gustav Heye Center near Battery Park in Manhattan. We got back just in time.

While I was standing outside the museum having a smoke, I met Raquel Chapa. Jeez, a skin face in the big city, things were looking up. She told us to be sure to go and hear Drew Lacapa, who was scheduled to entertain the people inside. Drew is a pretty good storyteller. I bet he could tell sad stories just as well as the funny ones we heard that night.

We rode the subways. It was an all-new experience for my son Joe. He hadn't subwayed before. I had done it lots of times, so I showed him my best secret for finding your way around. It consists mainly of asking a lot of people where something is and how to get there. After riding close with all those people I didn't know, I wanted to go home. That subwaying made me appreciate the quiet of the rez.

Joe and I were going to the Bronx to see the research branch of the National Museum of the American Indian. We found the building and met Terry Snowball, who showed us some of the things that were not on display at the Heye Center. I saw a lot of stuff and liked the way Terry put on gloves when handling certain items. I saw big drums and traditional Mide drums. We looked and left, caught the Manhattan Express, the bus. Joe found out where the Seinfeld restaurant was and we went there and, like tourists, took pictures.

On the way back to our hotel, we stopped at the American Museum of Natural History near Central Park. They have a lot of Indian stuff there. We saw a couple of the kind of birchbark baskets we make—nooshkaachinaagan. They even had a Mide bag unrolled with the contents visible, which I know is a disrespectful way to treat a religious object. We left. New York is a nice place to leave. I was glad to get home to the quiet of the rez.

My wife and I went to a bingo game at the Cloquet Community Center the other night. What I liked about the game was that we used
Ojibwe numbers. I won twice. I hope we can do this again soon,
maybe cribbage, too. Ashi naanan-niizh, ashi naanan-niiwin, ashi-
naanan-ingodwaswi, miinawaa niizhinoon ishwaaswi.

*QUESTION: Does he play slot machines?*
*ANSWER: They call him Keno-sabe.*

Fond du Lac Follies motored to the Black Bear Casino for Fond du
Lac Enrollees Day. The parking-lot event earned one moccasin from
this critic. Sure, there was free food. We each got a roll of quarters,
and there were cash drawings, but still it wasn't too good. We were
in the large white tent the rez uses for events like this. It was still
set up from the boxing and kickboxing events held in the evenings.
My family and I joined the employees standing in line for the free
lunch. We ate good and nodded at the occasional Fonjalacker that
passed by. The roll of quarters quickly disappeared inside those
Wiindigoo slot machines.

The enrolled members of the reservation were fed and treated
like the casino employees at the event. We all ate together and
listened for our names to be called for the cash drawings. We are
enrolled members of the Fond du Lac Band of Lake Superior Chippewa, not employees. We are the owners of that place. We don't just
work there. We should have a separate event, not something blend-
ed together with employee doings. How about celebrating a date important in Fond du Lac history, like the date the treaty was signed
that established the reservation? Or perhaps the date the perpetual
compact was signed with the state of Minnesota that allowed casino gambling? Why not during Peter DuFault Day, as we celebrate
a longtime tribal leader? Maybe the employees should be honored,
fed, and given cash drawings when they are working so hard during
the casino's anniversary celebration?

*QUESTION: Howdja know he was a wannabee?*

*ANSWER: He said his dad was a medicine woman,
and his grampa was a Cherokee princess.*

Clinton is part Cherokee? I snorted coffee out my nose when I read that in the newspaper. Once again, I ask, "Which part? Which part of the leader of the United States is Cherokee?" Clinton a skin? I don't think so. Could Clinton look a can of USDA commodity pork in the face without Secret Service assistance? Could Clinton go to a funeral, a birthday party, and a powwow all in one weekend? Could Clinton be on a HUD housing list for twenty-two years like my cousin Tiger? I don't think so.

Actually, Clinton is no different than the thousands of white people I've met who claim to be part Cherokee, so I guess he represents that wad of America. I believed Clinton on the Whitewater deal and the Monica Lewinsky doings, but this Cherokee thing is too much. Maybe I read the paper wrong. Maybe he is claiming to be part Jeep. Personally, I am glad that the word Anishinaabe is hard for a lot of people to say. Otherwise we'd have politicians all proclaiming they were part Shinnob, too.

My son Jim went to some doings out in the Dakotas. He met his friends from all over. One was a Lakota guy who had been visiting down in Diné country. They asked him how it was down there. He said, "Baaaaaaaaaaad." A Diné guy was also standing there telling stories about his visit to Lakota country. He said it was, "Rough . . . rough."

Along with forty-nine other people, I was selected to be part of a Minneapolis art project called Sculptures of Community Leaders. The subjects included activists, playwrights, politicians, writers, and a lot of people I don't know. I was honored to be included in such august company this August. When Fond du Lac Follies motored to Minny to attend the dedication ceremony, I found my head mounted on the bridge abutment. It kinda, sorta looked like me . . . I guess. It seemed like a lot of effort had gone into the project. All I can say is, I have been busted for sleeping under a bridge but never had my bust on one.

We have had many visitors to our little HUD house not-on-the-prairie this past summer. In addition to the usual drop-ins by relatives and friends, we have had visitors from overseas. Nadia, from Filipstad, Sweden, came back again. She came when we were making birch-bark baskets. Nadia jumped right in and learned how to gather the materials. She peeled some bark—birch and basswood. Nadia made a fanning basket and then began to experiment with different shapes and sizes. Now when the birch trees are peeled in Sweden, we will know who to blame—our primary Swede, Nadia.

Our back-up Swede came from the island of Gotland. Apparent-ly Annette took me seriously when I said, "If you are ever on this continent stop by." Annette also learned how to sew birch bark. We learned that people from Gotland call themselves Rauks and she was fond of saying, "Rauk and roll!"

Ann came from Oslo, Norway, because she had heard so much about Sawyer, Minnesota. While she was here she attended her first powwow. She walked around the circle at Mash here in Sawyer. We introduced her to the bingo games and slot machines at the casino. At first she was opening her purse, unzipping her wallet, and un-snapping her coin purse to play a quarter at a time. But after a while she was cracking the rolls like a real gambler. Ann made a beautiful basket and a lot of friends while she was here.

We also had some visitors from Southeast Asia this summer. People from Laos, Cambodia, and Vietnam came to see how the Fon-jalack skins live. We gave them the fifty-cent tour. We started at the Black Bear Casino, cruised through the housing compound, did a drive-by of the clinic, and wound up at Fond du Lac Community Col-lege. We got out of the vans and did a walking tour of the RBC build-ing. The visit wasn't complete until they had a look at Perch Lake and the wild rice growing there.

This visit was arranged by members of Women Against Military Madness (WAMM). As a Vietnam veteran, I was at first apprehen-sive about the Southeast Asians' visit. But after meeting them on my turf, I no longer felt that way. We fed them wild rice, berries, and maple syrup. They invited me to visit their homeland, but I told them bad things happened to me the last time I tried that.

*QUESTION: What do you call people who choose to live in the Twin Cities?*
*ANSWER: Citidiots.*

The U.S. Supreme Court is going to hear arguments and issue an opinion next year about our 1837 treaty rights. They couldn't buy it, so now they are going to try it, that government. Lest we forget, the state of Minnesota is a part of the United States. Now there are layers of lawyers arguing about my birthright. The birthright that includes treaty rights, the rights that were handed down by my ancestors to me. We kept our part of the treaty. We gave up the land in what is now Wisconsin and Minnesota. The Anishinaabe also reserved the right to hunt, fish, and gather in the lands we gave to the United States. Are we the only ones who kept the words in the treaty? I think so.

I worry about the Supreme Court deciding whether we have treaty rights or not. I know they don't hear many of the cases that are appealed to them. Why did they decide to hear this one? What is in those treaty rights that they want so bad? In looking at the history of the Supreme Court, I remember the case of the Cherokees. The Supremes agreed with the Cherokee people, but they still had to make that long walk to Oklahoma. Perhaps we will still lose even if we win the case in the Supreme Court. If the Supreme Court decides we no longer have rights according to the 1837 Treaty, I think it will also affect the rights in the 1854 Treaty. Then what? Does that mean no more moose hunting for Fond du Lac band members? Something very big is at stake here and I am wondering why the tribal governments are so quiet in this important case. Have our leaders been muzzled? Does gambling gold come with a trade-off? Has someone decided already that treaties are less important than gambling?

Commodity cheese now comes already sliced. What will that white man think of next? Why, this is the greatest thing since sliced bread, or something. The USDA program for distributing surplus commodities has been updated. We get frozen chicken instead of that canned stuff. There is frozen hamburger and we get real potatoes and onions, too. Sadly, I am sorry to report that commods no longer come with a Spanish lesson. The labels are now all in English. I remember when commods first came to the rez. I was just a pup. In those days, almost everyone had a garden in the yard. But since commods came, I don't see many gardens anymore. The rez has a gardening program, but I don't know how many people use it. I do see more people affected by diabetes, however. So, as health educators might say, is there a positive correlation between our commods diet and diabetes?

## 11.
# so sioux me

## 1999

Fond du Lac Follies motored to Madison, Wisconsin. It was part business but mostly fun. I had fun avoiding the gauntlet of casinos on my road trip. The first one I evaded was Black Bear, then Fond-du-Luth. I waved as I drove by the Majestic Pines and Ho-Chunk casinos.

I arrived in Madison with my frog skins intact and met David Young at Edgewood College. When he was giving me the fifty-cent tour of the campus, he pointed out an earthen mound shaped like a bird. I wondered about those old-time skins who built that, wondered what they would say if they knew a college had grown up around their work. David put me to work, and I visited his class that was studying short stories. I told them a couple of long stories. Shagg and Sandy White Hawk came into the room some ten minutes after the beginning. Do I dare say anything about Indian time? They just had to sit in the front row, too. It was good to see old friends among so many strangers.

The next day in Mad City I met some skin students from the University of Wisconsin. We talked and ate together. I didn't know any of them, but we recognized each other as being skins. I think we will remember each other's faces the next time our trails cross. Later that evening, we ate some of Shagg's deer-meat stew.

I wish I could say I avoided the casinos on the way home. I won a whole chunk of money at Ho-Chunk Casino, only to give it back at Majestic Pines. The rest of the trip was uneventful — except for that Wisconsin state trooper who followed me for about twenty miles. He was right on my bumper, so I know he was looking at the license plate. It says REZ CAR. Apparently I passed his visual inspection because he didn't stop me for a further check. I knew I wasn't break-

ing any laws, but just having a police car filling the rearview mirrors caused me to tense up. I relieved the tension by stopping at the
Black Bear Casino, where they were very kind to me.

My cousin Chuck Greensky and I were sitting here in this little HUD-
house-not-on-the-prairie when two bald eagles flew by the window.
Both eagles had white heads and tails. The smaller one was in the
lead as they arrived. The larger one had his mouth open as he dove
toward the other one. I don't know if that eagle scream was foreplay
or anger, but it looked like they were getting along while they sat in
the pine tree close to the house. Patricia and I went out on the porch
to get a closer look. The eagles stayed for a while, then left the same
way they came, still together, the smaller one leading. All three of
us humans said, "Miigwech." Thank you.

Fond du Lac Follies motored to Fond du Lac Tribal and Community
College in Cloquet. At the bookstore, I saw they had car incense for
sale. It was made to look like an eagle feather. What will that white
man think of next?

In Sawyer, the quiet little village on the rez, two of my granddaugh-
ters came to visit, Raina and Noonah. Raina, the eight-month-old,
arrived to spend a week. I hadn't seen her since she was a newborn
and now all of a sudden she was in a walker, driving her little car
around the living room and kitchen. We decided to call her Bineshiikwe after we got to know her. She once fell asleep on my chest. We
breathed together for as long as her nap lasted.

How can we account for the millions of dollars spent investigat-
ing and then trying to impeach the president? The huge government
monster seems to be consuming itself. Bill Clinton, Newt Gingrich,
and who knows how many others will fall before the beast is satisfied.
I get it, though. Bill Clinton is this year's O. J. Simpson. I think that
fine line between gossip and news has been crossed too many times.

As grandparents we knew why we were here. We were here to
take care of this amazing gift from the Creator. That little girl held
her arms up to be held whenever anyone came into view. Her spar-

kling eyes drew people to her. We took turns passing her from lap to lap, each of us making our silly baby noises. If we made the right sounds, she would reward us with a smile. It wasn't long before we got to know her little noises, too.

Televisions everywhere show and tell us the United States is imploding. We hear the harsh words every day on the news. The president is a liar, throw the man out of office. C'mon now, why is America so shocked by that news? In Indian country, almost every president has lied to us. Sometimes it seems like America elects a leader so they can destroy him. What kind of crazy sense does that make? It must be another indication that the country is going nuts.

Bineshiikwe discovered food while she was here. Bananas were a favorite and she could eat the little jars of baby food at one sitting. She would open her mouth wide and push her head toward the food. Two more favorites were crackers and ice-cream cones. She would scratch her itchy gums with those. The slap of a little baby's hands on the floor quickly became my favorite sound. When I heard that, I knew she was exploring this new world around her.

The news tells me we sent 450 cruise missiles to blow up things in Iraq. At $750,000 each, those are some loud, expensive explosions. I can understand why they used them, though. Cruise missiles have a shelf life like anything else and America wanted to rotate the stock, use the oldest first. Then, of course, we will have to order more missiles to replace the ones we used and all along the way a dollar is made. The cost of the bombardment of Iraq has been estimated at $500 million, a half-billion frog skins.

Noonah, our three-year-old granddaughter, also joined us in Sawyer. She came to visit her gramma and grampa. She politely told us she is no longer a baby and is now a little girl. She showed us her purse as proof, the purse that was filled with little girl things. Noonah showed Bineshiikwe the things she carried in her purse, carefully explaining what each item was for. The baby smiled because someone was talking to her. Noonah was a late talker, but now she talks clearly and constantly. She talked to the baby like they were two old birds at the bingo hall. The old people in the house smiled at the little ones.

With the cruise missiles and bombs, we have inflicted suffering on people on the other side of the world. With the touch of a button, missiles fly at treetop level until they reach their target and blow up, killing people and destroying things. Have we entered a new era called cruise-missile diplomacy? Do it the way America wants, or we will send explosives to blow up you and your house?

We had a good visit with our grandchildren. The laughter and loud noises are still echoing through this little HUD house. The grandchildren helped make this house a home. I can picture them telling their grandchildren stories about the times they visited their gramma and grampa.

QUESTION: *Aaniish gaa-ikidod giwiiw?*
ANSWER: *Gaawiin noongom niinimosh, nindayaan*
*i'iw mazinaabikiwebinigan odaanikanootage-wi-makakoonsim*
*aazhikwe-taagozi waabooz o we.*

Former wrassler and movie star Jesse Ventura is now the governor of the state of Minnesota. I will go on record as saying I voted for him. I wonder what he knows about the original people of this place now called Minnesota?

Our Tuesday night Ojibwe language class at the Cloquet Community Center is going great. We have a hard-core group that comes almost every time. We laugh and eat together. We play cribbage using Ojibwe to count our points while pegging. For me, relearning the language is filling an empty hole inside of me. I wonder where the rest of the Shinnobs are from this rez, or are they only Indians at per capita time? This is the best place I've found for learning more about Ojibwe.

My friend Walt Bressette died. I feel so sad that this man was taken from us while he was in the prime of his life. He was just fifty-one and he left a wife, children, and many grieving relatives. He was a Red Cliff Band of Lake Superior Chippewa member and was identified as an activist for treaty rights and the environment. I knew him better from the powwow circuit. We would show up at a powwow and were always pleased when we saw his craft stand set up.

One of my favorites from his rack of T-shirts was the one that said "I will snag no more forever." Walt was a patient, gentle man who always took time to visit with us. I will miss his funny stories and his opinions. I lost a friend like a great many others did. I am sorry that we lost Walt Bressette so soon; however, I believe that because of his actions and ideas, the next generation will have four Walt Bressettes, and the one after that will have sixteen Walt Bressettes.

We got a governor in this state with a loose-cannon mouth. Jesse Ventura seems to say whatever comes off the top of his head. In this day of mealy-mouthed politicians, his candor is a blessing, but it comes with a curse. His mouth is big enough to put both feet inside. He is beginning to remind me of another Ventura—that one was called Ace and he was a pet detective.

It is sad to say the governor is the product of a Minnesota education system that does not teach anything about Anishinaabe history. His recent statements about Anishinaabe people convince me he needs educating about us. The governor thinks we fish with two-hundred-horsepower Yamaha engines and fish-finders? Where the hell has he been? I have been spearing fish with my canoe for years. He further states that we should use birchbark canoes. Does he think white people are the only ones who are allowed to evolve? It sounds like he took one too many folding chairs to the head when he talks such nonsense.

His loose-cannon mouth got the Irish people mad when he said they were drunks. He made a watered-down apology. He has yet to apologize to the Anishinaabe people. So far, I am just going by what I hear in the news. I am anxious to meet the governor so I can take his measure.

My family and I have been downhill skiing. It's so much easier than uphill skiing. I started skiing when I was a young man and haven't done it for a decade or so. My old bones remembered how to get down the hill without falling. We make it a family affair, although my Dakota wife refuses to leave the bunny hill. Maybe after so many years of being married to an Ojibwe, she is used to things rabbit. My grandson Ezigaa was unsure at first, but over the weeks he has gotten better and better at it. I noticed a real improvement when we got him some ski goggles. I guess it helps to look the part of a skier. My old bones don't recover as quickly as they did when I was younger. We ski on Sundays and usually by Wednesday I can start moving normally again.

I was riding with a certain unnamed licensed driver from this house when she was driving in Minneapolis. It was on I-694 and it was rush hour just as it was getting dark. The cars in front of her stopped suddenly and she jammed on the brakes to avoid hitting the car in front of us. The rez car went into a slide when she locked up the brakes. Both of us were taking big bites out of the seat cushions. We slid to the left into the next lane and then to the right as she wrestled with the spinning steering wheel. Each slide was getting longer and quicker. The oncoming traffic managed to avoid us as we slid across their lanes. We did a long final slide onto the shoulder of the road. We could see the headlights of the oncoming traffic.

Then we were faced with the problem of how to turn the rez car around so we could go with the flow. There was a bridge and I was able to get the car up and back down and back again into the traffic. Now when she asks me if I want to go for a spin, I just say no. We narrowly avoided becoming a statistic.

I tapped trees and boiled some maple sap, but I had to leave the rest of the work to my family in order to jet to Rochester, New York, for some doings at SUNY-Brockport. I got on the plane in Deeluth (as my gramma used to say it) and had a short ride to Chicago. I had a couple of hours until the next part of the plane ride, so I went outside to have a smoke. I literally walked a mile for a Camel.

When I came back in, I went through the metal detector and the alarm went off. The security guard motioned me over for a wand search. I stood on the rubber pad as he passed the wand over me. It buzzed on my suspenders. I waited there with my arms stretched out in a crucifix position. The guard told me to turn around. I turned around and the man behind me was Henry Kissinger. I blurted out, "Henry Kissinger!" I guess I said it in case he didn't know who he was. He smiled and reached across to shake my hand. While shaking hands, in the best Henry Kissinger impersonation I ever heard, he said, "Thank . . . you . . . for . . . serving . . . your . . . country . . . in . . . Vietnam." I was so surprised by the meeting and greeting, all I could say was, "Yah, miigwech." I looked into his eyes, friendly but sad looking, I thought. His speech was measured and precise.

The encounter was a Boozhoo-Miigwech-Giga-waabamin kind of a thing, probably didn't last over forty-five seconds, but I felt good about the handshake and thanks. I wondered how he knew I was a veteran. Duh? Then I remembered I wearing the black jacket the Fond du Lac Reservation had given me. The screaming-yellow embroidered letters across the back say "Vietnam Veteran." The colorful rez logo sits in the center. Henry Kissinger had time to read my back. I am glad he decided to stop what he was doing to thank me. I felt like he was thanking all veterans when he shook my hand.

The rest of the airplane trip was full of thoughts of what I should have said and done upon meeting the former secretary of state. I could have given him a book and let him read about the Vietnam War from this grunt's point of view. I could have asked his thoughts about bombing for peace in Kosovo. I should have asked for an autograph or begged a passing civilian to take our picture. We could have signed a piece of paper together. Coulda and shoulda. I felt good about him thanking me, though. I arrived in Rochester where I put my feet on the ground, although I think my head was still in the clouds back in Chicago.

At SUNY-Brockport I met some folks who were putting on the doings. Margaret Blackman hosted the Native American Symposium. The presenters gathered at her house for a feast. I met Warren Skye Sr., a Seneca from the Tonawanda Reservation. I enjoyed telling stories with this seventy-six-year-old man.

We went to a Joanne Shenandoah concert and had front-row seats because we were part of the symposia. I finally got to hear Joanne Shenandoah in person. She and her sister Dianne sang to us and for us. Joanne spoke of a visiting writer from the Fond du Lac Reservation and dedicated a song for him. I felt honored to get that kind of recognition at a concert. My head swelled and almost snapped the knot in my headband; it was just hanging on by a scrap of cloth. After the concert I thanked Joanne. While hugging her up, I told her I met Henry Kissinger earlier in the day but that this hugging was even better.

We presenters stayed in a bed-and-breakfast while we were in town for the doings. It was called White Farm and was located on White Road, just west of the intersection of White Road and Redman Road. During a break in the action, I motored west for an hour to see Niagara Falls. As soon as I walked up to look at it, I had to pee. I enjoyed my brief visit to Viagra Falls and went back to the doings at Brockport SUNY. I met new and old friends at the doings. I flew back home, didn't see anyone like Henry Kissinger or Joanne Shenandoah. The next day, I was back in the sugar bush boiling maple sap. My wife says I always find excuses to leave home when there is real work to be done.

*QUESTION: What do Shinnobs call foreplay?*
*ANSWER: Are you awake?*

Without unpacking my suitcase, Fond du Lac Follies jetted on another trip. This time it was to the Institute of American Indian Arts in Santa Fe, New Mexico. Marla Redcorn brought me there as part of their gallery exhibit called "Seasons of the Woodland People." I wasn't on display or anything, just there to recite poetry. Pea drove me to the Duluth airport. We got to the terminal with plenty of time to spare. As usual, we had more time than money. We looked at the other early-morning flyers. I thought I recognized someone in the crowd going through the security system. "Pea, isn't that Walter Mondale?" I asked. "I don't know," said Pea. I threw Pea a Sawyer wave as I got on the plane. He threw me a nod.

Turns out it was Walter Mondale. I got a chance for a closer look as I was finding my seat. The former vice president was flying in the first-class part of the airplane while I was in the back with the commoners. I shook hands with him on the way by and he asked where I was from. When I told him the Fond du Lac Reservation, he remarked on what a good job the Fond du Lac Tribal and Community College was doing. I nodded but had to find my seat because I was blocking the aisle. What is it with this always meeting famous people when I travel? Last month it was Henry Kissinger, this month the former vice president of the United States. I wonder who it will be next month. Sherman Alexie?

Santa Fe was right where I left it last time, right in the middle of the desert. I met the folks from the institute and they treated me like I was a visiting writer. I couldn't help but notice the contrast between green New York and brown New Mexico. I toured the institute and saw much art. While there I met Dan Agent, Cherokee journalist, the former editor of the *Cherokee Advocate.* He told me stories about freedom of the press in Indian country. Dan wanted to run a free newspaper but is now the former editor because he was fired by his tribe, the Cherokee Nation in Oklahoma. Free press?

It felt good to be in Santa Fe. I didn't stick out in the crowd. There were many, many people who had brown skin and black hair, totally unlike Minnesota, where many, many people have blond hair. While in Santa Fe I met friends old and new. Ted Charles, a marine buddy from the old Corps, circa 1961 to 1964, came to visit. We told each other stories for hours and hours. The next day I went home. It didn't take long to get caught up on the rez gossip.

Sure enough, the next brush with fame was Sherman Alexie. When Dr. Bob Powless called from the University of Minnesota, Pea and me motored to Duluth to hear Sherman Alexie talk and read. I had wanted to meet this skin author ever since I read the title of his book, *The Lone Ranger and Tonto Fistfight in Heaven.* I enjoyed his presentation. At one point he used the now famous line from *Smoke Signals,* "Hey Victor." After the reading, we talked about writing for a while. Some of the audience members gathered in the Tweed Museum to meet Sherman Alexie, get their books signed, and get their picture taken with the author. At the reception, Pea and me guzzled punch and inhaled chocolate-chip cookies while Sherman Alexie greeted the people. Anne Humphries sang and played the guitar. Anne Dunn, her mum, was smiling as her daughter played the music.

I took a month off from writing
the Follies to make birchbark baskets.
So Sioux me.

Fond du Lac Follies has been motoring to the woods. Most of the time it is Pea and me, but sometimes others come along to select the bark for making fanning baskets. My grandson Ezigaa, nine years old, joined us one morning. Before we left he made sure we had drinking water because it was hot in the woods. He wore a long-sleeved shirt and long pants. He has been in the woods before and knew about mosquitoes and deerflies at this time of the year. I was glad he knew how to woods.

We found some good trees to use and I watched that boy to see what he has learned about gathering birch bark. He asked for some tobacco to offer thanks. I felt just proud that he remembered that part. He walked around the tree, examining the bark. When it met his approval, he used a knife to make the light initial cut. Ezigaa used his knife to cut deeper until the bark popped open. He then put his hands between the two layers and walked around the tree.

The bark made a cracking noise as it came off. The boy looked at the sheet of bark; he held it up to the sun to look for holes and weak spots. I just stood there slapping mosquitoes while my grandson gathered bark. At one point he was doing what I call the birch-tree dance, running from tree to tree saying, "Here's a good one, another one over here, and look at this one." I am glad my boy went to the woods with me. Now he has something he can teach his grandchildren when the time comes.

*QUESTION: Are you a full-blooded Indian?*
*ANSWER: Nope, the mosquitoes were really thick this year.*

Tom Goldtooth, a Diné who works with the Indigenous Environmental Network, stopped by in Sawyer for a visit. He was on his way to some doings at the Black Bear Casino and paused long enough to say "boozhoo." Then we had another visitor from the Southwest.

It was our old pal Sara Begay, Diné, from Page, Arizona. She came north to look at all of our green. After being in the desert and seeing all that brown, I can understand her yearning to see growing things. The last time Sareresa was in the area she worked at WOJB, that skin radio station in Hayward run by the Lac Courte Oreilles. Sara always brings her hearty laugh when she visits.

Her mom, Bernice Austin-Begay, makes things from flour sacks. My wife has an apron that says Blue Bird Flour on it. I myself have a pillowcase that says Blue Bird Flour. Funny, I have been dreaming of sheep as I sleep. Sara is a wannabe Shinnob, I think. Her e-mail handle is MuttonShinnob. She came to our Ojibwe language table one Tuesday night to continue learning Ojibwe. While we were there, a writer from the Duluth newspaper showed up. It was Jason Begay, Diné. Jeez, three Navajos in one week. I can go for months without seeing a Navajo and then three of them showed up. Hmmmmm.

Fond du Lac Follies has been motoring to powwows lately. It is a summer Sawyer skin thing to do. The rez car has been carrying us around. At the veterans powwow here in Sawyer, my wife set up her food stand, called Stand Here. She reported making over a thousand pieces of fry bread during the weekend. I sat in the shade and sewed birchbark baskets. The grand entry was just grand. We also motored to the powwow at LCO called Honor the Earth. This powwow was a gooder. I saw Chuck Robertson and Floyd Red Crow Westerman bellied up to a food stand, so I joined them for a few minutes. They were raffling off a car that was two years younger than the rez car. Of course I bought tickets, but I didn't win.

We traveled around the powwow circle sampling food until we got to Betty Jack's food stand. There we stayed and ate. *News from Indian Country* had a stand that was selling language books, newspapers, and posters. I learned that Fond du Lac Follies won the award for best column from the Native American Journalists Association. Paul, the editor from *NFIC,* had submitted the column and brought the award plaque home for me. I am always honored to be recognized by my peers.

Fond du Lac Follies has been motoring nowhere. Why? Maybe because the rez car tried to commit suicide. It happened this way. Me and Pea were going to roar to town to buy a part for something else that broke. The first quarter-mile of the trip was uneventful. The Troubles (to borrow a phrase from the Irish) began when we got to the tar road. We heard a loud thump. I looked in the mirrors and saw something lying on the road. I also saw a foot-wide trail of liquid following us. The liquid was coming from the car and told me we wouldn't make it to town, so I aborted the mission. We headed for home after I turned the car around. I came to that something that was lying in the road. It was the tapered end of the exhaust pipe. When I stopped to pick it up, I could hear the gasoline splashing on the road, could smell it, too. I figured out what caused the loud thump. The pipe had speared a hole in the tank.

The splashing gasoline made me think of every movie I ever saw that had an exploding car in it. I thought if the gasoline ignited, we would become part of the fireball. I was getting ready to yell "Eject" to Pea and do a dive-and-roll out of the car. His hand was on the door handle, too, as we roared home. I tried to outrun the trail of gasoline, speeded up and slowed down, swerved the rez car back and forth. We couldn't shake the trail of gasoline that was pointing right at us. We got home and shut the car off. Pea went out his door and ran about fifty feet. I did the same out my door. The car didn't explode so we were safe, but then quickly realized we had an ongoing toxic waste spill. The gas tank was gushing gasoline, looked like a shiny waterfall under there. It was pooling up. Pea said, "Full tank?" I had to say yes. While Pea got the jack out, I ran to find something to catch the gasoline.

While Pea was jacking the rear end up, a Chimook stopped by in his car. We had met him earlier at the powwow. After getting out of his car, he said, "Oh, working on your car?" Neither one of us answered. I found ice-cream pails, a coffee can, and a five-gallon gas can. Pea put the pails and coffee can under the river of gas. The civilian said, "Working on your gas tank?" Neither one of us answered. We used a plastic water bottle for a funnel. When the five-gallon gas can was full, I asked Pea if he wanted some gas. He said,

"Shore." I poured the five gallons into his car's gas tank. The civilian got tired of watching us and waved good-bye. That is when I realized the Chimook and his car were straddling our trail of gasoline. He had almost become part of our movie. After the tank ran dry, we drove to town in Pea's car. Same mission, same gas, different car. So now the rez car sits, a great hole torn in its bowels, while I call every junkyard within fifty miles looking for a gas tank.

QUESTION: *Why did you feel sorry for that white guy?*
ANSWER: *He didn't know his cousins.*

Well, it has been ten years since the Follies first appeared in *The Circle.* For this family, that would be about twenty-five rez cars, at least fifteen dogs, more than fifty powwows, forty seasons, and over thirty-five hundred sunsets and sunrises. Our grandson Ezigaa came to live with us, and brightened us like that ray of sunshine you sometimes see coming down from the clouds. He is nine going on nineteen and knows all the words to the songs of the sixties and seventies. Ezigaa has been looking for agates most of his life and last week found his largest ever. It is about the size of a softball.

On a professional level, I have had two books published and reprinted and had two plays performed. I sometimes wear the "author" headband. The video made by Mike Hazard and Mike Rivard is still being shown at film festivals around the country. On the rez, the gambling gold has fueled a building boom. I would guess over $100 million has been spent in the last ten years on building. We have clinics, offices, community centers, casinos, and hotels. The Fond du Lac Reservation is now one of the largest employers in Carlton County. We are buying squad cars for the sheriff's department and building our own tribal police department. Unfortunately, our constitution has not changed and our tribal judges can still be fired by the Reservation Business Committee.

Fall is coming to this rez in northern Minnesota. The ferns are dead, the maple leaves are turning from green to yellow to red. This has happened before. It was last year about this time. I am beginning to notice a pattern in these seasons.

I would like to tell you a ricing story, a story where the Anishinaabeg gather on the lakes and rivers to collect their annual gift—the wild rice. I would like to tell you about the happy crowds that came together at the boat landings to gossip and brag about their children and grandchildren. I would like to tell you how the jacket-cool mornings and T-shirt afternoons make me think of ricing. I would like to tell you stories about who fell in the lake this year, who broke their knockers or pole. I would like to tell you about the canoes coming back to the landing low in the water because of the weight of the rice. I would like to tell these stories, but I can't. The rice crop was not too good this year on this rez.

My son Joseph and I went to Dead Fish Lake to rice. I had looked at the rice during the first part of August and it looked good. The lake was full of growing plants, couldn't see any open water anywhere. Sometime between the time I looked and the time I went to rice, something terrible happened to the crop. The game wardens and biologists tell me the heavy rains flooded out the growing plants. We had to go to one of the other five reservation lakes that weren't flooded. Sonny Greensky was using his forty years of ricing experience to teach a new generation how to make rice. He had six students from Albrook School out on the lake. He laughed as he reminded them of canoe safety, how to climb back in—probably remembering all the times he tipped a canoe and fell in.

We tried going west to East Lake. It started out to be a typical ricing trip. Ezigaa helped me load the canoe on the rez car. Then I flooded the rez car, ran down the battery trying to get it started, hooked up the jumper cables to the rez truck, and cranked until the car started. Then we tried to follow the directions to the rice landing as given by my cousin Chuckles Greensky. Couldn't find the rice landing, ran into another Fonjalacker who couldn't find the rice landing either. I knew how to get to the north landing, so we went there and launched the canoe. As we got out there, it started to rain. We riced until we got good and wet, then came home. We were on the lake for about an hour, came home with half a sack of rice. It is good that we have a couple of sacks of rice left over from last year. As they sometimes say about baseball teams, wait until next year.

*QUESTION: What was the greatest thing before sliced bread?*
*ANSWER: Bread.*

*QUESTION: What was the greatest thing before sliced commod cheese?*
*ANSWER: Unsliced.*

My wife and I went for a drive the other day. Fond du Lac Follies motored to the Grand Casino in Onamia for the wedding of Tish and Chad. If you don't know who they are by their front names, that is just too bad. They were joined together by Jim Clark. There is white guy clock time, there is Indian time, and there is Follies time. We used up every bit of the Follies time and missed the ceremony. Pat and I got there in time to eat, so we were apparently still on time. We joined the wedding guests and Tish showed us where to sit.

Paul Day had a wireless microphone and was giving everyone a chance to get up and say nice things about the happy couple. When he thrust the microphone in my face, I did what any husband would do and introduced my wife. Pat talked about our marriage ceremony. She told how Jimmy Jackson joined us and some of what he told us about marriage and responsibilities. When the microphone came back to me, I offered the young couple some advice and suggested a division of labor. I said that I make the important decisions in our marriage: whether we should explore Mars or if Alan Greenspan should raise the interest rate. She makes the little decisions like what we will eat or how we should spend our time and money. Jim Clark said he makes the big decisions in his marriage, too. In forty years of marriage, he hasn't had to make a big decision yet, he told us.

After he handed the microphone back to Paul Day, Jim Clark came to our table to visit. He said he had a complaint about the Follies. I thought, uh-oh. What did I write that offended this Mille Lacs elder? He said the column was too goddamned short. He just gets started reading it and it is over. I promised to slip in a couple extra words for him. Jim Clark also told us about the language do-ings at Wigwam Bay. Every Wednesday evening at six o'clock or so they meet and talk Ojibwe. Everyone is welcome who wants to learn more, he said.

There was a lot of rice thrown around at the wedding, but it wasn't that ancient white guy tradition. It was just Shinnobs exchanging wild rice to eat. There was a small card attached to our gift of wild rice. It read, "Gimiigwechiwi'igoo maampiji giinawaa gakina-gidi-nawemaaganinaanig." In English it said, "We are honored by your presence, and hope that this small gift reflects our wedding as a joining together of all of our lives. —Tish and Chad."

On the way out of the Grand Casino, I learned the words for ten dollars. I put midaaswaabik in one of the slot machines and left it there. Let us hear a cheer for Tish and Chad.

The RBC gave the elders of the rez a gift this November. The require-ments were pretty simple: A person had to be over fifty-two and en-rolled in Fond du Lac. I showed up to get my gifts from the RBC. I was handed a pound of wild rice and a fifty-dollar bill. A grant of a Grant and rice, how nice, I thought. Is it election time already?

On Veterans Day, I was once again grateful that my life was spared during the Vietnam War. Fond du Lac Follies limoed in a limo, but that comes later in the story. First, Pea and me did the airport thing. He dropped me off in time to catch a Northwest flight to Minneapolis for the connecting ride to Detroit. I had been invited to speak at Michigan State University. The ride from Minny to the Motor City went all right. We took off and landed in the right plac-es. I met up with the people who gave me a ride from the airport to the university. I shook hands with George Cornell, who introduced me to the audience. George is a Vietnam veteran, so it was fitting since the reading took place on Veterans Day. I recited poems for the veterans.

I had to get up real early to connect with my flight back home. Because of the distance and time, no one wanted to drive me to the airport, so they sent a limo instead. The front desk called at 0400 hours to wake me up and the limo arrived at 0430. The Cadillac limo was long and gray. The driver said his name was John and he would take me to the airport. He said I could ride up front or in the back. I thought, when do I ever get to ride in a limo? I told John I would ride in the back. While getting in, I had time to look around to see if anyone saw me getting into a limo. Nothing, nobody on the streets at that time of the dark. What good is a limo ride if no one sees you?

I drank my coffee and read the newspaper during my limo ride. The soft leather seats felt pretty good. I wondered if I could get some for my rez car. I fiddled with all the switches and buttons to amuse myself in the back of that long, long car. After about an hour of limo time, we got to the airport. We had to park out in the third lane away from the curb because of the traffic, so no one saw me getting out of the limo, either. I did wait for John to open the door, however. At the Duluth airport, my wife met me. She handed me the car keys and asked me to drive the rez car. We talked about the limo ride as I drove her home.

# 12.
# smoking moccasins

## 2000

I don't like to admit it, but those Christmas lights are driving me up the pole. What do they mean? What is accomplished by stringing lights all around the house? What do the lights have to do with the birth of the Christ child? Are the lights supposed to help Santa Claus find the house? As I drive around the reservation, I see a lot of Indian homes that have the lights. I asked a Sawyer skin what he thought about the lights. He said all it means is some white guy convinced the skins they got to put the lights around their houses so he can make a profit.

In Duluth, the Christmas lights made some people angry. They put up thousands of lights but didn't win the lighting contest because their application was lost. Now they are out of the money because of a bureaucratic error. I smell a lawsuit somewhere. When I want to see flashing lights, I just go to the casino or wait for the cops to pull me over when they see my reservation license plates.

*QUESTION: What was the name of that new small drum group?*
*ANSWER: The Four Skins.*

One of my very basic rights is still being violated here on this reservation. I still don't have freedom of the press. *Nah-Gah-Chi-Wah-Nong, Di-Bah-Ji-Mo-Win-Nan,* the paper published by the Reservation Business Committee, has never printed opinion pieces. The editor further states that there are plenty of other places that will carry negative news about the reservation. It is our money that funds the newspaper and pays the salaries, but apparently we can only read happy stories. Spoon-fed or censored?

195

In my opinion, the rez newspaper should have carried the news about the RBC's attempt to disenroll a band member. I heard the skin was guilty of thinking of running for office. If it could happen to him, who else could get dis-membered? I saw the rez reporter/ photographer at the meeting. I would much rather read about something like that than the news that health and human services employees won yet another award from the BIA.

Our granddaughter Raina has been visiting lately. We call her Bineshiikwe and she is all of nineteen months old. I am amazed at how she moves. It has been over half a hundred years since I could move like she does. She was sitting on the floor. I said, "Come on, let's go." She planted her little fat feet on the floor and just stood up. I can't imagine myself being able to do that. I sat her down to see her do it again. She stood up after planting her feet. She caught on to the game and sat back down so she could stand up again. Amazing, I thought. Every time we had company I had to show them how that little girl could stand up. After a few times, she knew that game and would sit and stand on command, laughing the whole time. She got sticky after eating a piece of candy, so I washed her face and hands with a warm washcloth. When I was done, she looked at my eyes and said, "Thank you."

*QUESTION: How does an Indian find his way out of the woods?*
*ANSWER: He doesn't—he just sadly waits for urban sprawl.*

Reparations? Jeez, more and more folks who have been treated wrong are getting money—guilt money or something. I see other ethnic groups, other victims, being considered for reparations. Ahem, it was terrible what happened to those people and they should get compensated but, and there is always a *but* . . . what about the original people of this continent? When do we get our rebate checks, the reparations? According to my always-handy Webster's dictionary, one definition of reparations is "the act of making amends, offering expiation." *Expiate* means to atone for, appease, to extinguish the guilt, to make amends.

Now, it seems to me there is a lot to atone for, there is plenty to make amends for. The history of the dismal relations between the United States and us gives plenty of examples. Shall we run down the all-too-familiar list? The continent for one, the culture for another, the loss of language, the boarding schools, and the theft of land from the reservation. Am I the only one who remembers the story about how the Lake Superior Chippewa were supposed to get a dime a ton for the iron ore that was taken from northern Minnesota? And what about all that pine that was taken? Every time I walk in the woods, I am reminded of what happened. The stumps are still there from the big-pine days. Gambling casinos are not atonement.

It is time to make maple syrup, the crows told me so. The retreating snow in the backyard was another clue, as were the warm days and cool nights. I told stories to my grandson Ezigaa as we walked in the woods. I thought it was a good time to learn more Ojibwe. Thanks to Rick Gresczyk's books, we were able to use the language. The section called "At the Sugarbush" gave us the words we needed.

> Aaniindi ezhaayan? Where are you going?
> Iskigamiziganing indizhaa. I'm going to
>     the sugar bush.
> Nitam nimbiindaakoojige
>     nimiigwechiwi'aag manidoog. First
>     I make a tobacco offering and give
>     thanks to the spirits.
> Mii o'o negwaakwaan. This is a tap.
> Naadoobiin. Go get the sap.
> Chi-okaadakik wa'aw. This is a big kettle.
> Mii iskigamideg. It's boiling down.
> Eya,' bebangii. Yes, little by little.
> Mii zhiiwaagamideg. It's at the syrup stage
>     now.
> Gidaa-biindaakoojigemin. We should make
>     an offering.

I decided my kettle should have a name. The same cast-iron kettle that I use every spring for boiling sap, every fall for parching rice. Over the last fifteen years it has become part of the family. This is one version of the story I heard about that kettle. The kettle first came to the Anishinaabeg in the early part of the last century. There was a terrible smallpox epidemic at Sandy Lake, a lot of Anishinaabeg died. The kettle came here with a man who moved to Sawyer. He used it many seasons for boiling maple syrup and parching wild rice. He died, and his son owned the kettle. One day fifteen years ago, the son wanted to go to bingo. He sold me the kettle for thirty-five frog skins. So I guess the kettle's name is Bingo. Smallpox? Sandy Lake? Nah, Bingo.

The best part of this season was spending time with my grandson Ezigaa. This year, he wanted to learn how to carve a tap. We walked through the woods and found just the right size maple sapling. We sat by the fire and begin to make taps. I cut the sapling into tap-size lengths. I used my electric drill to make holes down the center. Then we carved. I made the tapered end and then watched as he carved his tapered end. We then carved the notched end that holds the milk jug. That boy's first tap was kind of rough looking, but I was able to smooth it down for him. He carved another, then another. I watched and felt grampa proud. Ezigaa's friends came by. The three boys wanted him to go with them to the community center. The boys asked him what he was doing. Ezigaa said, "Oh, just carving a tap for the sugar bush."

Ezigaa wanted to know what we were going to do with our newly made taps. I used my lips and pointed out some maple trees in the yard. I drilled one as he watched. The look in his eye when he reached for the drill made me smile. He drilled the hole at the right angle and depth, cleaned the hole of shavings. The boy used my knife and tapped the tap into the hole. The look on his face when the first drop came out made me smile inside and outside. He stuck out his tongue and caught the second drop of sap coming out.

Ezigaa went to the next tree and drilled and tapped that one, kept on drilling until we were out of taps. The boy strolled around, putting jugs on the taps we made. It looked like he was walking a little taller as he left to play with his friends. Sitting around the fire boiling sap sounds like hard work, but it isn't really. Once the fire is going and the sap is boiling, we just have to add sap and wood. While sitting around the fire with friends and family it is easy to tell stories. There is enough time for everyone to tell all the stories they want. Still, there is always more silence at the fire than stories. The sound of the fire and boiling sap tells its own story. The syrup I have at the end of the boiling makes it all worth it. I think the Creator likes us. We were given syrup again.

QUESTION: *Whadja hear at the rent-a-shaman's doings?*
ANSWER: *Take two smudges and call me in the morning.*

Fond du Lac Follies motored to the Cloquet Community Center for a gathering of Ojibwe language groups. Instead of the usual fifteen to twenty learners, I counted over eighty people who came to further their knowledge of the Ojibwe language. I'd call it a multinational event. I saw people from Gakaabikaang (Minneapolis), Ozaagiziibi-ing (St. Cloud), Odaawaa-zaaga'iganing (Lac Court Oreilles), Zhaa-ganaashiiwaki (Canada), Naagaajiwanaang (Fond du Lac), and my wife Pat from Bwaanaki (Dakota country). I saw a Navajo woman, Sara Begay, and she was speaking Ojibwe.

There were only six Fonjalackers there. The thought that immediately came to mind was where are all the rest of the Fonjalackers? I wonder and am perplexed as to why people stay away by the hundreds. We have good food at the language feasts, so that ain't the reason. Maybe there is something good on TV? A film about Indians perhaps? Whatever the reason or excuse, it has got to be pretty important to keep people away from learning their language.

I was honored to be asked to pray for the food. It was something we had learned there, so I felt comfortable saying the words. Then we lined up to eat, elders first. Of course, we had a couple of different kinds of wild rice dishes, and deer and moose meat. I like eating the traditional food of ancient Anishinaabe culture while striving to learn more of the sounds and words.

We were fortunate to have three language teachers all in the same room at the same time. Dan and Dennis Jones shared their comedy routine called "Braids and Brains" with the crowd. They took turns telling "groaner" jokes to the people. They made my cheeks sore from smiling so hard. I thought they should take their act on the road, any road. Personally, I think the entire Jones family should be commended for their efforts to teach the language: Dan and Dennis, the twins who share the same birthday, Lorraine, Dennis's wife, and their mom, Nancy, too.

Dennis Jones shared some language materials he uses when teaching Ojibwe. He is going to give us a quiz at the next annual gathering. So by next year we will be able to say (and understand) this phrase and thirteen others like it: Mewinzha gete-anishinaabeg gii-izhi-daagwag waaginogaaning. Noongom idash waaka'iganing izhi-endaawag.

Rick Gresczyk was there. He taught me how to say,

Gi gii jiimin,
Gi gii aazhoogaadeb,
Gi gii pookoshkaanan
        ndo'shkiinjigookajiganan.

Rick shared some thoughts about what he saw us doing. He said it was good to help each other learn the language. Rick taught us some songs that he has been using over the last couple of decades when he teaches Ojibwe. He had us all standing up marching in place while we sang the songs.

Then the language learners took turns introducing themselves. The language speakers from St. Cloud did a skit using the language. It feels good knowing that others are learning, too. I was just proud of Rachel, Fond du Lac's eight-year-old language learner. She introduced herself and smiled at all of us when she was done. She looked proud that she knew that much. Hazel, our sixty-seven-year-old learner, sounded good, too, when she introduced herself. Of the language learners from Fond du Lac, I would say half are under eighteen. There is hope for the future.

I felt proud to belong to the group that is preserving the language by using it. We feasted. I ate and ate until it hurt, then I ate some more. I think the people who came to the event learned some new words and phrases. I bet they got fired up about learning more. I felt that way. At home, when counting, we use Ojibwe numbers whenever possible, like during a game of Scrabble or cribbage. We are preserving the language by using it. I heard a lot of Ojibwe being spoken that night and am happy to say I understood most of it. Among the phrases I heard used were:

> Gi gii poogid ina?
> Ninzhaabokaawiz.
> Gaawiin gegoo giziindime'on.
> Aapichi nin-gitimagoz gikendimaan iye
> Anishinaabemowin.

*QUESTION: Gigii poogid ina?*
*ANSWER: Geget gosha, apane na go nimaazhi maagoz?*

Fond du Lac Follies motored to Rainy River Community College with my son Matthew and his partner, Jackie, for a writers workshop and reading. Matthew was playing the part of bodyguard/driver and Jackie was the attack chick. The workshop was in the afternoon and we had a few hours to play until the reading, so we went to Canada for lunch. Right away we looked suspicious to the authorities. Who goes to Canada for lunch? Matthew drove the rez car up to the bridge and we stopped for Canadian Customs. The man with the uniform asked us a few questions about whether we were carrying guns or drugs. We told the man no, although I did mention having a Buck knife. When he heard that, we were invited over for a search of the rez car. We parked and stayed in the vehicle as instructed. The Canadian Customs man came and looked in the front seat of the car. He kneeled on the seats and looked around. When he stuck his hand under the front seat, I thought . . . you're a braver man than I, Gunga Din. I don't even put my hand under there.

When he was done with the front, he searched the rear seat. He looked through each compartment of my briefcase. After that he opened the trunk to look inside. In addition to the usual items— spare tire, jack, jumper cables, extra oil—there was a cardboard box. He picked it up and looked inside and asked me about it. I told him it used to hold books. There was an invoice inside. He looked at the invoice, put it back in the box, and set the box back down. He closed the trunk and told us we could go.

We were walking down the main drag of Fort Frances when we ran into Dan Jones, the language instructor from Fond du Lac Tribal and Community College. We swapped lies and stories while standing there. After eating a Canadian steak, we motored back across the international bridge. At U.S. Customs, the man on duty asked about the license plates on the car that say REZ CAR. He asked where we were from, how long we had been in Canada, and what we did there. We told him we were from the Fond du Lac Reservation, as were the license plates. We told him about the Canadian steak and where we ate it. He smiled and waved us through.

We stopped for gas on the American side and I was going to put something in the trunk. I moved the box the Canadian Customs guy had looked at. Under the box was a gun. What? A gun? Were we international arms smugglers and didn't know it? I looked at the gun and then remembered where it came from. It was a $CO_2$ pellet gun that I had confiscated from my grandson. A few months back I had put the pellet gun there so he couldn't find it again. The Canadian Customs guy couldn't find it, either. We had unknowingly carried the pellet gun across the international border twice. I guess I will not be crossing the border again for a while.

*QUESTION: How militant was he?*
*ANSWER: He used nothing but AIM toothpaste*
*on his Indian Health Service smile.*

My friend and almost-relative died. Artist George Morrison spent many years on earth doing his art. He will be long remembered in Grand Portage and the world. My sympathy is extended to the family. My son Joseph just had a son and named him Joseph

Anthony Northrup. My son Joseph was named after his great-grandfather, and now so is his son. As one spirit leaves, another arrives in my life.

Fond du Lac Follies motored to the Fond du Lac Tribal and Community College to take an Ojibwe class taught by Dan Jones. In the class we learned how to construct proper sentences in Ojibwe. Here are some of my sentences:

1. Enji-niibing noongom, mii a'aw gwiiwizens izhinikaazod Ezigaa gaa maajii-ozhitoonan nooshkaachinaaganan.
2. Wii piindaakojige gwiiwizens jibwaa maniwiigwaased waabang.
3. Ezigaa gii ikido, "Giishpin bimoseyaanh noopiming nin'gaa ashaamnaa ezigaag."
4. Nin gii piinjwebinige Niizho-giizhigad ishkwaa Eshpabidi'iw ingodwaak-waabik n'gii miin'ig Ishkwaa-aname-giizhigad.

1. Because it is summer, that boy called Ezigaa starts to make fanning baskets.
2. He will offer tobacco before gathering bark tomorrow.
3. Ezigaa said, "If I walk in the woods, I shall feed wood ticks."
4. I voted on Tuesday after the chairman gave me one hundred dollars on Monday.

Every time I learn a new word or phrase, I think that America's assimilation policies are not working. We are still here, still being Anishinaabeg just as hard as we can. We are speaking Ojibwe and learning more of the language daily.

At this time of the year, we gather birch bark to make fanning baskets for wild rice. I am grampa-proud of my ten-year-old grandson Ezigaa. Last year he sewed a small basket, but this year he wanted to make a full-sized one like his grampa. First I showed him how I make an awl using a stick and a nail. The boy made three of them. He picked one to use as his personal awl. I carved some notches so it fit his hand. Then we went to the woods and looked at hundreds of trees before we found some good bark for our purposes. Ezigaa learned this part of the process last year, so he was on familiar ground. We fed the mosquitoes, deerflies, and wood ticks while we were in the woods.

I selected a good piece of birch bark. It was General Custer yellow on the inside. I showed him how I lay out the basket and bend the birch bark, and where to put the holes for the corner stitches. He used the awl he had made to make the holes. While he was sewing up the corners, I could hear him saying over and over, "Tight and flat, tight and flat." He was repeating my words about how to sew birch bark using strips of basswood bark. The boy showed a lot of concentration as he was making the basket. I think his hands got tired, so he would take frequent breaks and then return to his sewing.

It took him about fifteen hours to finish the basket. It didn't look too much different than the ones I make. He sold it to his gramma. Ezigaa also made a small one that he sold to a girl in Vienna, Austria. He is now waiting for his check. Welcome to the adult world, gwiiwizens; we are all waiting for a check. He is working on his next basket. I am grampa-proud because that boy is learning things that he can teach his grandchildren. A friend pointed out that making birchbark baskets is all bark and no bite. I will be making baskets for another month and so will that boy, Ezigaa.

The veterans powwow was held here in Sawyer. I ate at my cousin Chetty's food stand. Then I ate there again. Powwow cuisine right here in Sawyer, and it will happen again at the Mash powwow next month. This year I was impressed with how clean the powwow grounds were kept. The clean-up crew should be commended for their work in keeping our little corner of the earth so clean. Fellow marine and Vietnam vet Ray Earley and I set up our perimeter in the shade and observed the passing crowd. We told war stories and invited other vets into our perimeter to sit and tell a few stories. As usual the ground was littered with grenade pins, empty C-ration cans, and dud artillery shells by the time we were done refighting the war.

This year's powwow honored all veterans. The reservation gave us all a pound of rice. One veteran I know wouldn't go up to get his rice because the chairman was handing out the packages and shaking hands. At the risk of looking a gift rez in the mouth, what happened to the presents we used to get? This year we had to buy the powwow T-shirts. I wish I had waited for the second day because they were half price then. I am wondering how next year's powwow will happen.

Fond du Lac Follies motored up deadly Highway 2 to a summer camp operated by members of the Red Lake Nation. Eugene Stillday of Ponemah invited me up there to tell stories to their campers. There must have been over a hundred children at the Norris Camp, an old Civilian Conservation Corps (CCC) camp about seventy miles north of Bemidji. As the postcard says, it wasn't the end of the world, but you could see it from there.

My grandson Ezigaa and I motored up Highway 2 until we got to Bemidji. We turned north toward the camp. We didn't really get lost. We were just exploring a part of the state that we hadn't seen before. Eventually we found the right road through the swamps. And I thought we had big swamps around Sawyer. These way-northern Minnesota swamps make ours look like a damp stretch of grass. These were real wetlands that went on for miles and miles.

As we motored along we talked. "Noozis, mino-giizhigad noongom." "Geget gosha, zaagaate." As we continued along we told stories. Well, okay, it was mostly me telling the stories. I had a captive audience, although I was competing with a Game Boy. "Nashke, migizi!" Too late, couldn't get a picture of the eagle. "Nashke iwedi waawaashkeshi." Too slow, got a picture of the deer's hind end. "Nashke iwedi zhede." Got the picture of the pelican.

By my reckoning we were eighty miles from the nearest C-store. That would have been a bad place to run out of gas, smokes, or batteries for the boy's Game Boy. At the beginning of my storytelling session I introduced myself in Ojibwe. Ezigaa provided the translation into English. I am glad that the boy is learning the language, too. We made the trip home without meeting any grain trucks, logging trucks, or tourists. In Bemidji I got some new batteries for the Game Boy.

Chicago. Fond du Lac Follies motored to Chicago for the 11th World Conference on Tobacco OR Health. I was invited to open the proceedings. What an opportunity. I thought I would introduce myself in Ojibwe. I had learned that much during the Tuesday night language sessions on the rez. "Bangii eta igo ni'nitaa Ojibwem idash, ninga gagwejitoon ji ojibwemoyaan," I thought.

I worked with Cliff Kennedy on how I would use my ten minutes. He owns the agency that was coordinating this part of the evening program. That is when I learned that this convention was big doings, three to four thousand delegates from 165 countries gathering at the Hilton hotels in the Loop. I called Vic Swan and asked if he would like to sing a song for all of those people. He thought it might be a good idea, so he gathered his fellow singers: Steve Blake, Ray Jackson, Larry Long, and Jim Northrup III. We were scheduled to perform in the International Ballroom. They had a stage with those thirty-foot convention screens on both sides. There were chairs set up for 2,500 people; another ballroom had another 2,500 chairs. It had those big screens, too. Big doings, indeed.

We rehearsed in the afternoon in that huge ballroom. The singers and drum sounded good in that space. Cliff Kennedy put together a series of images that were projected on the big screens. He used some images from the film made by Mike Hazard and Mike Rivard called *Jim Northrup: With Reservations.* He used still photos and live video feeds, too. Big doings, indeed. At the appointed time, Vic and the singers sat around the drum and began to sing. The sound of the singing and the drum got everyone's attention. They sat and listened as images flashed on the big screens. I thought of how the drum and singing were heard in this very same place hundreds of times, for hundreds of years. Big doings, indeed. As the song ended, I walked out to the stage and introduced myself in Ojibwe. My sounds were translated into English and then into the languages of those people from around the world. That felt good. I was glad the sounds of Ojibwe were returning to Chicago.

After the introduction, I said in English, "Welcome to my continent." There was a split second of silence followed by laughter followed by applause. When they were done, I said, "Stay as long as you want, everyone else has." They laughed again. Baapiwag, I thought. I told the delegates that I am Anishinaabe and only speak for myself. I told them there was a difference between tobacco and aasemaa. I recited poetry about wild rice and birch bark. As long as I had the microphone, I told them about powwows, a feeling-good time of the year because you get to see relatives you haven't seen for a while, get to lie about your children and grandchildren: "Yup, my boy is a hunter, went hunting the other day. He shot a deer, the bullet passed through, hit a duck on the other side, the duck fell in the lake, which scared a fish that jumped in my canoe. Yup, my boy is a hunter." As I finished talking, the drum sound came back up again. My last words to the delegates were, "Miigwech bizindawiyeg. Thank you all for listening to me."

After our part of the convention doings, we met delegates from many different countries. I remember shaking hands with people from France, Poland, Scotland, Norway, New Zealand, England, Mexico, and Germany. After escaping from the crowd, the Shinnobs went outside to have a smoke. While we were standing there, two Americans came walking up. One of them said to my son Jim, "Hey Chief, you got a smoke?" I watched my son's face go from a storytelling smile to stone instantly. He told the guy, "What makes you think I would give you a smoke?" His eyes looked dangerous, I thought. The two guys thought so, too, and one apologized as they turned and walked away rather quickly.

The next morning the Shinnobs strolled across Daley Plaza to Mickey D's for breakfast. We were all gawking at the tall buildings. It reminded me of what my grandfather Joe Northrup once wrote about Shinnobs visiting a city: "They got the roof of their mouths sunburnt." It was Chicagooey with the heat and humidity. I must have seen ten thousand faces I didn't know. The noise made me long for the quiet of back home. I missed the pines and poplars of the rez. I drove home. Giiwedaa, I thought. Let's go home.

Some of the leaves near the top of the maples are turning orange. I saw other maples that had red leaves. I usually see these colors in this order when ricing season is over. The chilling winds and cool evenings are a reminder that winter is coming.

We had a good wild rice season this year. As I tell my grandson Ezigaa, the Creator likes us; we were given manoomin (wild rice) again. This year is a teaching year. There were quite a few people who wanted to learn how to make wild rice. I was happy to share what I know about rice.

*QUESTION: What is the funniest thing you heard lately at your casino?*
*ANSWER: "Them Indians act like they own this place."*

Fond du Lac Follies motored to Cloquet to attend the tribal court proceedings. The doings were held in the tribal council chambers. There was a lot of decorum going on in there. It looked like a courtroom. They had Judge Blue Dog sitting in front, flags behind him. There was a court reporter tap-tapping on her skinny typewriter. Of course there was a prosecutor and defendants. The entire Fond du Lac police department was there in force, all four officers. The witnesses were sworn and gave testimony just like in a courtroom off the rez.

The judge identified the file number and the defendant's name. The prosecutor and the defendant went into a back room, where they played let's make a deal. When they came out, they told the judge the details of the deal. Judge Blue Dog then passed judgment and arrangements were made for payment of fines. It looked like any courtroom. It was very efficient. The only cloud on the judicial horizon is the history of the court. The last two judges were fired by the Reservation Business Committee. They wouldn't do that to Judge Blue Dog, or would they?

Fond du Lac Follies jetted to New York City. Because I am a Vietnam veteran who writes poetry about the war, I was invited to come to Albany, New York, for a tribute to Native American Vietnam vets. I was honored to be asked. Colette Lemmon set up the whole deal. She arranged to meet me in Grand Central at the information kiosk. We got on a train and went up the Hudson River valley. I had only read about this place before, so I was getting my eyeballs full of history.

Colette lives in Pleasant Hollow, New York, and that is where I met the dog, the turtle, and her housemate Dennis. Their home is in the Catskill Mountains south of Albany. The next morning we motored to downtown Albany, where the New York Vietnam Veterans Fine Art Gallery is located, the site of the doings. Inside the museum, they had an 81mm mortar as part of their display. I turned the elevation crank and also cranked the tube around to a different azimuth. I looked at the practice shells and saw the fins located on the base of the shells. I remember finding fins like that lying in a crater after we got mortared by the enemy.

I met Joe Curry, a Seneca who had spent twenty years in the military. He showed me the memorial he had constructed in memory of his brother Wilbur, who died in the La Drang valley during the Vietnam War. The memorial consisted of a rifle with bayonet attached. There was a helmet with a camouflage cover on it. There were red beads and feathers that were attached to the helmet. A pair of dog tags was also hanging from the rifle. I could tell that Joe Curry had spent a lot of time making the memorial. I could tell how Joe felt about his brother Wilbur.

We had a visitor here at the World Headquarters of the Fond du Lac Follies. Hannah Piironen came from Helsinki to stay for a week. She came to learn about the Indians, so I took her ricing. With Hannah, my Scandinavian collection was almost complete. A few months later, Annette from Copenhagen came by with Pam Johns of St. Paul. We drank coffee and talked about my collection. I have had visitors from Norway, Sweden, Finland, and Denmark. My Southeast Asia collection is already complete since I had visitors from Laos, Cambodia, and Vietnam.

The following is a salute to mothers. I am really early for Mother's Day or really late, take your pick. It is a story about my maw and her teeth. She got her smile from town when her birth teeth got tired and died. "What? I got pyorrhea?" she said when told by the dentist that her teeth were loose in the sockets. The dentist pulled her teeth, then fitted her for the false teeth. "Jeez, pyorrhea? Diarrhea is bad enough," she told us when she came home. She never did take to those teeth. She carried them in her apron pocket and would only put them in for company or when she had to go somewhere. Around the house, she smiled at us with only her eyes.

One evening, after all day with six kids in a small house, my dad wanted to go look for deer. He told maw he would warm up the car while she got ready. He sat in the car revving the motor to remind her he wanted to go . . . now . . . *Rrrmmmm, Rrrmmmm.* Maw did a quick draw into her apron pocket and her hand came out toothless. She looked around the room. She saw some kids in front of the TV, some chasing each other, some just sitting there. She told the kids to help her find her teeth. She wasn't smiling when she said it. *Rrrmmmm, Rrrmmmm.* Five kids went in seven directions as they scrambled to help find the teeth. She stood in the middle of the room directing the search for the missing smile. *Rrrmmmm, Rrrmmmm.*

Wahbegan, a little round-headed four-year-old boy, continued watching cartoons as the search swirled around him. *Rrrmmmm, Rrrmmmm.* The five searchers couldn't find the teeth. They were already looking where someone had just looked. It was a small house. Maw stood there, pointing with her lower lip to show where to search next. *Rrrmmmm, Rrrmmmm.* Wahbegan caught maw's eye. She was wondering why he wasn't searching. He slowly turned his head and gradually smiled at her. He had her teeth in his mouth. The adult teeth looked large in that little four-year-old face. *Rrrmmmm, Rrrmmmm.*

I don't remember exactly how it happened, but maw got her teeth, took her apron off, walked out the door, and got into the car. I'd like to think she gave Wahbegan a gentle caress on the head that knocked the teeth into her hand as she walked by. The five searchers in different parts of the room looked at Wahbegan. He was sitting there smiling at them all with his own little teeth. Maw was going to help tip over a deer to feed all those teeth in that house.

Fond du Lac Follies motored to Washington, DC, for the Marine Corps Birthday and Veterans Day doings. I traveled with two other marine grunts from the Vietnam War. Ray Earley and Walter Stafford had both served two tours in the war. We cruised to D & C in a conversion van, so there was plenty of room for all of us. So much room that Ray brought his two sons, John and Zac. Getting to DC was easy; we hung a left in Chicago and a right in Harrisburg, PA.

Along the way we stopped at Denison University in Granville, Ohio. I was invited to read from my works at the college. At the end of my reading, I passed a birchbark fanning basket through the crowd to show them what I make all summer. Ray pointed out what the audience was doing with my basket. They were putting money in it like they were at church. I laughed and stopped them from putting any more money in the basket. I did keep the nine bucks that was collected, however.

We left Ohio and drove through West Virginia where it is real skinny. After several hours, we stopped at Carlisle, PA. We drove onto the U.S. Army post. Carlisle was where my grandfather Joe Northrup attended boarding school for a while. We went to the U.S. Army Military History Institute, where they had some records from the boarding school. I found my grandfather's name in one of the books. The county museum was closed, so I was unable to find any pictures of my dad's dad. During our visit there we found the graves of some of the children who had died while at the boarding school. We offered some tobacco while we were there. The headstones had names and tribes on them. The saddest ones I saw were the ones marked Unknown.

Eventually, we hung a right at Harrisburg, PA, and motored to the nation's capital. I don't know if it is a seasonal thing, but it seemed like there were four semitrucks for every car we saw on our drive across the country. We set up camp at a Days Inn motel in Arlington, just about a grenade throw away from the Marine Corps memorial. We went to the Wall. This was the first time for Ray and Walter, so I was able to help them find names and make rubbings. We hung around the area and talked with a lot of other marines. Since it was the 225th birthday of the Marine Corps, we wished each other a happy birthday. I told most of them they didn't look a day over two hundred.

VFW Post 3150, Arlington, Virginia, was the site of a spaghetti feed for out-of-town visitors like us. We ate and thanked the hosts. Later there was a reading of the commandant's birthday message. The oldest and youngest marines present cut the Marine Corps birthday cake with an NCO sword provided by one of the visitors from Minnesota. We ate good. We thanked our hosts for their hospitality. We later made a stop at the Smithsonian Air and Space Museum. It wasn't very far from the hole in the ground that will be the National Museum of the American Indian.

*QUESTION: What did Geronimo say when he jumped out of an airplane?*
*ANSWER: Meeeeeeee.*

# 13.
# Brown-Bellied sapsucker

## 2001

Fond du Lac Follies has been motoring a lot lately. Once again, I met myself on the freeway near Hinckley. I waved. We were both late. There was a highway patrolman, but that comes later in the story. I was invited to the University of Wisconsin-La Crosse to tell stories because it was Native American Heritage Month. I actually think all months are Native American heritage months. I drove through Red Wing, Minnesota, on my way. Just seeing the name on the road signs reminded me of the time in the 1950s when I was last in Red Wing. As I drove by the huge administration building of the state reform school, I took a memory trip back to when I was a resident of Jefferson Cottage.

Reform school wasn't too bad; it was just a bit stricter than the boarding schools I had attended. I spent nine months of my teen-age years in that place. I was found guilty of aggravated buffoon-ery with intent to mope. While I was there I met a lot of guys I had known in boarding school. There were a lot of Indians from the other reservations there also. It took about nine months to get my attitude adjusted.

After I got out my probation officer told me if I didn't stay in school, I would go back to Red Wing. I didn't want that, so I stayed in school and graduated in 1961 from Carlton High School. They told me I was one of the few Indians in the state who had graduated from high school. At the time, it seemed like there were only two choices. One was the boarding school/reform school/state prison trail and the other was the boarding school/reform school/military trail. I am glad I chose the military trail after high school.

As I was remembering my time in Red Wing, a siren came on

and red lights began flashing in my mirrors. A highway patrolman stopped me and asked me why I was speeding. I told him my story about being locked up there and how I wasn't paying attention to my driving. He listened and gave me a warning ticket. At that point, I learned something new. The trooper told me it was illegal to have my eagle feather (or anything) hanging from my rearview mirror. I thanked the trooper for the warning and continued motoring.

QUESTION: *What did your uncle Wayne E. BuShoe*
*say about wearing long underwear?*
ANSWER: *Yellow in the front, brown in the back.*

Birchbark Books was another place I motored to last month. Louise Erdrich owns the bookstore that is located near the west end of Franklin Avenue. She asked if I would come down and help her celebrate the opening of the bookstore by reading from my works. She has been my inspiration ever since I started writing, so it was an easy decision to make. I was honored to be asked. The audience was small but enthusiastic. I noticed that most of the audience members bought books, so it was a good one. Louise and I used our limited Ojibwe vocabulary to have a limited conversation in the language.

Fond du Lac Follies motored to a rez in southern Minnesota to attend a ceremony, a ceremony that was being used long before there was an America. I would say that the ceremony is proof that assimilation didn't work with all of us. The ceremony was done by a medicine man. He had a helper who brought a hand drum and his voice to the place. The ceremony was used to end a period of mourning. I watched the doings closely because I had never seen it done before. I had heard about this particular ceremony and I was glad to be taking part in it. A family from Canada drove eleven hours to attend the ceremony. During one song, the helper was singing and I heard a woman's voice behind me singing along. We are used to hearing male voices, and the feminine voice added to the beauty of the song. I could smell burning sage and tobacco. There was a strong feeling that we were all gathered for one purpose in the crowd of two hundred who came to the doings.

The giveaway began. The two sisters who set up the whole thing were standing in the front of the room. They were surrounded by thirteen star quilts, a Beaver State blanket, and a Pendleton blanket. They had towels and T-shirts and other household items. One of the sisters gave away her jingle dress. People came up one at a time as their names were called. The family had a year to prepare for this giveaway, and when the two sisters were done, everyone in the room had a gift. After the giveaway we all ate together. I ate walleye, chicken, and ham. I ate like my stomach thought my throat was cut. I ate until it hurt. I was glad to be included in this celebration of life. As I was sitting there I thought, yeah, America, assimilation didn't work. The people are still finding strength in their ceremonies.

Well, my oldest son, Jim, did it again. He took part in Wegner Auto's Annual Traditional Blizzard Sale. The last time he did this was a few years back. This is the twenty-fourth year of the Blizzard Sale, which is held near Pierre, South Dakota. People stand in line for days to get good prices on all sorts of cars and trucks. My boy began the line on a Wednesday afternoon. The showroom doors are closed until 8:00 AM on Saturday. He said he came prepared by dressing in his warmest layers. Jim is a construction worker so he is used to being outside in the winter, but this time he said it was really cold.

He brought some creature comforts to the proceedings. He had a radio, a TV, and a tape player. Jim's wife, Lisa, kept their warm van parked nearby so he could warm up as needed. Jim had a charcoal grill, and he said he was eating all the time. Some of the other thirty people in line came up to cook on his grill. They kept their meat frozen in a snowbank. The temperature was twenty below zero on those long cold nights. The wind was also a factor — no trees to stop the wind, you know.

My son said he recognized a couple of people who had stood in line the last time he attended the sale. There were skins from South Dakota and a few from the Twin Cities. Jim stayed in line all of those hours and, just before the doors opened, he traded places with his wife, Lisa. She was warm and she made the dash inside to put her hand on the truck they had been looking at. It was a big black Ford pickup SuperCab with four-wheel drive. There was enough room in the truck for Lisa, his son Jimmy, and his daughter Jaelisa. For Jim, the whole event was over pretty fast. He said by 0830 Saturday morning he was in a motel shower warming up. Jim brought his new Ford truck back to the rez to show family and friends what standing in the cold can do for you. Outside we were smiling and nodding, but inside we were saying . . . Giiwanaadizi ina?

> Imbaashkizige apane jachaamoyaan.
> I have an orgasm every time I sneeze.
> Awegonen mii mooyah? What are you
> taking for that?
> Gaawiisagang. Pepper

Fond du Lac Follies motored to the Black Bear Casino to attend the quarterly open meeting of the Reservation Business Committee. The doings were held in the bingo hall, the site of so many spoiled dreams. According to a report from the Fond du Lac Development Corporation, we have some money. To put it in understandable numbers, let us look at it this way. Our total assets are $168.05. The liabilities are $2.18. Now add six zeros to those numbers and you will understand where we are.

I learned that Fonjalacker John Smith is the new chief of police for the Fond du Lac Reservation. Congrats, John. I also learned this sovereign nation is thinking of issuing driver's licenses for the people.

> QUESTION: What's the gambler's responsibility at the casino?
> ANSWER: To move the coins from one slot machine to another.

The spring nights in northern Minnesota are cool. The days are getting longer; the place where the sun rises is traveling north. In the mornings, I hear the crows. That means two words to me: sugar bush. I can see the snow shrinking in the backyard. There is a brown collar of last fall where tree and dirt come together. I checked my taps, need to make some more. I don't know what happens to them. I always have to make some each spring. I have three grandchildren gracing this house now, so I will have help. My son Jim, his wife, Lisa, and their two children moved back to the nest for a while.

Ezigaa went with me to the woods to get the maple sticks that will become taps. I broke trail through the knee-deep snow. The boy followed me, and Biindigen, his dog, followed him. We cut the sticks into the right lengths for taps. He is getting good with the bow saw. That evening we sat at the kitchen table and made taps. When I drilled out the center of the sticks, Ezigaa used a wire to dig out the shavings. When he was done he would hold the new tap up to the light, blow through it, and say the sap could flow through that hole. Noonaa, all of age five, also used a wire to clean the shavings from the drilled holes. Niiwin, the eight-year-old, couldn't join in. He was doing homework.

On these warm days and cool nights, I can almost feel the sap flowing in the trees. We will thank the Creator for the gift of maple sap. Once again it will be storytelling time around the fire as we boil the sap down into syrup and sugar cakes. I will have a captive audience of three grandchildren. I can already see Aaron Ezigaa roll his eyes back and ask if I am going to tell the same stories again. At that point, I will invite him to tell a story. This is one of my favorite times of the year. We are still doing what generations of Anishinaabeg have done through the centuries.

Me and the rez car were headed home on I-35. I had spent the day in the Cities and it was time to return to the quiet of Sawyer. Just south of Harris, Minnesota, the rez car said "Gaawiin." No. It was emphatic and dramatic. A great cloud of steam suddenly appeared in all my mirrors. I knew it was coming from the rez car. Radiator hose, I thought. Then I remembered I had a spare hose in the trunk. I wanted to grab a microphone and yell, "Mayday, Mayday, we're going in." Then I remembered I didn't have a microphone.

I coasted into a C-store in Harris. They had what I needed to get back on the road again. I fired the rez car up and watched for leaks. No leaks, so I got on the road. Oh-oh! The hose came off as I was turning onto the freeway ramp. I steered off the road and knew I'd have to crawl under the car again. I reconnected the hose, replaced the lost coolant, and got in to start the car. It spun but didn't fire up. Then I knew I was in trouble. It was getting dark. Using just body language and my glove as a cell phone, I asked a passing civilian if he had a phone. He did. I called my son Jim, gave him my location.

I got in the car to wait. The sun was now down and it was getting chilly. I remembered I just happened to have a military surplus green woolen cape in the back seat. I wrapped up and waited. Three hours later, my son arrived for the rescue. We couldn't fix the car there, so we dragged it off the freeway to the bait shop owned by Les Carpenter. I left him a note and continued my trip home. Later Jim used a dolly and dragged the rez car home. Now it sits, waiting for the mechanic and a new place to break down.

Ishkigamizige-giizis. I just call it the woods. It is where my maw, my grammaws, and all the grammaws before them came from. I am going home when I go to the north woods. The Shinnobs in this HUD house are excited about going to the sugar bush. We have been hearing the crows for a while now. The returning birds let us know it is time to make maple syrup. Eagles, crows, swans, ducks, and some I don't know are flying about. I looked in the mirror and saw a brown-bellied sapsucker looking back at me. The moving birds keep me looking up to see what comes next as winter fades and spring comes blooming in. Before we went into the woods, we gave the three grandchildren the standard lecture: "We are quiet in the woods because this is the deer's house and we are just visitors. See the tracks?"

At first the snow is thigh deep to adults and waist deep to the grandchildren. The snow has butt prints where someone tipped over. One day I used snowshoes to make trails. I waded from tree to tree, breaking trail for a train of grandchildren. One is carrying milk jugs, one is carrying taps, and one is just watching, trying to keep up. Using a brace and bit, I drill a hole at a slight upward angle into the maple tree. Using an always-handy twig, I clean out the shavings. One of the kids hands me a tap and I *tap-tap* it into the tree. We watch to see if the sap comes through the tap. I hang the jug on the tap. With some trees, the sap pulses out of the tree, like a heartbeat almost. The kids make O-shaped mouths when they see the sap coming out like that. We got about 130 trees tapped but are bragging 150.

What I like about going to the woods is I have to walk slow. That is good because it gives me a chance to appreciate what the Creator has given us. When we went to gather the sap the kids got the standard lecture. "Spilling sap is a felony, anyone spilling sap spends a night in the box. Oh, wait a minute, that's from *Cool Hand Luke.* Just be careful with the sap. Remember, we are quiet in the woods." The laughter of the children breaks the quiet rule as they run from tree to tree, laughing, wanting to be the first to empty a full jug. "Watch out for the deer poop," one little voice cautioned.

We brought the sap home and built the fire. I like to build a base of hot coals using dry maple. Every time I go to the woods I look for dry, standing maple. Cadillacs, I call them. The Cadillac of firewood. After the bed of coals is ready, we add more dry wood and then stack split firewood around the kettle. At first as it heats, the wisps of steam come off in a tentative way. As the sap gets hotter, the steam comes rolling off, seemingly happy to be free.

The Shinnobs are drawn to the kettle like a magnet. As more people join the circle around the fire, each one looks around for something to do. One takes charge of the balsam branches that are used to keep the sap from boiling over. Another takes responsibility for the fire, keeping it fed and roaring. One tells stories. Once again, there is time for everyone to tell a story. At one point we had fourteen humans and two dogs sitting there. The fire roars on and we are reminded that we are just one of the generations that have sat around such a fire watching sap boil down. We are bathed in wood smoke.

After about seven hours of kettle time, the syrup comes off the fire. We are careful as we carry the hot syrup into the house for the final boil and filtering. Now I have jars and jars of dark maple syrup. This has been a good learning season for the grandchildren. They learned to be quiet in the woods, to respect the gifts we have been given. They also learned the way we make syrup, how to make the taps, how to drill the trees, how to collect the sap and boil it into syrup. Another seasonal cycle of the Anishinaabeg cycles through. We are blessed to be a part of it. We thank the Creator for the gift of syrup. N'miigwechiwendaan.

Fond du Lac Follies motored to the Palace at Cass Lake. We were in town to help celebrate the graduation of fourteen Anishinaabeg from Leech Lake Tribal College. The high point for me was hearing an eleven-year-old boy speak and translate Ojibwe. Okay, it was my grandson, Aaron Ezigaa. I was grampa-proud as he came up to the podium and used about twenty sentences to introduce himself. When he was done, I also spoke Ojibwe and the boy told the people what I was saying in English. The graduates will forget the advice I laid on them, but they will remember that boy speaking Ojibwe. In closing, I borrowed a line from Chuck Robertson Sr. and told them not to sign any more god-dammed treaties.

It was a cloudy day when I went to the woods on the north side of the rez. Somehow while walking about I zigged when I should have zagged and got twisted around. I wasn't lost. I knew I was still in northern Minnesota. I just couldn't tell where I had parked my truck. I walked in many directions looking for the road. I fed many mosquitoes while walking. I used all the woodsman tricks I knew to find the right direction. I studied the clouds to see which way they were moving. That didn't help. I listened for the sounds of cars and trains. It sure was quiet in the woods. I saw airplanes flying over, but that didn't help because they fly in any direction. I didn't look for moss on the north side of trees because I think that only works for Boy Scouts. After a couple of hours, I was tired. I was also embarrassed. It has been years since I got twisted around in the woods. I was glad that I was alone, didn't want to be leading someone astray while my internal compass wasn't working. I finally popped out of the woods about a mile from my truck. I drove home and took a nap, a very long nap.

Fond du Lac Follies is now motoring in a 1964 Corvette Stingray. The rez car license plate looks good on the silver machine. My wife, Patricia, won the sports car in a drawing at the Black Bear Casino.

She had eight tickets in on the drawing, but we are bragging just one. The first time I saw a picture of the '64 Corvette Stingray was on a moonlit night at An Hoa, South Vietnam, in 1966. The night was bright enough to read a newspaper or magazine by the moonlight. The marines were writing letters and sharing their reading material and I saw a picture of the '64 Corvette Stingray. I thought that someday I would like to own a car like that. Well, someday happened. We met the insurance man at the casino where he took pictures and took our money for the insurance. We drove to the reservation licensing bureau and the rez car plates were officially transferred to the Corvette.

It is somewhat scary to drive that powerful machine. The hardest temptation is when the road is clear in front. Just resisting the impulse to push down on the gas is difficult. We drove that car for about two hundred miles. Pat was going to take my Aunt Beeb for a ride when we noticed a strange noise coming from the vehicle. It was a sound that was in between a tapping and a knocking. We shut the car off. We talked with Pete Defoe about the car, and he said the reservation would get the car fixed for me. In the meantime, I am driving the rez van while the Corvette is in the shop. It looks like another long two weeks before I can drive it again. The mechanic from Jerry's Auto Electric thinks the noise is coming from the torque converter. Now I have to figure out how to carry a canoe on that Corvette. Ricing is coming up soon.

QUESTION: *What is yet another Shinnob snagging line?*
ANSWER: *Wanna go ricing? You bring your knockers, I'll bring my pole.*

Fond du Lac Follies motored to Perch Lake to inspect the Fond du Lac Navy. All three vessels were there. Admiral Chaz Tuna gave me the tour. Chaz isn't really an admiral. We just call him that because it makes him happy. He is actively cutting and removing moose-ears and lily pads from the lake. Both plants compete with the wild rice for nutrients, water, and sunshine. The rice was standing tall and thick. It was goldish-green as it waved together in the wind. My son Matthew was along shooting a video.

The first vessel we saw was the airboat, with a big, beefy V-8 motor that spins an airplane propeller for propulsion. Admiral Chaz fired that thing up and we buzzed across the lake. The Admiral steered the vessel with two vanes behind the propeller. We skimmed over places that would take a long time to get through in a canoe. Other than the noise, it was an enjoyable ride. The airboat is called the SS *Go Fast.* I guessed we were traveling at thirty miles an hour or more. The air-boat goes through the moose-ears like they aren't even there.

While skimming along we saw several blue herons taking off. We watched an eagle family in the middle of flying lessons. A large bald eagle was showing a smaller one how to soar in the wind. When the big one banked and dove left, the little one did the same thing, same angle on the wings, learning. Ducks were exploding in all directions.

Admiral Chaz took us to the vessel that is used for harvesting the plant debris. This was a genuine paddle-wheeler. It uses a sickle cutter on the front and a series of conveyers to cut and gather the plant material. When the vessel is full of plant debris, the Admi-ral takes it to the shore and dumps out the debris. The SS *Paddle-Wheeler* is the largest vessel in the fleet. The last boat in the Fond du Lac Navy is the SS *Cookie Cutter,* as the Admiral calls it. This nar-row boat mounts two huge counter-rotating propellers on the front to move the craft through the water. The propellers also cut swaths through the vegetation.

The reservation has invested a lot of money to make growing con-ditions better for the wild rice. This is the second year of the project to protect the gift from the Creator. I was glad they picked a ricer like Chaz to be the Admiral. Are we the only rez that has a navy?

I will never forget September 11, 2001. I had one of the best days ricing I have ever had in almost forty years of ricing. My godson Zac and I went to East Lake to harvest wild rice. We were invited by the people of East Lake to come and share the gift from the Crea-tor. Once again the people were displaying the Anishinaabe trait of generosity.

I lost my canoe at the beginning of the season, but one day while

I was on my way to Superior to replace it with a new one, I came by former legislator Willard Munger's motel and noticed a couple of aluminum canoes in the yard. I stopped and asked Willard's son if he wanted to sell one of them. He said no but was willing to rent one for a couple of weeks. So, I had a canoe for ricing. It is nice the way things fall in place.

My old pole had also seen one too many seasons, so my son Jim repaired it. He replaced the crutch end and the pole end. Early in the season we went ricing at Dead Fish Lake here on the reservation. The rice beds looked good from the rice tower, but once we got out on the lake we quickly realized the rice worms had started harvesting before we got there. My son Matthew and I took a look at the Moose Horn River, but the rice wasn't ripe. There were a lot of worms there, too, which is how Zac and I ended up at East Lake.

The Four Oaks drum group has been staying here since early July. They go out on the weekend to sing at powwows but return here to the World Headquarters of the Fond du Lac Follies to rest, rebuild, and refurbish their vehicles. Tony Sayers, Bill Sayers, David Manual, and Zac are the singers. While they were here they tanned a hide, worked on my sister's house, and made themselves useful. Some of them went ricing and they learned how to make wild rice without machines. They took their drum to the community center and sang powwow songs. My son Jim made a dancing pit, and they are taking turns dancing on the rice. While one dances, another one sings and plays a hand drum; it makes the dancing easier. Zac made a fanning basket to use on the rice. This was his first time making rice like this.

The bright red of the maple, brighter red of the sumac, and yellow of the birch trees remind me of why I am glad to live in northern Minnesota. The Norway pines have some brown needles and I expect to see the orange of the tamarack trees soon. After looking at different shades of green all summer, it is a visual feast in the woods now. I like to go out to the Ditchbanks area of the rez and listen to the quiet. When I am in the woods, I know my relatives walked the same ground, paddled the same lakes, and felt the seasons change as I do. I feel connected. I like to bring Ezigaa to the woods with me. My eleven-year-old grandson likes to look at stuff in the woods. Some blueberry bushes reminded him of all the berries he picked last summer and he told a story about berry picking. Together we watched a hawk that was hunting. We didn't say anything, just watched him flying. It is peaceful in the woods.

So, the Gov came to the rez. Yup, that's right. Former wrassler and movie star and current Minnesota governor Jesse Ventura came to our reservation. He spent the day and evening here, touring and talking. I later learned that Fond du Lac is the first reservation he has visited since becoming governor of Minnesota. There were about forty people in his entourage. Assistants, police, and newspeople were in the group. They traveled in a big white bus accompanied by many, many police cars.

Fond du Lac Follies motored to the new reservation school to see the Gov. I got to the school and started walking the halls. I met Chairman Peacock along the way and he pointed me in the right direction. Then I saw the Gov. He was standing in a hall with his entourage. It was easy to pick him out of the crowd. I saw a tall, bald-headed man surrounded by normal-sized people. He was at least a head taller than everyone else. When he came walking by me, I gave him a hand salute, from one veteran to another. He returned my salute, reached over, shook my hand, and told me, "Welcome home." I said, "Eya,' miigwech."

The newspeople wanted a photo op and the Gov asked if they wanted the school in the background. He came walking back up the sidewalk to where I was lounging against the railing. He stood next to me. So, there we were, shoulder to shoulder. Well, actually it was shoulder to elbow. I asked the Gov if he ever read the Follies. He said he might have once or twice in *The Circle*. I told him if he had read the right issue, he would have seen where I confessed to having voted for him. He laughed and thanked me for the vote. I noticed that he had a five-o'clock shadow behind the right ear on his famous bald head.

The cameras got their photo op. The governor continued on his tour of the rez. I toured the rez on the way back to Sawyer. I got home and the moccasin telegraph, in the form of my sister Doris, reported there was a feast with the governor scheduled for that evening. She said the social hour was a half-hour long beginning at 1800 hours. We went to the Black Bear Casino bingo hall, where everything was set up for a feast. We picked out a strategic table (close to the food and close to the drum) and waited for the Gov. Chairman Peacock got up and started to speak. The podium was set up under the G-ball sign, ningaabii'inong. He told us what was going to happen and when we would eat. It was a feather in his cap to have the Gov visit Fond du Lac before any of the other reservations in Minnesota. He was beaming.

There must have been 250 Fonjalackers in the bingo hall. The tall man walked in and the crowd responded with a standing ovation. His charisma machine was set on stun as he wowed the crowd. He knew he was walking into a friendly house. The governor was presented with a veteran's song, gifts, and applause from the Fonjalackers. Then the feast began. The feast consisted of wild rice and some other stuff. We ate good.

The governor spoke from prepared notes and said he gets in trouble with the unprepared part of his talks. He gave us several messages about September 11. One was hope: "No one will destroy our freedom," and "We will not fail." And another was patriotism: "I believe in America," and "We will stand united." The Gov answered a few questions from the gathered Fonjalackers. When he didn't know the answer, he said so. The Gov told us that airplanes from Duluth were guarding the state of Minnesota during that terrible time in September. When Jesse Ventura walked out, Leland Deebe and I, two Vietnam vets, gave him a hand salute. The Gov returned our salute using his index finger. He came over and showed why he couldn't give us a regular salute in return. The Gov had a handful of asemaa, tobacco.

*QUESTION: What is Shinnob Viagra?*
*ANSWER: One part blueberry, one part moose meat,*
*one part wild rice, one part commod pork, one part maple syrup,*
*one part bacon grease, and 94 parts Fix-a-Flat.*

Fond du Lac Follies motored to Brainerd to participate in the Environmental Grantmakers Association annual retreat. I was invited to recite poetry. The doings were held at Madden's golf resort on Gull Lake. Too bad I'm not a golfer. The first person I recognized there was Winona LaDuke. We talked about dead raccoons (in Ojibberish). Later at the evening feast I saw a guy who is usually on my TV. It was Bill Moyers, a keynote speaker for the event. We met at the dessert table. I said, "Boozhoo." "Fine, I'm fine, thank you," he answered. Either he misunderheard me or he doesn't know as much Ojibwe as he thinks. Vic Swan brought a drum to the doings and with three others, Bill Sayers, Larry Long, and Zac, sang two songs for the people. I did my part in between the songs.

My son Jim moved back home to work on the reservation's new school building. He and his wife and two children were living in an RV and he was promised housing by the people in tribal government. That is all he has to shelter his children from the weather—promises. Jim built a waaginogaan, a domed lodge, for his family to live in while waiting for housing. It is about twenty feet by thirty-five feet, with an eight-foot ceiling. The waaginogaan will have a stove and a window.

Jim has hung a door on the structure and the door has a deadbolt lock on it. Whoever heard of a deadbolt lock on a waaginogaan? He also has electricity and a ceiling fan. I hope he gets a house before it gets to be thirty below. I don't want my grandchildren sleeping in the cold. We shall see how this plays out. I don't think we need to have Fond du Lac people living as their ancestors did when we have $100 million in the bank.

*Anishinaabe Syndicated* was designed and set in type by Judy Gilats at Peregrine Graphics Services. The text type is Eidetic Neo and the display face is Eidetic Neo Omni. Printed by Sheridan Books, Ann Arbor, Michigan.